Class, Ethnicity, and Social Inequality

MCGILL-QUEEN'S STUDIES IN ETHNIC HISTORY
Donald Harman Akenson, Editor

Class, Ethnicity, and Social Inequality

CHRISTOPHER McALL

McGill-Queen's University Press
Montreal & Kingston • London • Buffalo

© McGill-Queen's University Press 1990
ISBN 0-7735-0716-7

Legal deposit second quarter 1990
Bibliothèque nationale du Québec

∞

Printed in Canada on acid-free paper

This book has been published with the help of a grant
from the Social Science Federation of Canada, using
funds provided by the Social Sciences and Humanities
Research Council of Canada.

Canadian Cataloguing in Publication Data

McAll, Christopher, 1948–
    Class, ethnicity, and social inequality
    Includes bibliographical references.
    ISBN 0-7735-0716-7
    1. Social classes.   2. Ethnicity.   3. Equality.   I. Title.
    HT609.M38 1990   305   C89-090470-7

Contents

Preface

Class and ethnicity have long been key and, in the case of class, hotly disputed conceptual tools for the dismantling and understanding of societies. Processes of labour migration into the old established industrial heartlands since the Second World War, and rapid urbanization and industrialization outside those heartlands, have led to the increasing juxtaposition within the same social environments of ethnically distinct groups. In the context of a competitive labour-market, in which the boundaries between ethnic groups can come to coincide with occupational or class boundaries, opposition that arises on the basis of the latter can come to be "seen" in terms of ethnicity, since ethnicity by definition relates to manifest differences. Hence social relations can only too easily degenerate into "ethnic" conflict, particularly when fuelled by racist propaganda. For some, therefore, ethnicity is the mask that conceals class and prevents people from acting in the name of it. For others, inter-ethnic conflict can be resolved through greater tolerance of the "other" and an increase in intercultural awareness. As one moves towards the right, ethnicity comes to be the "glorious" fact that has to be more or less belligerently protected by, for example, the "voluntary repatriation" of immigrants.

The aim of this book is to face up to the reality of class and ethnicity and their apparent opposition to each other as bases for identity and political action in the context of inegalitarian societies. The book is divided into four parts. In the first part I present different theoretical approaches to class and ethnicity, and in the second, the role of class formation and ethnogenesis at different historical periods and in different social contexts. This leads, in part three, to a discussion of class, ethnicity, and nationhood in which I look both at the idea of the "nation-state" and at the role of ethnicity in the context of colonialism. Finally, I advance an interpretation of contemporary society in which ethnicity is no longer opposed to class but is presented as one of the ways in which social inequality expresses itself and ensures its own survival.

Ethnicity has been peculiarly neglected and underestimated on the left, and my intention has been to confront the question of ethnicity from that perspective. If the left is traditionally defined by virtue of its will to reduce or eliminate relationships characterized by material social inequality, it has been less preoccupied by the various forms of consciousness and collective identity that have been a part of those relationships. The opposing tradition in social science is equally definable by virtue of its more supportive position in relation to existing social inequalities – structural functionalism, meritocracy, and socio-biology being cases in point. That tradition has expended much energy in attempting to neutralize the Marxian concept of class, which directly calls those inequalities into question. Instead, it has placed considerable emphasis on shared value-systems and various forms of collective identity – including ethnicity – as alternatives to class in the determination of social action. In this book I suggest that the classic Marxist neglect of ethnicity as an important social phenomenon is unsatisfactory, as is the rejection of the Marxian notion of class in non-Marxist tradition. Inasmuch as actors persist in acting in the name of ethnicity, and inasmuch as such action contributes to the maintenance or the elimination of social inequalities, then ethnicity is a phenomenon that those who seek to eliminate or reduce social inequality cannot afford to ignore.

One of the main problems in the domain of ethnic relations is that the plethora of detailed area studies and short theoretical pieces in specialist journals has given rise to a field that is fragmented at both the practical and the theoretical levels. Attempts to create unitary texts frequently succeed in doing little more than bundling the fragments together without establishing the links between them. There is a need for more elaborate presentations of the field from differing perspectives so that the overall issues can be more readily grasped, debated, and resolved. This book sets out to be one such presentation.

The book originally provided the basis for a course of lectures on class and ethnicity, and subsequently a graduate seminar on ethnicity in industrial societies, at McGill University. I have benefited greatly from the many exchanges and discussions that took place among the class and seminar participants during that two-year period. In addition, I would not have been able to undertake the process of revision without the careful and constructive comments of those who took the time to read through the manuscript in its early stages and discuss it with me. I particularly want to thank Linda Dawe, Tom Dunk, Mikhael Elbaz, Peter Gutkind, Minoo Moallem, Frances Mooring-Aldridge McAll, Philippe Planel, Rolande Pinard, Jérôme Rousseau, and Philip Cercone and Susan Kent Davidson of McGill-Queen's University Press.

Finally, I would not have been able to produce this book had it not been for a post-doctoral research fellowship generously provided by the Social Sciences and Humanities Research Council of Canada.

CHAPTER ONE

Introduction

The problem posed at the outset is as follows: to take a selective look, first, at what has been said about class and ethnicity, and second, at the interplay between class and ethnicity in different social contexts and at different periods, with the aim of finding out what the relationship between the two might be in the overall context of the generation and maintenance of social inequality. This implies the formulation of a theoretical model in which class and ethnicity as concepts are satisfactorily defined both in themselves and in relationship to each other within the context of a specific theoretical goal: if we can begin to understand how social inequalities reproduce and intensify themselves, then we can be better placed to put an end to them.

The logic of the argument is not dictated simply by opposition to inequality but by the necessity of moving towards fundamental social transformation. The problem as formulated may appear to be a fairly simple one, but in fact the whole question of social inequality is a sociological minefield. If we begin by asking about the relative significance of class and ethnicity in the determination of social action – in other words, about the relative significance of our Englishness or Frenchness or of our petty bourgeois or working-class social origins in the determination of the actions that we undertake – we at once find ourselves bogged down in the sociological mire. To ask the question "What is the relative significance of class and ethnicity in the determination of social action" is, in sociological terms and without further qualification, meaningless.

Class, for example, has been defined in as many ways as there are interests to be defended, whence the difficulty of attempting to arrive at common definitions and even of maintaining meaningful arguments when the opposing interests in question are not taken into account. But however it has been defined, it is none the less and invariably an essential conceptual tool in the understanding of inequality. Class is a concept that allows us to organize difference by grouping things or people into different categories depending on their resemblance or non-resemblance to each other according to certain criteria (and we are free to choose whatever criteria we like).

There, at least in part, is the problem of class. To say that there exists a class of plants that we will agree to refer to as trees is not the same as saying that there exists a class of persons we will refer to as a class. Class itself doesn't tell us anything about why the class exists in the first place. It has to be systematically linked to a particular set of persons or objects. In other words, the problem of class is that of the constant coming and going between its use as a "simple class concept" (in Weber's terms),[1] that is, its purely classificatory use, and its use as a generic concept or an ideal type within the context of a given theory. In the latter case, what is meant by the concept "class" differs necessarily from one theory to the next. What Marx means by it, for example, is indissociable from the theory of society and history he puts together in *Capital* and elsewhere. Equally, what either Weber or Dahrendorf means by class is related to his particular and distinctive way of conceptualizing society. The meaning of class is in fact so context-dependent that it makes no sense to talk in terms of the relationship between class and ethnicity unless we specify what theoretical construction or constructions we are referring to.

"Ethnicity" is equally likely to disintegrate in our hands the moment we attempt to get hold of it. Not only does it vary wildly from one conceptual system to another, but the very phenomena to which it tends to refer as a simple class concept are themselves inherently vague. In terms of everyday usage, we all know what a class is – in terms, for instance, of a "class" of objects, or a "class" of offenders. The concept has a precise meaning even if the criteria for classification can vary from one instance to the next. Ethnicity, on the other hand, as a simple class concept, is much less precise. If, for example, I maintain that in my case "ethnicity" means my Englishness, I would be considerably at a loss if someone were then to ask me what I mean by Englishness. Yet being English is not the same as being Welsh, which suggests that there is somewhere a set of patterns for action or ways of being that concretely represent what Englishness is supposed to be.

In attempting to bring together class and ethnicity, therefore, one would appear to be bringing together the inherently context-dependent and the inherently vague. They are both, however, key concepts in any discussion that takes social inequality as the general problem that is being addressed. Ethnicity, for all its vagueness, relates to the way in which people identify themselves as either belonging or not belonging to particular ethnic groups, and is therefore of central importance to the way in which people socialize, vote, fight, co-operate, or otherwise translate their beliefs into action. At the same time, we cannot understand social phenomena without classifying, particularly in the context of social inequality. The problem is not, of course, just a conceptual one but one that results from decades of trench warfare between assailants and defenders of the status quo whose inability to agree about concepts is directly linked to their inability to agree about the form that society should take.

The first phase of the argument that follows consists of a selective review of existing opinion about the significance of class and/or ethnicity. The point of this review is to understand what each individual theorist (or school of theorists) understands by the concept in question. I start from the premise that concepts only mean something in the context of the theoretical construction in which they are formulated, and that it is therefore necessary to present the principal characteristics of a theory prior to considering the precise meaning of a given concept within that theory. In the case of Marx we have little choice in the matter since it is simply impossible to extricate his theory of class from the body of his theory of society, if for no other reason than that he never actually got round to addressing class as a distinct problem.

It is equally important to situate Weber's notion of class in the context of his understanding of society, and indeed particularly so, in that the way in which he defines concepts can create the impression that we need look only at those sections of *Economy and Society* that relate to the concepts we are interested in. As I suggest in discussing Weber's concept of class, there are a number of themes that run through *Economy and Society* that have to be taken into account if we are to grasp the significance of the concept for Weber.[2] Even in the case of Parsons, for whom class is a thoroughly marginal concept, it is necessary to know what the theory is in relation to which class is considered to be marginal.[3] If, therefore, the general problem throughout this section remains that of coming to an understanding of the significance of class and ethnicity for the generation and maintenance of social inequality, specifically it is necessary to look beyond class and ethnicity themselves as concepts to the different theoretical wholes in which they have meaning.

This leads to the second aspect of the selective review of existing opinion, which is that of the principles of selection on which the review is based. As two key concepts in a key area of sociological argument, both class and ethnicity independently and in combination have generated an extensive literature. It has not, however, been my intention to treat a representative sample of everything that has been said about class and/or ethnicity, were that possible. The overall aim of the book necessarily determines the principles on the basis of which existing opinions are to be selectively reviewed. I take the theorist's attitude towards the maintenance or the termination of existing inequalities as the key criterion for the selection and organization of the opinions that are to be discussed.

In my presentation of critical attitudes towards inequality I take as representative the theoretical tradition stemming from Marx, both in its original Marxian form and in its various contemporary manifestations. In my presentation of non-critical attitudes I begin with Weber and continue with a selective discussion of a number of theoretical approaches that can be loosely grouped together as non-Marxist. In the former case, all the theoretical formulations start out from the premise of the unacceptability of the inequalities that are generated under capitalism, and they can be related to each other as so many different formulations operating in terms of the same overall objectives. In the latter case there is no such consensus against inequality. That does not mean that on occasion Weber or even Parsons may not allude to the desirability of greater equality (Weber)[4] or the unacceptability of the intergenerational transmission of inequality (Parsons),[5] but the core principles on which their work is based are either neutral or supportive in relation to inequality (cf Dahrendorf),[6] and they therefore set out in a different direction and with a different aim from those of Marxist theorists.

If the overall aim of this book dictates the selective principles on which the review of existing opinion is based, it also necessarily predetermines the kind of attitude that I am likely to have to the different opinions that are being reviewed. My basic assumption is that, in large part, the significance of opinions lies in their bias. There is thus no point in my attempting to conceal my own. You are forewarned that there is a built-in prejudice in the argument in favour of all those theorists whose attitude towards social inequality is systematically hostile.

In the central part of the book I adduce evidence relating to class, ethnicity, and social inequality in different places and at different times. The intention is to allow us to assess the various theories presented in the first part and, if necessary, to arrive at a more satisfactory theoretical formulation. The kind of information used depends on the social and historical context. In the case of the existence or otherwise of class in non-capitalist societies, the evidence is adduced mainly from ethnographical accounts and historical reconstructions of such societies. In the case of ethnicity and boundaries in the practice of social anthropology, the source material is mainly social anthropological. As the focus moves in from the past and the periphery towards class formation and the emergence of capitalist relations of production, then on into the heartland of contemporary industrial capitalist societies, so the source material is derived more from social history and sociology.

Again, the bringing forward of evidence is a question of selecting from an immense field of material to illustrate certain ways in which the phenomena have been and can be presented. At the same time the various ethnographical, sociological, and historical accounts are themselves constructions that are placed on the peoples and events they describe.

Each of them constitutes a "theory" of what was or is happening at the particular place and time in question. It is thus not strictly correct to suggest that we are moving from theory to description in moving from the first to the second part of the book. It is rather that in the first part we are concerned with general theories that seek to put forward general explanations concerning what happens across a range of different societies, whereas in the second we turn to accounts of those different societies themselves.

The movement in these central sections is not just one from the periphery and the past to the centre and the present, but also one in which the destinies of class and ethnicity come to be increasingly intertwined. Again the logic of the presentation is subordinated to the overall aim of the book. The presentation of the evidence is intended to demonstrate how productive relationships (and therefore class relationships in Marxian terms) can coexist at different times and places with different kinds of perceived relationships at the level of social identity and action. The basic sociological aim is to look for consistent patterns, across different societies and through time, in the ways in which collective social identity (in the form, for example, of ethnicity) and class relationships (in the Marxian sense of class) fit with each other. It is on the basis of those emergent patterns that I turn to the final section.

The final section addresses two principal problems. On the one hand, those who are critical of existing inequalities and who operate within the Marxian tradition tend to write off what people *perceive* as their relationships to each other – when not conceived in class terms – as of secondary importance to their "real" class relationships. Ethnicity is exactly such a set of perceptions in that it has no apparent relation to class, which is, in Marxian terms, the engine-room in which real inequalities are generated. Ethnicity and the related phenomenon of nationalism, therefore, have some difficulty finding a foothold within Marxist theory other than in the form of gigantic red herrings that somehow have to be nullified by increasing class consciousness.

Non-Marxist theory, on the other hand, is as much preoccupied with reducing the significance of class (in its Marxian guise) as Marxist theory is with reducing that of ethnicity. In non-Marxist theory, value-systems tend to have pride of place as the generative factor in social action and relationships. Ethnicity thus comes to be one of a series of core explanatory concepts, inasmuch as ethnic belongingness and value-systems can be considered to be closely related. Class, however, is presented as largely non-explanatory and tends to be used as a merely descriptive way of classifying people according to some criterion or other that is itself of secondary importance in the context of social action.

On one side the barricades are manned in the name of class without ethnicity, and on the other in the name of ethnicity without class. And yet, when we look at the social contexts in which racism or nationalism come into play against the background of pronounced class divisions in Marxian terms, or where, as in long-established class societies, privileged classes gradually transform themselves into in-marrying, self-protecting, and self-aware collectivities with a strong sense of common culture, identity, and origin, the impression remains that on both sides of the barricade there is a theoretical inadequacy.

If, in my view, one cannot come to an understanding of the way in which inequality is generated without a theory of class along Marxian lines, it is equally evident that we will never be able to understand how inequality is maintained unless we have a theory of ethnicity. We need to move towards a theoretical formulation in which class and ethnicity are related to each other as constituent concepts, corresponding to observable relationships in the world.

PART ONE

Class versus Ethnicity:
Manning the Barricades

CHAPTER TWO

The Hostile Opposition of Interests: Class in Marx

Marx's theory of class is indissociable from his theory of production and relations of production. I therefore begin not by looking at class itself but at the best single presentation of his more global theory of capitalist production and its antecedents: volume 1 of *Capital*. In beginning with *Capital* one is also in line with the prescription of Marx and Engels in the *German Ideology*, where they attack the young Hegelians for attempting to understand society solely at the level of ideas. For Marx and Engels, consciousness derives from activity in the world. So it is not from law, religion, or philosophy that one should set out to understand the world but from the activity of real people and their relationship to each other in specific social formations and at particular epochs.[1]

Marx makes a similar point in the *Introduction to the Critique of Political Economy*, although in this case it is not the young Hegelians but political economists who come in for criticism. They at least are primarily concerned with the activity of living subjects, but for Marx, even though that concern might be preferable to the philosophical speculations of the Hegelians, it is still inadequate to limit oneself to the subjects themselves in a society divided along class lines and in which individual activity is determined by class position. At the same time it is impossible to start from class, in that class itself is inseparable from the relations of production and the process of production that underlie it. To understand class, and ultimately society, it is therefore necessary to begin with production.[2]

In any society people have to produce in order to survive, and in any society individuals exchange what they produce according to their needs.[3] Such exchange may be based simply on the production of surplus or on the specialization of given producers in producing specific items for exchange. In the simplified form of exchange, producers confront each other as producers, both having a surplus of some item that the other wants. There is no mystery attached to this process. The amount of each item offered or accepted in exchange depends on the amount of work that went into producing it, collecting it, or bringing it to the point of exchange. The generalization of such relations of exchange necessarily gives rise to the existence of markets in which producers can meet each other to exchange. It also gives rise to the situation in which producers come to know from past experience how much of any given commodity they are likely to get in return for what they bring to the market. The development of such a conventionally established set of exchange rates or relative values in turn serves to obscure the fact that commodities are exchanged for each other as the embodiments of the labour that went into them. Exchange in the market thus comes to be seen as a relationship between the objects that are exchanged rather than between the people who produced them in the first place.

The generalization of such exchange relations leads to a further development, in which one particular commodity begins to stand apart from the rest such that the market values of all other products come to be measured in terms of it rather than in terms of each other. This takes the process of mystification one stage further, in that a relationship between producers that had come to be seen as a relationship between products now comes to be seen as a relationship between the individual product and the universal equivalent, which might be any easily transportable and generally available commodity such as cattle or slaves.

The final stage in the mystification of exchange as a relationship between direct producers comes with the development of a particular kind of universal equivalent, which in itself has no use value except in so far as it can be exchanged for any available commodity. That universal equivalent is, of course, money, and it can quickly cease to be in any real sense the equivalent of the commodities whose relative values it symbolizes, inasmuch as the labour that it embodies, as the debased product of royal mints or state-controlled printing presses, ceases to bear any relation to its face value. What remains a relationship between producers (or producers and non-producers) comes to be seen as the realization of a given product's money value, according, for example, to demand for that product in the market-place.

In this simplified evolutionary sketch of exchange, the exchangers themselves are now in a more or less complete state of mystification, or rather, their attempts to understand what it is that underlies exchange and rates of exchange is complicated by the apparent role of money. The existence of money creates further possibilities. Hitherto producers have arrived at the market to sell in order to buy, that is, to exchange their products. It is equally possible, however, to arrive on the market-place to buy in order to sell. All that this presumes is that the would-be buyer is possessed of sufficient money in the first place to be able to buy. This poses no problem for the theory of exchange if the money received by selling only exceeds that advanced in buying by the amount of value added to the commodity by the seller (who might, for example, have bought it in one market and carried it to another for sale). But it is more difficult to explain where an individual realizes more money from the transaction than could possibly be accounted for by the labour that he may himself have expended between buying and selling. It cannot be the case that he simply buys cheap and sells dear, since other sellers would soon start doing the same and he would be forced to buy as dearly as he sells.

This is essentially the conundrum posed by capitalist production, where the capitalist uses his accumulated capital to buy raw materials on the market and subsequently sells them transformed into commodities at a profit over and above what they cost him as raw materials and beyond the normal return for any labour that might have been expended on their transformation. Marx's answer to this conundrum is that there is one commodity on the market that, in being used, creates new value, such that its purchaser can then realize the value thus created in the form of profit. That commodity is labour-power, or the capacity of an individual to work for an agreed period of time and in return for the receipt of a money payment.

It is fundamental to Marx's theory of value that value is reduceable to and created by labour. So if I can persuade someone to work for me for less than the value that they create (what they create being realizable by me on the market in terms of money), I will have realized the apparently impossible feat of using money to make money. I then have the choice of either consuming the difference and finding myself with the same amount of money as I had originally advanced; hoarding it; or returning to the market with my increased funds to repeat the process, although now in the position of being able to buy a larger amount of raw material and a greater quantity of labour-power to transform it. It is in this latter context that the money – in Marx's terms – becomes capital, and the process of production to which it gives rise a capitalist mode of production.

In the *Introduction to the Critique of Political Economy* Marx criticizes the capitalist economists for attaching too much importance to the individual as a unit of analysis when we need to look not only beyond the individual to his class position but beyond class to the process of production that underlies it.[4] It is interesting, therefore, that in *Capital* the analysis turns on the interactions of individuals in order to explain the development of money or the origin of capital, but they are individuals drained of their individuality, being rather the representatives of different categories of producers or of classes of producers and non-producers.

For Marx, the existence of a class presupposes the existence of another class from which it is differentiated and to which it is opposed. Where direct producers exchange with each other and any opposition is limited to the exploitation of parallel or complementary ecological niches at the local level, from which none of the groups involved benefits at the expense of other groups, there are no classes, inasmuch as there is no broad division of society into opposed interest groups. Where, however, the process of hiring wage labour becomes generalized across a social formation such that a large number of individuals are involved in the hiring of workers and are able to sell what those workers produce for more than it cost to hire them in the first place, and where they use the money thus accumulated continually to return to the market in order to buy raw materials and the labour-power necessary to transform those materials into commodities, there necessarily come into existence two opposed classes of capitalists and workers.

The central part of the first volume of *Capital* relates to what happens once the purchaser of labour-power and the labour-power thus purchased disappear behind the factory gates – in other words, the process whereby labour-power creates value for the capitalist.[5] First, the capitalist uses his accumulated capital to buy the machinery and the raw material that is to be used in the process of production. Second, he presents himself on the labour-market to buy the labour-power necessary to do the work. We have already seen that what the capitalist pays for the labour-power and what he receives for its product are not the same, and that this is the source of the accumulation of capital that makes the capitalist what he is. If we look more closely at this difference, we find that what the capitalist pays for labour-power is equal to or greater than the cost of reproduction or subsistence of that labour-power, that is, the cost of the necessities of life both for the individual workers and for their families. What he receives for the product on the market is determined both by what he originally paid for the raw materials and machinery used in production and by the value that has been added by the labour-power to those raw materials in the process of transformation. It is this added value, realized in its money form, that is split into that part which goes to pay the costs of the subsistence of the work-force and that part which makes up the profit of the capitalist. The goal of the capitalist is to maintain, and if possible to increase that part of the value created that goes into his pocket rather than the worker's.

Workers thus work partly to acquire the means of their own subsistence and partly to produce surplus value for the capitalist. Their working day is made up of (what is for them) necessary labour on the one hand and surplus labour on the other. Inasmuch as there is a certain fixity to what is necessary for the subsistence of labour-power, any extension of the working day will directly benefit the capitalist. The capitalist will therefore do everything he can to increase the length of the working day. However, there are evident limits to such increases, not the least being that each day is restricted to twenty-four hours and that within those twenty-four hours some minimum amount of time has to be devoted by the workers to eating and sleeping, and this apart from any pressure that may be put on the capitalist by organized labour to reduce working hours.

So the capitalist is forced to find ways of increasing surplus value other than by increasing the length of the working day. This can only be achieved by reducing the amount of time that the worker spends working for his own subsistence and thereby increasing the time that he spends working for the capitalist within the fixed span of the working day. This can be done by increasing the productivity of the individual worker, a process that starts with the elementary division of labour and specialization within the process of production, and continues with mechanization, where the same amount of labour expended leads to increase in output. This in itself does not increase the value created but rather spreads the same amount of value across a greater range of products. However, it does give rise to two results. First, it gives a competitive advantage where other capitalists have not mechanized to the same extent, such that the innovating capitalist can undersell his competitors while still realizing a greater quantity of surplus value than they do in relation to the same number of workers. This advantage, however, will only last as long as the other capitalists do not introduce the same changes. Second, the cheapening of the individual product through increasing productivity will, if sufficiently widespread, cheapen the cost of the necessities of life to the worker and therefore reduce the cost of labour-power to the capitalist, thereby increasing surplus value.

This is the arena in which the struggle between the two classes of workers and capitalists takes place within the capitalist mode of production, with the capitalists doing all within their power to maintain and extend the length of the working day and, failing that, to increase that part of the working day in which the worker works solely for their benefit, and organized labour in turn doing all in its power to improve the terms on which it sells itself to capital. Inasmuch as the bulk of all production in a given society takes place along capitalist lines, the struggle between the contending classes of workers and capitalists becomes the dominant class confrontation in that society. This does not mean that there are not other class confrontations within the same society but only that they come to be marginal.

Marx, for example, distinguishes between the "ruling class," the *Mittelstände* (literally, "middle-status groups"), and the "working class," where the ruling class is composed of the industrial bourgeoisie and the landed aristocracy, and the middle-status groups of small farmers, artisans, small manufacturers, and small traders.[6] But the landed aristocracy, although they were still over-represented in the power structure of early nineteenth-century Britain, were increasingly marginal to the central opposition in that society between the working class and the industrial bourgeoisie. The middle-status groups are also marginal to this conflict except in so far as they include elements that are liable to be drawn down into the working class. The working class is also distinguished from the possessing class and is therefore by definition the non-possessing or the non-propertied class.[7] This latter distinction relates directly to the historical conditions that lead to the existence of a working class prepared to sell its labour for less than the value that it produces.

Those conditions are simply that there should exist a part of the population that does not itself possess the means whereby it can produce what is necessary for its own survival. It has direct access neither to the land that could be used for its subsistence nor to the equipment and raw materials that could be used to produce the commodities that then could be exchanged for the necessities of life. The pre-condition, therefore, for the existence of the opposed classes of capitalists and workers is that the former should have accumulated sufficient funds to set the capitalist process of production in motion and the latter should have been removed, for example, from whatever land they might have possessed and have no alternative but to sell their labour-power in order to survive. It is this lack of alternative that provides not only for the initial development of the capitalist mode but also for its continuation.

There are two ways in which the necessary conditions for the development of capitalist relations of production (that is, the relationships between capitalists and workers) can be brought into existence. The first is that of piecemeal development within a particular social formation; the second occurs where the conditions of existence are forcibly imposed from the outside. In the first volume of *Capital* Marx outlines the process whereby in Britain a population primarily involved in agricultural production was gradually removed from the land (or the land removed from them) subsequent to the demise of feudalism.[8] They were ultimately replaced by capitalist tenant farmers hiring wage-labour and producing for the market, a form of agricultural production that cannot easily coexist with a subsistence-oriented peasantry – except where the latter are confined to economically marginal lands – if for no other reason than that it was much more profitable for the landlords, who were thus keen to get rid of their (often insolvent) peasant tenants. This development succeeded in removing a large part of the peasant population from the land and thus forced them into the towns in search of work, at the same time creating the very urban market that the capitalist farmers needed for their produce. The third element in this process was the fledgling capitalist manufacturer – the difference between him and the existing small masters being only one of degree[9] – who could meet the rising demand for work on any terms that he chose to name.

The opposed classes of workers and capitalists thus come into existence after a long process of brutal separation of the agricultural producers from the land. However, that process of separation once completed, it is economic necessity rather than brute force that keeps the system in operation – according to Marx – since the working class has no choice but to sell itself to capital on capital's terms, more particularly since it is surrounded by a reserve army of labour consisting of the surplus population in the countryside and the unemployed in the towns, who will accept any terms as preferable to none.[10]

If the first volume of *Capital* allows us to look at class within and in relation to the capitalist mode of production, the *Communist Manifesto*[11] and the *Eighteenth Brumaire of Louis Napoleon*[12] allow us to see class in action. The *Communist Manifesto* – as befits a political manifesto – is of a different temper from *Capital*. The coming into existence of a working class under capitalism is presented as part of a historical process that will eventually lead to the overthrow of the class of capitalists and the appropriation of the state and the means of production by the proletariat. The bourgeoisie have therefore come into existence with the very class that will destroy them, but at the same time they are also in continual conflict with other status groups and class fractions. They are in conflict with the old landed aristocracy, for example, and with the "middle-status groups: the small manufacturer, the small trader, the artisan, the small farmer," all of whom "are locked in struggle with the bourgeoisie in order to ensure their survival as middle-status groups."[13] But the bourgeoisie is itself rent into fractions, each of which is in conflict with the other, while the different national bourgeoisies fight over international markets. The picture presented by the *Manifesto* is therefore one of generalized conflict within and between classes, but the principal and historically necessary and portentous conflict is the struggle between the progeny of capitalism itself, the two opposed classes of proletariat and bourgeoisie.

The *Eighteenth Brumaire* looks at events in France between February 1848 and December 1851 in the light of class struggle. The different contending parties were the proletariat, the landed aristocracy, the industrial and commercial fractions of the bourgeoisie, the army, the Church, the peasantry, the petty bourgeoisie, and, above all, Louis Napoleon, who reinforced his position by buying support from the "disreputable classes" – the lumpenproletariat, among whom Marx includes discharged prisoners, vagabonds, and pickpockets.[14] In the background was the conflict between the two main fractions of the ruling class, the landed aristocracy and the bourgeoisie, although that conflict was marginal to the events that took place from 1848 to 1851. In 1848 the Paris proletariat was defeated by the combined forces of the army and the "disreputable" classes (organized as a mobile guard) backed up by, among others, the bourgeoisie, the petty bourgeoisie, and the Church. Subsequently, the petty bourgeois democrats were defeated by the bourgeois party of order, which thereafter emerged as the dominant party in the legislative National Assembly in the second half of 1851. But the parliamentary experience of the bourgeoisie was an unhappy one, the more so since it prevented them from concentrating on the accumulation of surplus value, and by December 1851 they had connived at their own downfall in the form of a *coup d'état*.

If, in Paris, the various classes are locked in struggle with each other, the mass of the population, the peasantry, remain on the periphery, but with the more conservative among them giving their support to Bonaparte. It is in relation to the peasantry that Marx comes closest to giving a definition of class: "In so far as millions of families live under economic conditions that separate them from other classes in terms of their way of life, their interests, and their make-up, and that place them in hostile opposition to those other classes, they make up a class. In so far as there exist only local connections among small farmers, with the similarity of their interests not giving rise to any broader sense of community, national association, or political organization, they do not make up a class."[15] So the peasantry both is and is not a class. It is a class inasmuch as it is composed of a mass of families in similar economic and social circumstances whose interests are opposed to those of other classes, but it is not a class inasmuch as the individual peasant smallholders never leave their own restricted locality and weld themselves into a broad political unit.

It is just this state of self-awareness as a class that Marx and Engels in the *Communist Manifesto* describe as coming into existence within the working class, by virtue of its being concentrated in the great centres of capitalist industrial production, and that in *Capital*, volume 1, is referred to as the *Selbstgefühl der Arbeiter*, the "self-awareness of the workers."[16] According to Marx in the *Eighteenth Brumaire*, the French peasantry *are* a class in the sense that they share the same class position, and they may even be *aware* of themselves as a class (although Marx does not dwell on the point), but they are incapable of *acting* as a class, being scattered across the French countryside and easy prey at the local level to the manipulation and control of state bureaucrats. It is not so much class consciousness that is important for the existence of class but the political action that flows from that consciousness.

If we piece them together Marx's works (including those where he collaborates with Engels) provide us with a theory of class based on an unravelling of nineteenth-century relations of production. Not the least of the assumptions underlying that theory is that it is the relationship of individuals to the process of production that determines their social being. And not only are social and class position determined by that relationship, but also the consciousness one might have of one's position. Or rather, one's consciousness is determined by one's class position which is itself related to production. It is for this reason that the bourgeois classical economists are described in the third volume of *Capital* as being incapable, because of their class-bounded consciousness, of understanding the process whereby value is created in production, just as their predecessors were incapable of conceiving of profit as being anything other than the natural and just return on capital advanced, rent as the just return for land-ownership, and wages as the just return for labour.[17]

Apart from the central position occupied by production and the different kinds of appropriation built around production, a further general characteristic of Marx's theory is that of historical necessity. This is set within a theory of history in which human society in its beginnings is conceived of as having been relatively egalitarian and communistic, and in which it will, eventually, return to a state of classlessness, having passed through several millennia of class struggle.[18] Thus bourgeois society is a stage in this development that follows necessarily from the breakdown of feudalism and will result, necessarily, in the construction by the proletariat of a classless society.

At the centre of Marx's theory of society and history is thus the notion of a gradually unfolding conflict in which the primary units of conflict are not individuals, nor localized associations, but classes. There may be conflict within different classes – between, for example, different sections of the working class or different fractions of the bourgeoisie – but those conflicts are themselves overshadowed by and secondary to the global conflict between bourgeoisie and proletariat. Classes are defined in the *Eighteenth Brumaire* in terms of the "hostile" (*feindlich*) opposition of interests.[19] They are not definable simply by what distinguishes them from other classes but by embattled opposition to one another, a war of positions in which a loss for one side can only be a gain for the other. Class is thus a central concept in Marx's theory of society, linking together the themes of the determinant role of production and the historical necessity of the struggle between classes leading to the overthrow of the bourgeois order.

CHAPTER THREE

Neither Central nor Absent: Class in Weber's Economy and Society

In *Economy and Society* Weber seeks to understand and explain human action.[1] There are two principal ways in which action can be understood: as a concrete case where two or more individuals act towards each other on the basis of certain specific motives, or as a pure type of action. The study of history, since it is concerned with the explanation of events, is concerned with the first of these alternatives, the elucidation of concrete cases of action. Sociology, by contrast, is concerned with pure types of action – that is, it abstracts from concrete actions those aspects that are sufficiently common to warrant our speaking of pure types. A sociology that seeks to understand thus aims to distance itself from the individual and idiosyncratic aspects of the concrete and produce a series of refined categories and concepts that can serve as classifications of action. We need, therefore, to start by looking at the concept of action itself, which has come to be of central importance to an entire school of non-Marxist sociology.

For Weber, sociology should be principally concerned with the acting individual (as a pure type), inasmuch as individual action is socially oriented, that is, oriented towards the behaviour of others. Just as Marx begins with the encounter between producers meeting to exchange and places primary importance on the material aspect of that exchange, so Weber also begins with an encounter, but of a kind different from that considered by Marx. What interests Weber is the motivation underlying the encounter, the different motivations providing the means for categorizing actions.

Weber distinguishes among four principal kinds of motivation for action. The first is action accompanied by calculation on the part of the actor in terms of a particular end or goal. In other words, the kind of action that is undertaken is dictated by the goal that is sought. The actor calculates that a given action is the best way of achieving the intended goal. The action is, therefore, "rational" in terms of the goal. The second type of action is undertaken on the basis of values rather than ends. Both these types of action are rationally justifiable and explicable in the light of either the achievement of a specific goal or a system of values. They result from a process of rational calculation that serves as a basis for the action. In the two remaining cases there is no such rationality behind the action. The first of these is based on emotional response. It refers to any non-self-conscious action towards others that results from emotions such as anger or affection and that is explicable in the light of such emotions and because they are not the result of any prior calculation. The fourth and final pure type relates to habitual action, which is equally undertaken unself-consciously and without prior reflection.[2]

These four kinds of motivation, relating to goals, values, emotions, and habit, underlie the four pure types of action. They are "pure" in that they are refined out from the mass of concretely observable actions and do not necessarily correspond to any one of those actions. In other words, there may never have been a purely goal-rational action, but rather all actions represent a mix of two or more of these four types. But this does not undermine the classification, since it is necessary – in order to understand action – to distil out the various component motivations, so that in our subsequent attempts to understand action we can assess them in the light of what we know to be the fundamental component motivations.

There is another way in which these four types are out of key with concrete action, which is that we frequently act in a state of only semi-awareness of our own motives. Actions may be classifiable as goal (or instrumentally) rational, where the actors themselves may be unconscious of the rationality underlying the act or may not have rationalized the act to themselves beforehand.[3] The pure type of wholly (and therefore self-consciously) rational action may be only marginally present among concrete actions, but this does not prevent sociology from classifying such actions in terms of pure types of motivation, which themselves are refinements of the confused and semi-conscious motivations that accompany any given action.

This breaking-down of social action into its main component motivations is as basic to Weber's theory of society as relations of production are to Marx. It brings up a primary distinction that is present throughout *Economy and Society*, that between "rationality" and "irrationality." The distinction has its basis in the four pure types of action.[4] The first two, goal- and value-oriented action, are based on rational forms of motivation, in that the actors rationalize their actions in terms of an immediate goal or a system of values. The second two, emotional and habitual action, are irrational, in that the action is not the result of rational calculation but rather of non-reflective response to emotion or habit. There is a further distinction between goal- and value-rationality that is of importance for the following analysis. Value-rationality is considered to be substantive, in that it is the substance of an action that is rational in terms of values. The goal- or instrumentally rational act, by contrast, is not rational in itself but only in so far as it leads to the achievement of a goal. Such acts are therefore not substantively but only formally rational, in that a form of action has to be gone through in order to attain a desired goal.

These distinctions between rational and irrational action, and between substantive and formal rationality, are the foundation stones on which the edifice of Weber's theory of society is constructed. They signal that for Weber – and for a sociology that seeks to understand social action – collectivities must be seen as collectivities of acting individuals.[5] The four pure types of motivation of individual action (in relation to other individuals) thus remain of central importance even in discussion relating to large-scale collectivities. To demonstrate the role of these concepts and pure types in Weber's subsequent analysis, I look at four areas that play a major part in that analysis: economy, law, administrative organization, and religion.

In all these cases the distinctions between rationality and irrationality and between formal and substantive rationality are central. There is a dominant theme in which the sequence of different kinds of social formation through history is viewed as a development from irrationality to rationality. In production, for example, there is at one end of the scale the mode of life of peasant producers, who year after year repeat the same work-cycle on the basis of a traditional adaptation to the habitat in which they find themselves. In so far as any particular task in which they may be involved is dictated by tradition, peasant production is essentially irrational.[6] What is true of small-scale peasant producers is also true of other subsistence-oriented peoples, whether they be nomadic pastoralists, hunter-gatherers, or settled agriculturalists.

At the other end of the scale is developed capitalist industrial production. Here we find fully elaborated formal rationality: the process of production is the result of prior calculation by the capitalist and leads to the realization of a goal in the form of profit, which in turn is the basis for the accumulation of capital. There is thus nothing "irrational" about the capitalist process of production, since it is subject to close and continuous calculation. It is also formally rational in that its rationality is not to be found in the process as such but only in the process as the form that has to be gone through for the achievement of the goal. It is this element of pure, formal rationality that distinguishes capitalist production from prior or alternative forms of production, and such rationality can be reduced to the notion of calculation. The capitalist calculates beforehand the quantity of capital that is in his possession and repeats the same calculation after the cycle of production is completed. In the difference between the two figures lies the whole rationale of the capitalist system of production.

Weber makes a distinction between organizations based on capitalist rationality and what he describes as "budgetary units," which can run from the household or the extended family to the courts of princes or the domains of feudal lords.[7] In the latter case production is for consumption by – and the subsistence of – the budgetary unit itself, whereas in the former case production is oriented towards profit. Budgetary units, however, contain the seeds of a more rationalistic form of production wherever they produce a surplus and dispose of that surplus on the market, it being the market that allows for the development of capitalist accounting and the capitalist system of production.

The distinction between rationality and irrationality is thus central to Weber's conception of economic action and is set in an evolutionary perspective. The formal/substantive distinction also has important impli-cations for such action. Capitalist production is an example of formal rationality since it is instrumentally related to the realization of particular goals. However, any economic action which has its *raison d'être* in a system of values rather than in a set of goals to be achieved is not formally but substantively rational.[8] For example, the reorganization of an industrial enterprise so that the workers will have an equal say with management in the organization of production, in line with certain social-democratic values, is substantively rational in terms of those values. It may, however, be formally irrational, in that the realization of the goals of the enterprise – where there is no change of ownership and where the goals are under-stood to be profitability for the owners – can become problematical, given that profitability may be dependent on the maintenance of relations of domination. There is, therefore, a distinction maintained by Weber between the formal rationality of capitalist production and the formal irrationality (which can be another way of saying substantive rationality) of alternative ways of organizing production, along the lines, for example, of social-democratic or socialist value-systems.

The history of legal systems, administrative organization, and religion are also set in the evolutionary sequence of irrationality-rationality. Along-side the increasing rationalization of production and of economic action, Weber considers that systems of religious belief and of law were required to change in accordance with that rationalization. Law, for example, goes through a series of stages, leading from "charismatic legal revelation" through "empirical creation" and "finding" of the law, and its subsequent imposition by secular or theocratic powers, to, ultimately, its systematic elaboration and the professional administration of justice.[9] There is thus a development towards rationality and away from the irrationality of early legal systems, which might be typified by trial by ordeal or the consulta-tion of oracles. This development is not, however, something internal to law itself but rather reflects the changing demands that developing ration-ality in economic action makes upon existing legal systems. In Weber's terms, such development requires a legal system that provides a sure basis for capitalistic calculation, not only because the right of property on the basis of which the calculation is made has to be guaranteed and protected in law, but also because the character of any possible legal decision concerning any aspect of the productive process has to be known in advance and allowed for within the calculation.[10] Rational capitalistic accounting requires the existence of a rationally formulated and coherent body of law.

This is equally true of the form of administrative organization that is required by capitalism, which again needs to be predictable, dependable, and instrumentally rational to be the most efficient means of achieving the required administrative goal. Parallel to the rationalization and the systematization of the law there has developed an administrative system that fits these requirements: bureaucracy.[11] Bureaucracies do not operate merely on the basis of blind tradition, as in the case of patriarchalism or patrimonialism, where authority is traditionally vested in the head of a household or extended family, nor are they constructed around the charismatic qualities of exceptional individuals (who have authority by virtue of that charisma), but operate rather according to a set of established rules.[12] Ideally bureaucrats act in accordance with those rules, are paid a fixed sum on the basis of the fulfilment of the tasks that are assigned to them – and hence should gain no advantage by abusing their position – and are promoted within the hierarchical bureaucratic structure according to how well they meet the technical requirements of the different levels. The bureaucracy remains a structure of domination in which individual bureaucrats are subject to the authority of those above them, with ultimate authority being vested in the person occupying the highest position, but the basis for that authority remains a system of rules.

So, just as capitalism requires a predictable and instrumentally rational legal system, it also requires a dependable and efficient bureaucracy. Weber further suggests that a developed bureaucracy also requires capitalism as the most rational way of providing the fiscal basis for its own existence.[13] Bureaucracy itself represents the splitting-off and independent development of the calculating, planning, recording, and administering that necessarily accompanies all productive activity. The picture that Weber presents us with is thus that of a set of institutions and structures developing in parallel along an axis running from irrationality to rationality, with, as the central feature of this development, the coming into existence of a formally rational mode of economic action based on capitalist accounting. The study of religion is no exception to this general presentation.

If ethics and economic rationality have generally been mutually exclusive, there are two religious systems that have managed to combine the two, Protestantism and Judaism. In Judaism, believers behave ethically towards their co-religionists (and their behaviour is therefore substantively rational, being based on the tenets of Jewish law) and according to strict economic rationality (and therefore non-ethically) towards gentiles. In Protestantism, by contrast, substantive and formal rationality in economic action are combined, in the sense that the success of such action is taken to be a sign that the successful individual is in possession of God's grace and is assured of salvation.[14] Economic action for Protestants is both the instrumental means for the realization of profit and for the accumulation of capital, and, in so far as it is successful (and the resulting profit is not dishonestly come by), is in itself an assurance of salvation.

Both Judaism and Protestantism are somewhat exceptional, although Judaism is less so, since a distinction is made between formally and substantively rational economic action involving non-believers and co-religionists respectively. Protestantism, though, represents an isolated example of a rational, ethical religion growing up alongside the development of rationalistic capitalist enterprise. It is exceptional in that the bourgeoisie – and capitalism, according to Weber, has existed in one form or another at many periods in history[15] – has traditionally been non-religious, given the general incompatibility of ethics and economic rationality. And where the modern period has seen the birth of capitalist manufacturing and the coming into being of an industrial proletariat, that proletariat also tends to be non-religious (being involved in a capitalistically rationalized form of production) except where it has substituted a belief in a socialist millennium for the old religions and the belief in salvation after death that characterized the oppressed strata of the past.[16]

Protestantism excepted, therefore, formal rationality tends to displace religious belief. There is consequently a polarity in the sphere of religion that parallels that in other spheres (for example, economy, law, administration) and in which there is a progression from irrationality in religious belief and economic action at one end to the development of rational ethical religions, or the displacement of religious belief altogether, and of formally rational economic action at the other. There is a different kind of polarity within those social formations in which rational forms of religious belief are the preserve of a privileged intellectual stratum – or a stratum that has the leisure to be intellectual – and irrationality is the characteristic of the lower strata. In China, for example, Confucianism led to the coexistence of a rational, bureaucratized intellectualism at one level with the popular maintenance of irrational cults and magical beliefs at another.[17] Rationalized bureaucracies have always frowned on such irrationalism among the lower orders but have none the less encouraged it as necessary for the upholding of their authority over those same strata. Another kind of polarity has existed between social strata in relation to salvation religions, which have traditionally, although by no means always, been adhered to by those whose lot in life is insupportable without the assurance of a measure of improvement in the life to come. Upper strata have tended to be more preoccupied by justifying and rationalizing their privileges than by seeking the assurance of salvation, although here again Protestantism manages to interpret present privilege as the sign of the possession of God's grace and therefore the assurance of future salvation.

Weber's theory of society is thus a theory of action, and his theory of action is reduceable to an overriding opposition between irrationality and rationality. This opposition itself becomes the basis for a theory of the historical development of institutions, of belief-systems and – at a fundamental level – of economic organization. It also provides the basis for one kind of distinction among the different strata within an existing social formation. All this leads up to the principal question to be asked in this chapter concerning the role of the concept of class in Weber's theory of society and history.

If the great progress of history has been one that began in the mists of traditionalism and irrationality and has laboriously dragged itself up to the heights of capitalistic rationality, and if religion, law, administration, and economic organization have all been transformed in the process, class, to some extent, stands apart. In Marx's theory of society and history, class is both central and absent, in the sense that class struggle is the driving force behind history but the theory of class itself remains relatively unelaborated. In Weber's theory, by contrast, it is neither central nor absent. It is not central in that the focal point of Weber's theory and analysis lies elsewhere (in the rationality and irrationality of social action), but it is not absent either in that it occupies a relatively significant position in the analysis.

For Marx, class is essentially a relationship between producers and nonproducers, in which the latter appropriate the surplus production of the former. These two opposed groups constitute classes and have existed in the variety of forms that have characterized such appropriation through history. For Weber, production and relationship to production is only a part of the question. He distinguishes three kinds of class: "property classes," "commercial classes," and "social classes."[18] Class situation for Weber is reduceable to a set of shared conditions of existence, or the extent to which a given set of individuals can command goods and services on the market. In so far as such individuals are able to command relatively more goods and services than others and at the same time have the possibility of attaining positions of high standing, and – it is presumed – of thereby achieving inner satisfaction, they occupy a positively privileged class position, as opposed to everybody else, who is negatively privileged.[19]

The single most important way of having privileged access to utilities, or goods and services – and "goods" are defined by Weber as being the advantages of present or future use to be obtained from non-human objects, while "services" are those obtained from human agents[20] – is through the possession of property, which explains the importance given by Weber to the "propertied" class. The propertied class uses its property to provide itself with an income that does not derive from its own productive or commercial activity but from the activity of those who are obliged to pay to use that property. It then uses the various forms of "rent" it receives to consolidate its privileged position as an acquirer of the most expensive goods and services, of the most costly status privileges (for example, private education), and to gain control of the formation of capital itself in production, frequently controlling the nomination of personnel to executive positions. At the other end of the scale are the "negatively privileged" property classes, who have less than no property, being either in debt, bankrupt, or unfree. In between are what are described as the "middle-status classes," which include those who possess property but not such as can provide them with an income from rent – for example, small peasant freeholders, craftsmen, and small-scale entrepreneurs.[21] This analysis of Weber's concept of the propertied class suggests that there are two ways of approaching his concept of class. There is the sense in which class situation is reduceable to the ability to command goods and services, to achieve social standing, and to arrive at a state of inner satisfaction, although it is not clear what this state of inner satisfaction is supposed to consist of. And that situation is itself determined by one's relation to property.

A commercial class as opposed to a propertied class is one whose conditions of existence, and therefore class situation, are not determined by property but by the productive or commercial activity in which the members of the class are involved, or by the services that they provide.[22] Here again there are negatively and positively privileged classes, with, at the top, entrepreneurs, merchants, bankers, and some highly skilled workers and sought-after professionals, and, at the bottom, skilled, semi-skilled, and unskilled labourers, with various other categories in between.

Weber suggests, therefore, that there are two principal determining factors for class situation: one's property (or lack of it), and one's professional, commercial, or productive activity in the world, irrespective of property. The third and final category in Weber's threefold distinction is "social class." A social class is made up of the "totality of those class situations between which individual and generational mobility is easily possible and typically takes place."[23] Where, for example, a negatively privileged property class can become a negatively privileged commercial class by giving up its rack-rented smallholdings and finding employment as unskilled labour in the town, then there can presumably be said to exist a social class that includes the impoverished rural tenant and the unskilled urban labourer.

Weber distinguishes among four principal social classes: the working class; the petty bourgeoisie; propertyless intellectuals, highly skilled white-collar workers, and civil servants; and the large-scale property owners and the privileged. Individual mobility among the four classes is restricted, but generational mobility among the first three is relatively easy, while some mobility is allowed between the third and fourth.[24]

There is one further important distinction in this review of concepts, that between class and "status group." Class includes all those individuals who fall within a certain bracket, whether they are aware of it or not and whatever the criteria of selection.[25] A class is not a group but simply a classification, although under certain historical circumstances it may become more than that. A status group, by contrast, is a collectivity that chooses to think of itself as a group and is recognized by others as such. Whatever the basis for its existence (and it can easily overlap with class in that large landowners, for example, as a fraction of the privileged property class, might regard themselves and be regarded as a status group), its "groupness" is established through and maintained by a shared style of life that separates members from outsiders. Where that style of life is expensive, the status group is *de facto* restricted to the rich. Where it can only be acquired through a costly and privileged education, it may be restricted to those who were born rich. But it may have other bases independent of wealth and equally selective – for example, hereditary charisma or monopolistic appropriation of power. Indeed, the boundaries of status groups may as easily cut across those of classes as coincide with them.[26] We have, therefore, a set of concepts relating to different kinds of collectivities, which may be self-conscious status groups, all-embracing social classes, or specific kinds of class, based, for example, on property. Before further evaluating these concepts, we need to look at the way in which they are used in that part of *Economy and Society* that is concerned with historical analysis rather than conceptual definition.

I suggested above that the concept of class in Weber's theory of society is neither central nor absent, in that it plays only a subordinate role in the theory while still occupying an important position in the definition of concepts. This statement needs to be explained and justified. Class struggle, which is the driving force in Marx's theory of society, is for Weber only the possible *consequence* of particular kinds of class structure. The difference between positively and negatively privileged property classes can under certain circumstances give rise to class struggle, but that struggle is only a result of class situation, which itself follows from the concentration of property on the one hand and the separation from property on the other.[27] Property (particularly property that constitutes the means of production) is also important for Marx, but is itself the outcome of, is maintained by, and will be dissolved through class struggle. One might say that Marx sees property as a form of class struggle. For Marx, therefore, class and class struggle are factors from which consequences flow, while for Weber they are only consequences of other primary factors.

The place of class struggle in Weber's theory of history is thus different from its place in that of Marx. Weber identifies three main phases in the history of class struggle: between debtors and creditors in antiquity, particularly where a city-based warrior class reduces the surrounding small farmers to a state of debt-bondage; over the means of subsistence in the Middle Ages; and under industrial capitalism, over wages.[28] But in none of these cases is class struggle *necessarily* present. On the contrary, it is only likely to arise where the nature of the given class structure is transparent to those who do not benefit from it, such that the consciousness that they have of their common class situation may lead to rational association, rather than just "acts of intermittent and irrational protest."[29]

For Weber, a given society may be divisible into classes, and class struggle may follow at particular moments in time as a form of rational action by the negatively privileged. Class struggle is thus considered to take place as a specific historical event, although it remains of significance for sociology since in any class society there is always the potential for such struggle. Apart from the primacy or non-primacy of class struggle, however, there is also the relationship among class, status, and the market. It is notable that the three phases of class struggle all relate to conflicts in the market, whether in the ancient money-market between creditors and debtors, in the medieval commodities market, or in the modern labour-market. This brings us back to Weber's definition of class, which relates above all to one's ability (or otherwise) to command goods and services in the market. For Weber, "class situation is ... ultimately market situation."[30] But the existence of the market is itself the solvent of ancient traditional and irrational modes of economic life and the basis on which economic "rationality" (if this word can be understood in a value-free sense) was eventually to triumph in the form of capitalism. At the same time, legal systems have developed, from their origins in regulating differences of status (and laying down scales of rights and penalties depending on status, such that all were unequal before the law) to regulating (supposedly) free contracts between equals.[31]

The rational systematization of the law leads, therefore, from status to freedom of contract.[32] The rationalization of economic action has led from traditional subsistence practices to capitalist production for the market. And inasmuch as "class situation is ... ultimately market situation," the development of the market has necessarily given rise to the development of class. So class has a place after all as a by-product of the long march of humanity towards rationality, and since Weber makes the distinction between "status societies" and "class societies," one can presumably speak of a historical development from status to class, although such a development does not exclude the existence of status groups in class society. This, therefore, gives us a different theoretical perspective on class to set alongside that of Marx. But there is a further element in the distinction between their two concepts of class, one that also serves as a characterization of their entire theoretical constructions, which is that for Weber class is a *situation*, while for Marx it is a *relationship*.

CHAPTER FOUR

The Spectre of Class in Non-Marxist Social Science

In this chapter I look at the work of two sociologists whose concepts of class are opposed not only to that of Marx and contemporary Marxism but also to each other, in that one of the two writes explicitly to demolish the other's theories. We need to keep in mind, therefore, the dual distinction that on the one hand characterizes their work as non-Marxist and on the other sets their two approaches into mutual opposition within the current of non-Marxist social science. Talcott Parsons' work belongs to the school of social theory that characterizes itself as structural-functionalist. Ralf Dahrendorf's is less easily classifiable, unless one labels it a form of defused class-conflict theory.

For Parsons the social system is a structure composed of interacting individuals, and if we wish to understand how that system functions as a system, we have to go about doing so at the level of interaction.[1] This takes us back to Weber, but Weber is more concerned with individual motivation in social action and tends to see interaction as the sum of the individual motivations that led up to it (which might be instrumentally or value-rational, affective or traditional, or a combination of any of these).[2] In addition, Weber reduces collectivities to the aggregate actions of the individuals who compose them, and his analysis is thus too historically oriented to posit the existence of a self-contained social structure outside time as a functionally integrated unit.

Parsons' problem is not so much individual motivation as how the conflicting interests of the actors in a given social system are conciliated with one another to the extent that the system is able to exist in the first place. The articulation of this problem follows on a series of assumptions. First, there is assumed to be an entity, however one chooses to define it, that can be described as a "social system." The notion of the system requires us to conceive of a boundary surrounding it such that everything falling outside the boundary does not belong to the system and everything within it is in some kind of closed systematic relationship. Second, in so far as a system exists, its existence must be assured by the elements of which it is composed, and those elements must be functionally integrated with each other and must each contribute to the maintenance of the system's existence. The final assumption is that all actors act for the optimization of gratification.[3] How, therefore, does the self-interested motivation of the individual actors within a system lead to system maintenance rather than system destruction?

The answer is that there exist restraints or curbs on individual gratification such that certain kinds of gratification-seeking behaviour meet with rewards and others with sanctions. Individual actors who would otherwise seek total system-destroying gratification at the expense of everyone else, are socialized to seek gratification but only in so far as it does not interfere with the gratification of others. This necessary process of curbing gratification begins in childhood and continues in school, but is also present in every subsequent case of interaction, in that if someone seeks gratification at my expense, I will react in the way that best prevents him or her from succeeding.

The question arises of how he or she and I know what we can get away with, or rather, since we may know from bitter experience, of what establishes that one kind of behaviour rather than another is to be rewarded, for example, by compliance. If I seek to optimize my gratification, it is because I have certain needs or wants that are themselves rooted in my personal background and preferences. In Parsons' terms, these are "need-dispositions" and they have their basis in the "personality-system." At the same time, I not only have a status or position in society, which might be "ascribed," as heir to a throne, or "achieved" as a ticket-collector, but in my relationships with others I am required to play a role on the basis of that status, which might be doing nothing or collecting tickets. In so far as people expect me to do nothing or collect tickets, they can be said to have role-expectations concerning me, which I may or may not satisfy. So, in that society is reduceable to a collection of statuses, there must exist a system in which those statuses relate to each other as roles and in which everyone has role-expectations of everyone else. This is referred to by Parsons as the "social system." The nature of those expectations cannot be said to lie in or emanate from the statuses themselves, but rather relates to a set of shared values, particularly in so far as the playing out of those roles meets with reward or sanction. This set of shared value-orientations constitutes the "cultural system,"[4] and it is this system of values that is inculcated by the primary and secondary processes of socialization in the family and the school, and is internalized to produce the need-dispositions of the individual actor.

Thus when I interact with someone else, I have certain notions of what my role in the interaction should be and what I may get out of it in terms of my own gratification, as well as expectations about the role and intentions of the person with whom I am interacting. Both our sets of expectations are rooted in a shared system of values such that there is a concordance between the two that makes our interaction and mutual comprehension possible. If either of us does not act in accordance with the other's expectations, that lack of compliance implies the non-acceptance of the same value-system and, in many cases, the breakdown of the interaction. If individuals consistently fail to act in the expected way, they become, in Parsons' terms, "deviants,"[5] and if a group of individuals starts to act and react in a way that runs counter to the established value-system, they can come to constitute a deviant subgroup and may even come to threaten the value-system itself. We need, therefore, to consider the nature of the value-system, or cultural system, from which the individual might deviate in the first place. Granted that a group of individuals, or even a whole society, may operate according to a shared set of values, in what do those values consist?

Parsons relates values to value-orientations and considers that different roles in society are played out according to different value-orientations. His classic example is that of the physician and patient.[6] Physicians (ideally) give all those suffering from the same illness the same treatment, irrespective of their personal status or qualities. In so far as they live up to this ideal, their approach is "universalistic" – that is, the same for everyone. The opposite case would be one of particularism. Physicians (again ideally) remain affectively neutral in their relationship with patients. Surgeons, for example, have difficulty maintaining the necessary objectivity when operating on relations or acquaintances. The relationship between the physician and patient is further characterized by "functional specificity" – that is, the specific skill of the physician resolving the specific problem of the patient, as against the more diffuse kind of relationship that the physician might have with kin or neighbours. The relationship is also one – on the physician's side – that is based on the achievement of skills and qualifications rather than on having been born qualified, as in the case of the heir to a throne. Finally, the role of the physician is supposed to be oriented towards the collectivity rather than the self.

The ideal pattern of value-orientations underlying the role of physician is thus one of universalism, affective neutrality, specificity, achievement, and collectivity-orientation. Any role in society has a set of value-orientations that are shared by the various actors with respect to it. In the physicians' case, this means that physicians will ideally attempt to bring their action into alignment with the relevant values, and the patient will assess the physician's competence in the light of those values. If different roles in society are based on different combinations of these "pattern-variables,"[7] Parsons none the less suggests that in any society certain combinations are dominant and that rewards (in material and status terms) will tend to go to those whose action in any given role best corresponds to that society's dominant value-orientations.[8] In individualistic industrial societies, for example, the dominant "clustering" of pattern-variables is related to universalistic, functionally specific, affectively neutral achievement, which means that the greatest rewards go to those who achieve most through their own efforts in specific fields while remaining affectively neutral and non-particularistic. In other societies the emphasis may be on being born great rather than on achieving greatness (ascription versus achievement), or on particularism rather than universalism. What Parsons would seem to mean is that in industrial societies those who, in material terms, achieve most, achieve most because they achieve most. In the light of this conclusion I turn to Parsons' consideration of class.

Parsons is not particularly interested in class as a way of thinking about collectivities in society. He concedes that the distinction between upper, middle, and lower class can be useful, but he considers that the traditional dividing lines between, for example, middle and lower class have become blurred by the high wages paid to the labour elite.[9] It is, as a result, difficult to say with any certainty who is to be included within which class, which somewhat reduces the usefulness of the concept. He is more interested in the concept of social stratification and in putting forward a theory of stratification based on the theory of action as outlined above. He does not, however, altogether abandon the concept of class, but incorporates it as a subsidiary concept within his theory of stratification.

The outward sign of high status, according to Parsons, is wealth measured in terms of possessions. There are two main kinds of possessions: instrumental possessions and possessions as rewards.[10] Instrumental possessions are those productive or performative facilities that are accorded to the individual actors who have shown themselves to be the most efficient as performers or producers. In other words, possession of the means of production (or performance) is accorded by society to those who are considered the best able to use them. Rewards, on the other hand, are accorded differentially on the grounds of performance. Those who perform the best receive the most. Top performers are thus given the instrumental facilities (which may be in the form of property) to carry on performing, and simultaneously get the highest rewards for their performances, while those who are the least successful get no instrumental possessions (no ownership of the means of production) and low rewards.[11] Society is, therefore, stratified according to success or failure, not simply success or failure to become wealthy or high-ranking but rather success or failure in the eyes of society and in the light of that society's values.

This brings us back to the nature of the value-orientations that lead to the differential distribution of rewards, or rather, the nature of the process of evaluation of performances. Parsons distinguishes between evaluation on the basis of qualities and on that of performances. Quality refers to what one *is* in terms of achieved or ascribed status, while performance is what one *does*.[12] Quality therefore relates to status and performance to role. Evaluations of quality and performance revolve around four kinds of standard, any one of which may be dominant in a given society: the performance itself, which may be evaluated in terms of achievement, or universalism as opposed to particularism; goal-orientation and realization; system-integration; and quality-ascription.[13] North American society in the early 1950s was not, according to Parsons, dominated by goal-orientation as it had been in wartime, where the whole effort of society had been concentrated on the realization of specific goals.[14] Indeed, goal-orientation was the last of the four except in specific sub-systems within the system, such as the industrial enterprise. The dominant standard was one of universalism and achievement in performance, and consequently those who achieved the most, in whatever field that achievement might lie, received the highest rewards. System-integration, in the form of the loyal bureaucrat, and quality-ascription, typically in the form of those who transmitted knowledge and skills (for example, teachers), both rated lower in a performance- and achievement-oriented society.

Social stratification, therefore, in the form of the differential distribution of wealth and status in American society in the 1950s, is, according to Parsons, the result of differences in performance that give rise to differences in reward according to evaluation in the light of certain standards. It is the result of, or alternatively requires, a high level of social mobility and equality of access to social services, so that no performers start out from a position of disadvantage with respect to others. In practice Parsons admits that there is some transmission of advantage by successful individuals to their children, although he suggests that research is required to know precisely to what extent such transmission exists.[15]

"Class status" for Parsons refers to the combination of statuses that any individual may have, in occupational terms, in the various associations to which he or she may belong, and as a member of a more or less extended group based on kinship.[16] Class, therefore, is used, in association with status, to encapsulate the variety of statuses that any individual may occupy, against the background of social stratification. If, for Marx, class is a relationship centred on the process of production, while for Weber it corresponds to a situation or position in relation to market opportunities, for Parsons the situational aspect of class has been expanded to include all the principal "situations" in which individuals find themselves, but at the same time class is further marginalized as a concept. For Marx, it is central. For Weber it is peripheral and secondary to the great movement of history towards rationality. And for Parsons it is relegated to the category of the useful, a form of honourable retirement. Class for Parsons is far from being the motor of history. It is an alternative and not very enlightening way of classifying groups of actors whose actual status and differential access to rewards are based on considerations that have nothing to do with class.

Superficially and explicitly, Dahrendorf's theory of society defines itself in opposition to Parsonian structural functionalism since it places conflict and class conflict at the centre of the analysis and claims to present society in a state of constant change. Structural functionalism concerns the maintenance of value-systems and the bringing of deviants into line with those systems. There is thus an apparent stasis in Parsons' system, whereas there is an equally apparent non-stasis in Dahrendorf's, whose entire system is constructed around conflict.

However, before looking at what Dahrendorf means by class, it is important to underline a certain similarity between his and Parsons' approaches. In two articles, one written before and the other after *Class and Class Conflict in Industrial Society*, Dahrendorf puts forward views that correspond – to say the least – to those of Parsons. In "Homo sociologicus" he describes individuals as having "positions" and "roles."[17] An individual may have the position and role of teacher, and in playing that role will have internalized the role-expectations that society has with respect to teachers. In so far as individuals conform to those expectations, the expectations are thereby reinforced, while if they fail to conform they are classed as deviants and are liable to be sanctioned. However, if a sufficient number of teachers fail to conform, the expectations may change. This is close to Parsons' structural-functionalist view of society, in which individuals have specific statuses within the social structure with particular functions attaching to those statuses in the form of roles.

Dahrendorf is also close to Parsons in his theory of inequality, as outlined in the former's 1961 article "On the origin of inequality among men." He describes inequality as resulting from conformity or non-conformity with the norms prevalent in a particular society: those who conform most closely to the norms come out on top.[18] This is roughly the equivalent of Parsons' saying that given societies have given sets of standards that serve as the basis for evaluating performance and, therefore, the ranking and rewarding of individual performers. Dahrendorf, however, introduces a small refinement that resolves the question of who evaluates or who decides who is in conformity with the norms and who is not. The norms are upheld by force, imposed through legal sanctions by those who wield power.[19] The law can thus serve as a means for the hierarchical ordering of society into conformers and non-conformers, inasmuch as legal sanctions can be brought to bear on the latter, and, presumably, threaten everyone else into conformity.

So we have progressed beyond Parsons to the extent that power and authority have been brought to bear, but we should not forget the substantial identity of views that exists between Parsons and Dahrendorf. Both present a social system broken down into the individual positions (or statuses) and roles of which it is composed, and one in which those positions (or statuses) are ranked hierarchically according to established norms (or value-orientations). Both, therefore, present a theory of society based on the individual actor, and a theory of inequality based on positive and negative evaluation.

In *Class and Class Conflict in Industrial Society*, the notion of power and authority again predominates, while roles, role-expectations, and norms recede into the background. Before we look at Dahrendorf's use of the concept of class, we need to consider certain assumptions that he makes concerning the nature of society. For Dahrendorf, contemporary industrial society is "post-capitalist."[20] A capitalist society is one in which ownership and control of the means of production are in the same hands. This may have been true in the nineteenth century, where the typical industrial enterprise was directed and owned by the same individual (or group of individuals), but it is no longer the case. Ownership and control have been split up, and the owners have withdrawn into the background, leaving the control and direction of industry in the hands of managers. At the same time, according to Dahrendorf, the concentration of ownership in the hands of the few is being broken down. He cites United States society in the late 1950s, where 8 per cent of the population were reported to own shares.[21] This he considers to be a substantial proportion, although he fails to break down that 8 per cent into those who own only a few shares and those who own a large number.

So we no longer live in a capitalist society, since the archetypal working capitalist entrepreneur, the nineteenth-century mill-owner, for example, is hard to come by. But there is another way in which society has changed since those early days of industrialization, where Marx seems to have been right in his portrayal of an overriding confrontation between the two classes of capitalists and of workers, and that is in terms of social mobility. According to Dahrendorf, there is now an increasingly high level of such mobility, facilitated by an educational system that distributes individuals according to their capacities, although he admits that the research necessary to establish the extent of that mobility remains to be done.[22] In addition, absolute deprivation in advanced capitalist societies no longer exists, having been replaced by relative deprivation.[23] That is, most workers are no longer on or below the poverty line but may still consider themselves to be deprived relative to others.

The original capitalist class has thus been broken up into owners and professional controllers; ownership is filtering down to the lower levels; the original working class has been split up into the skilled, semi-skilled, and unskilled; absolute deprivation no longer exists, and individuals from whatever social background are likely to be propelled up to one or other position on the hierarchy according to their capacities – Dahrendorf tends to avoid the subject of those who should necessarily be propelled down-wards by the same logic. This is an optimistic view of a society transform-ing itself in the direction of equality of opportunity, rewards and positions conferred according to merit, and generally a more equitable distribution of wealth. Again, it is one that would be endorsed by Parsons, who draws attention to the end of the concentration of great wealth in a few hands (in the United States) through aggressive taxation policies, and simultane-ously the disappearance of an oppressed class of workers through the benefits accruing from trade-union organization.[24]

Within this global conceptualization of society Dahrendorf develops his concept of class, and it is notable that – as in the case of Parsons, and because we are in the world of theory rather than in the vulgar world of empiricism – the argument is not over-encumbered with factual illustra-tion or support. Indeed (and Dahrendorf is explicit on this point), in many cases the necessary research has not been done, and there are therefore few facts to support the argument. While this is unfortunate, it does not – according to Dahrendorf – undermine the conclusions formulated, since these are based on what, after all, we know to be the case,[25] or if we did not know it before reading Dahrendorf, we know it afterwards.

The old classes of nineteenth-century industrial society no longer exist. Instead we find a wide variety of groups in a permanent state of conflict with each other. The root cause of conflict is not the possession of or sepa-ration from the means of production but rather the relationship of authority and subordination that has always existed within associations of individuals between those who possess power and those who are subordinated to it. Dahrendorf describes these groups as "classes," or rather, "classes as conflict groups."[26]

The concept of class as conflict group is a peculiarly hybrid product of Weberian and Marxian forebears. The "imperatively co-ordinated asso-ciation," which is, for Dahrendorf, the association within which class conflict takes place, derives from Weber, being a translation of Weber's *Herrschaftsverband*. But whereas for Weber the particular structure of dominance so characterized tends to emerge at all stages of history, whether legitimized through rules, or tradition, or charisma, and will inevitably emerge in even the most democratic organization where the coming to power of any group will always lead to the development of a "structure of domination," *herrschaftfliches Gebilde*,[27] this tendency is distinct from his notion of class. In addition, Weber always maintains a distinction between classes and groups, inasmuch as class for him is a descriptive category referring to all those who occupy a certain position with respect to the command of goods and services on the market but do not necessarily have any consciousness of themselves as a group. So Dahrendorf has wedded the alien notion of "class as conflict group" to Weber's own notion of the "imperatively co-ordinated association." The conflictual aspect of class derives directly and explicitly from Marx, but it is made into the attribute of the thoroughly non-Marxian conflict groups opposed to each other within, and on the basis of, associations characterized by the differential distribution of authority.

The typical imperatively co-ordinated association for Dahrendorf is the industrial enterprise, with production workers subordinated to the authority of supervisors and managers.[28] These two groups constitute classes within the framework of the enterprise. The resemblance between this conceptualization and the Marxian concept of class is, however, superficial. For Marx, the confrontation between workers and management in any given factory is to be understood as a localized confrontation between representatives of the two broader classes of workers and capitalists. For Dahrendorf, however, class groups only exist within the bounds of the particular factory. The internal class affiliation of any individual depends on where he or she happens to be at a given point in time. A worker who is elected to sit on the board of directors, for example, ceases to be a member of the class of workers and becomes a member of the class of director/managers.[29] Class affiliation is simply a question of the side that one happens to be on at any given moment in the structurally localized conflict between groups. When the worker and the manager leave the factory, they leave their factory-based class affiliations behind them. If they do not participate jointly in any other associations, they are without any specific class relationship to each other until they once more step inside the factory gates. Alternatively, if they both happen to be members of a chess club, and if the worker happens to be on the executive while the manager is only an ordinary member and therefore subject to the executive's authority (according to the rules of the club), their class positions of the factory are reversed for as long as they may be involved in club activities.[30]

This leads to a central point in Dahrendorf's conceptualization of society: the congruence that existed in nineteenth-century industrial society between class conflict and overall social stratification no longer exists, precisely because individuals can occupy a variety of class positions in relation to each other depending on the particular associations in which they find themselves.[31] For Dahrendorf, this overturning of what had earlier been the case is symbolized by the possibility of managers' being "mere citizens" outside the workplace, while workers may be members of Parliament.[32]

This lack of congruence between class conflict and social stratification reduces the likelihood of the overturning of the established order by a part of the population that might find itself in a position of subordination in every association into which it enters, as in the case of the working class in the nineteenth century.

That individuals come to occupy a variety of different social positions in relationship to each other, and the consequent development of cross-cutting ties among them, were insights dear to the heart of a number of social theorists in the 1950s.[33] This is one of the central features of functional-conflict theory: far from being necessarily threatening, conflict can be considered to reinforce an existing social order where there is no one over-riding confrontation, but rather changing patterns of alliance and opposition within a multitude of localized conflicts. In spite of his rebuttal of functionalism and structural functionalism, therefore, Dahrendorf's presentation of class conflict is in many ways a paradigm of functional-conflict theory. Society operates through conflict at all levels and in all its parts and has always done so; what is more, its cohesion is guaranteed by the variety of localized class conflicts in which individuals find themselves. Dahrendorf would evidently agree with Marx's and Engels' characterization of the history of all societies as the history of "class" struggle,[34] but his agreement with that sentiment would be as hollow as his entire attempt to pass off *Class and Class Conflict in Industrial Society* as in some way a twentieth-century development of Marx.

The principal accolade that Dahrendorf bestows on Marx he offers because Marx developed a theory that faced up to and attempted to account for social change, particularly inasmuch as Marx discovered the importance of "conflict groups and their clashes as forces that make for change."[35] In terms of parentage Dahrendorf places his own theory in the Marxian tradition because he also sees change as the characteristic state of any society and class conflict as the motor of change. That element in Marx's theory of class conflict, however, that implies and requires social change is absent from Dahrendorf's theory. For Marx, class conflict necessarily leads to radical structural change, inasmuch as the conflict of interests between classes in a given social formation provides an impetus towards the resolution of that conflict for the benefit of one or other of the classes, depending on their relative strengths. Inasmuch as industrial capitalism has itself brought into existence a working class that increasingly comes to constitute the bulk of the working population, and in that the working class is concentrated in centres of industrial production and is in a position to become aware of itself as a class and act as a class – in a way that scattered agricultural producers have rarely been able to do – there is no doubt in Marx's mind about the eventual outcome of the principal class conflict under capitalism. Class conflict for Marx cannot be static, since the nature and relative strengths of the classes in conflict are continually changing.

Dahrendorf equally claims that his theory of class conflict presupposes or presents society in a state of continual flux, although, since there is no longer any overriding opposition between classes that cuts across society, changes brought about through conflict are localized and piecemeal and lead to gradual change rather than to the revolution prophesied by Marx. One would presume that Dahrendorf simply reduces to localized, isolated instances of association the global opposition that Marx had generalized across society. But even at the localized level the nature of the class conflict is of an order different from that of Marx. Relationships of authority and subordination are political in nature rather than economic, and class conflict based on such relationships does not necessarily imply a conflict of material interests. For example, class conflict in Dahrendorf's chess club, involving executive authority and membership subordination, takes place around and within consensus over a set of rules that limit the former's authority and require the latter's subordination to permit the functioning of the club. The membership could, therefore, continue to conflict with their executive *in aeternum*, but if such conflict always falls within the bounds of the rules, any change that takes place need only be a change of personnel (in executive positions). Although that is precisely what Dahrendorf understands by "structural change,"[36] the formal structure of the club itself and the nature of the class conflict it contains (in his terms) remain unaffected.

This brings us to the core of Dahrendorf's approach to class, class conflict, and social change. He uses Schumpeter's image of a bus to sum up one aspect of his notion of class. A bus may always be full, and yet its complement of passengers always changing.[37] Equally, in a period of social mobility, or, in a chess club, of periodic elections, the persons occupying different class positions can be continually changing while the classes remain the same. His theory of social change is thus really a theory of social mobility, according to which more people are changing places more frequently. The theory gives us no indication of how the places themselves might change.

Underlying these various non-Marxist approaches to class is a common theme that one might sum up – to misquote the *Communist Manifesto* – by saying that they are haunted by the spectre of the Marxian concept of class. That they should be so haunted is not surprising, given that the Marxian conceptualization of class is linked to the necessary overthrow of an existing order and has continued to play a central role for those who see themselves as standing to benefit from such an overthrow. The Marxian concept of class and the derived concept of class in Marxism[38] have been, and continue to be, omnipresent and powerful, and if we wish to understand the curious place that class occupies in the various non-Marxist theoretical systems we have been looking at (present and yet peripheral in Weber, secondary in Parsons, trivialized and localized in Dahrendorf), we have to realize that Marxist theory constitutes not only a different way of understanding the world but one that necessarily involves the reordering of the world that it seeks to understand. The claims of a Parsons or a Dahrendorf to be value-free and objective social scientists seeking to understand (but not to change) society only make a virtue of their unwillingness to see society changed, and the will not to change society is no less an active *engagement* on their part than the will to change it is on Marx's. We need, therefore, to understand that behind the different theoretical approaches of non-Marxist and Marxist social science to the concept of class is a diametrically opposed set of views concerning the desirability or the non-desirability of a certain kind of radical social change.

CHAPTER FIVE

Theory and Experience: Class in Contemporary Marxism

By "contemporary Marxism" I refer, obviously enough, to a body of thought that derives its principal inspiration and orientation, whether explicitly or implicitly, from the work of Marx. The form that that orientation can take, however, is subject to considerable variation. It can consist of an empirical study of contemporary or past social conditions within the general framework of a Marxian approach – that is, using the concepts elaborated by Marx as the basic tools for understanding society without necessarily attempting to question or refine those concepts. Alternatively, it can be more specifically concerned with refining Marx's concepts, or those concepts that derive from Marx within the Marxist tradition, to bring them into closer alignment with contemporary capitalist society. The latter constitutes a classic theoretical approach in which the inadequacy of existing theory as an explanation of phenomena serves as the starting point for the proposal of alternatives, even if those alternatives consist simply in the refinement or adjustment of existing concepts. These, therefore, constitute two distinct approaches in contemporary Marxism, which can be classified broadly as empirical and theoretical, although it is preferable to think in terms of an axis running from one to the other rather than of a clear-cut distinction between the two, with any given work lying at some point along the axis.

This distinction is not only a useful way of classifying different approaches but is present and evident within the approaches themselves, inasmuch as the more empirically minded accuse the theoreticians of cabbalism and abstractionism, while the latter accuse the former of mindless empiricism and the misuse of concepts. In the one case, clarity of definition would seem to be lost in a welter of detail, while in the other the detail and complexity of an existing formation can easily be sacrificed to the rigidity of definition. Between the chaos of empiricism and the rigidity of abstractionism there lies a middle way in which an attempt is made to introduce sufficient flexibility into the theory and its constituent parts for it to be able to account for the complexity of phenomena.

The distinction between empiricism and abstractionism is particularly acute in the case of class, which can be seen either as a concept within a theoretical construction that serves to identify a particular collectivity (as against other collectivities) or as something that is inseparable from the experience of the people so classified. In the following discussion, I consider several approaches to class within Marxism that can be placed at different points on the axis.

E.P. Thompson's definition of class at the beginning of *The Making of the English Working Class* provides one eloquent point of access to the empirical approach, that is, to the notion of class as experience: "By class I understand a *historical* phenomenon, unifying a number of disparate and seemingly unconnected events, both in the raw material of experience and in consciousness. I emphasize that it is a historical phenomenon. I do not see class as a 'structure' nor even as a 'category', but as something which in fact happens (and can be shown to have happened) in human relationships."[1] He concludes: "Class is defined by men as they live their own history, and, in the end, this is its only definition."[2] According to Thompson, therefore, to understand class we should not abstract ourselves from the concrete but immerse ourselves in it.

The Making of the English Working Class illustrates what Thompson means by class. It is an attempt to understand the process of class formation that accompanied the development of capitalist relations of production in late eighteenth- and early nineteenth-century England, and does so by examining in detail the various movements for reform, protest, and association on the part of artisans and of the new and growing class of skilled and unskilled factory workers. The coming into existence of the working class is not, however, portrayed as arising out of changed or changing relations of production in any straightforward way but as a painful and long drawn-out process that has its roots in the eighteenth century but only reaches fruition in the 1830s and 1840s. By this time a working class can be said to exist, for there is evidence that a sizeable proportion of the working population was coming to an awareness of its own condition as an exploited class and acting in consequence. Up to that point there had been many outbreaks of protest among particular groups of workers and directed at particular developments (notably at their own displacement by machinery), as well as a variety of reform movements and subversive plots against the government, the latter frequently the work of *agents provocateurs*. These scattered outbreaks of protest were the forerunners of concerted and self-conscious working-class action, and therefore of the coming into existence of the working class itself. They also have their roots in the food riots and popular protests of the eighteenth century.

Thus for Thompson the transition to capitalist relations of production is not simply of theoretical interest as a stage in a sequence of conceptualizable modes of production, or more particularly – which is frequently the case in Marxist theory – as a problem for such conceptualization precisely because it falls in between two historical periods that are broadly characterized as "feudal" and "capitalist." If the feudal and capitalist modes of production consist of a particular articulation of the forces and relations of production, the problem is how to characterize the transitional period between the two. From the empirical viewpoint such theoretical problems reduce the content of history to a set of empty categories.[3] The transition from feudalism to capitalism cannot be understood by juggling concepts and ironing out contradictions within theory, but rather by gleaning from the records of the time what was actually happening to the mass of craftsmen who were displaced by machinery, or the different categories of independent or semi-independent weavers who were gradually brought under the control and on to the premises of the capitalist entrepreneur, or the large number of peasant smallholders forced off the land and into the cities (whether of English or Irish extraction) and who came to make up a reserve army of labour that could be used to force down the wages of unskilled labourers and factory workers. Behind all the different movements of workers and technological developments are the living conditions of the workers themselves in the urban environments of the early nineteenth century, where those who could afford a horse lived as far out of the town as the horse could carry them.[4]

The separation of the producers from the means of production that, according to Marx and Marxist theory, lies at the heart of the development of capitalist relations of production can easily become just a convenient formula that "explains" why the working class under capitalism is forced economically to sell its labour power to capital in order to survive, without the necessary intervention of any coercive force. In an empirical approach to class, however, it becomes the lived experience of peasant producers thrown off their holdings, or seeing those holdings reduced to such an extent that they are compelled to work for whoever is prepared to employ them and for whatever he is prepared to pay.

This is the principal strength of the Thompsonian approach: it seeks to replace the empty categories of theoretical abstractionism by describing what it means to live in a period of transition to those who find themselves no longer in possession of the means by which they might ensure their own survival. It is still, however, for all its empiricism, a work of Marxist theory, in that the construction placed on the period of history that it studies is Marxist (or at least Marxian) in inspiration and orientation. To state that "class is defined by men as they live their own history, and in the end, this is its only definition" may serve to highlight the fact that collectivities act in time and space irrespective of what theoreticians think about them, but this position can also come to conceal the premise on which the discussion is based: that of the theoretical construction placed on society and history by Marx in which class and class struggle have a central position as *concepts*. To say that the only satisfactory definition of class is the lives of those of whom it is composed undermines the status of the concept of class within Marxian theory. Concepts cannot be defined by what they refer to in the world but only in relation to other concepts within a theoretical system.

This is symptomatic of a tendency on Thompson's part to suggest that inasmuch as it is the working class that defines itself through its own experience, the task of the historian should be to allow that experience to speak for itself, and the impression left by *The Making of the English Working Class*, with its attention to detail, is that Thompson has succeeded in that task. However, this impression masks the fact that the book is a carefully pieced-together construction placed on a particular period, and a work within the framework of Marxist theory. The subject-matter of a book can no more speak for itself than can those who are considered to make up a class define that class through their own action.

If Thompson represents an approach to class within Marxism that seeks to free it from the restricting bonds of theory and let it define itself via the recreation of the experience of class in history, there are equally Marxist approaches to contemporary society that attempt to go directly to the reality of class in a capitalist society. The work of Miliband and of Westergaard and Resler both constitute refutations of the prevailing orthodoxies in non-Marxist social science that suggest (à la Parsons) that social stratification is now based on evaluation rather than on any other criteria, or (à la Dahrendorf) that inequality of opportunity is now becoming a thing of the past. In order to bring about this refutation, Miliband places himself, and dangerously so in Poulantzas' view, on enemy terrain, in that he uses such bourgeois concepts as that of "elite," which has no status in Marxist theory.[5] Miliband's refutation is based on the existence of a ruling class (in Britain), which he identifies not so much on the grounds of its position as a class within capitalist relations of production but on that of the personnel of which it is composed.[6]

According to strict Marxist theory, individual social position and role are inseparable from class position, which is itself structurally determined according to the dominant set of relations of production. Thus, for Marx, individuals do not meet as individuals in the labour-market but as the personifications of capital and labour, and it is only at that level that any contract between them involving the sale or purchase of labour-power can be understood. On such theoretical grounds, therefore, in order to discover who belongs to which class, it is first necessary to discover their objective relationship to the dominant confrontation (in capitalist society) between capital and labour. This is particularly the case for state bureaucrats, whose class position can only be known if one can properly understand the role of the state in relation to the dominant mode of production. This theoretical preoccupation is diametrically opposed to non-Marxist theories of class, where classes tend to be reduced to the sum of the individual positions of the actors of which they are composed.

Miliband, while placing himself within the Marxist tradition, adopts an approach to class that is in many ways close to that of non-Marxist theory. The ruling class, which is a concept that has its place within Marx's own theory of class, is not identified on the basis of its role in the maintenance and reproduction of capitalist relations of production but on that of the close kinship and cultural ties that bind together top-ranking businessmen, bankers, army officers, civil servants, and politicians. That there is a ruling class can be seen from the far-reaching horizontal mobility between the top places in each of these hierarchies.[7] Class, therefore, comes close to being defined (in Weberian terms) as that collection of statuses and positions within which intragenerational mobility is easy and possible. Dahrendorf is in some ways closer to strict Marxist theory than is Miliband, in that he maintains a distinction between class as a category and the individuals of which it is composed, claiming, for instance, that an individual who is elected to a club's executive changes class within the context of the club. Dahrendorf's class bus continues on its way irrespective of who gets on and off.

That the grounds for Miliband's demonstration of the existence of a ruling class are questionable is evident from the fact that Raymond Aron can argue, from a non-Marxist perspective, that the contrary is the case, inasmuch as some of his closest acquaintances are high-ranking civil servants, bankers, and businessmen and that, far from being in agreement with each other, they are often in total disagreement and open rivalry.[8] If interpersonal solidarity and social connections are served up as the stuff of class, then nothing is easier than to dismember the class thus assembled by showing that X and Y do not talk to each other any more and are not married to each other's second cousins, which are approximately the bases on which Aron demonstrates the non-existence of a ruling class.

What Miliband says, however, concerning the persons who occupy the highest positions in private and state bureaucracies and enterprises in Britain is demonstrably true. They do share a common culture, education, and accent, inhabit the same residential areas, belong to the same clubs, attend the same churches, and shoot on the same grouse moors, and they are thoroughly interrelated. In Weberian terms Miliband could be said to focus his attention not so much on the constituent elements of class as on the trappings of a status group whose boundaries may or may not coincide with those of class. And we may come across precisely the same trappings among some professionals, certain academics in the older universities, and the remnants of the old landed aristocracy, none of whom rules but all of whom know somebody who does. From a more Marxist perspective, however, one could say that Miliband draws our attention to a neglected and important aspect of class – the mechanisms of ruling-class solidarity – but fails to give adequate emphasis to the link between that solidarity and relations of production.

Westergaard and Resler also reject cabbalistic theorizing and also write specifically to refute prevailing non-Marxist orthodoxy.[9] In spite of certain superficial changes, and in some cases – for example, the introduction of the National Health Service – more than superficial, the core assumptions of British society have not changed and are non-negotiable.[10] These core assumptions concern the existence of private property in whatever form, but particularly in the means of production; the retention of surplus income from such property after costs, wages, and so on have been paid; and the maximization of such surplus income, that is, the pursuit of profit. It is precisely because these assumptions are non-negotiable that the role of labour in the three-cornered management of the economy by the state, capital, and labour is reduced to a war of attrition in which its position is continually undermined by the reinforcement of capital's position by the state.

Westergaard and Resler's argument is aimed mainly against the notion that there has been any serious move towards equality. Welfare payments tend to represent a higher proportion of income at a lower level, but in many forms, that of family allowances, for example, are equal across the board.[11] Income differentials between the different socio-economic categories of unskilled, semi-skilled and skilled manual, clerical supervisory, low-grade professional, professional, and managerial have remained largely unchanged over a period of forty years, except that low-grade professionals have seen their position eroded, and clerical workers have seen their pay and conditions slip down below the level of semi-skilled manual grades.[12] This relative long-term stasis in differentials has been accompanied by the retention of major shareholding in the hands of a small minority, particularly in Britain and the United States, and the guarantee in the form of inheritance that present inequalities will necessarily be transmitted to the next generation, the latter factor giving the lie to Parsonian notions that wealth is in some sense a reward bestowed by society in return for achievement.[13] The central features of the argument concern, therefore, the existence of private property, particularly in the means of production, and the maintenance of that property across generation boundaries in the form of inheritance; the role of the state in consolidating the position of capital, to the detriment of labour; and the evidence for the continuation of low levels of social mobility in spite of everything that Dahrendorf claims on the basis of his impressions. Statistics do not bear out those impressions, but serve on the contrary to underline the continuity of the boundary between manual and non-manual categories, which few manual workers succeed in crossing.[14]

In *Class in a Capitalist Society* Westergaard and Resler are as little preoccupied with a theory of class as Miliband or Thompson. They are concerned rather with demonstrating that Britain is still a rigidly class-divided society, in spite of the claims of non-Marxist social science. As far as the nature and boundaries of the classes are concerned, they do not go beyond classical Marxist theory and therefore leave unanswered many questions about where class boundaries are held to lie, particularly with respect to upper management and the bourgeoisie, or clerical and manual workers. Does the solidity of the manual/non-manual divide represent a class boundary? The problem is that class boundaries cannot be deduced from the experience of class, just as the ruling class cannot be defined according to its personnel or the working class reduced to what it means to be a member of the working class. While it is important to concentrate on the realities of class or the experience of class in a capitalist society, it is also necessary to clarify the reality of what one is looking at. As far as Marx is concerned, class remains assumed rather than precisely defined, and these empirically oriented studies tend to share that assumption.

As an example from the more abstractionist end of the spectrum of contemporary Marxist theory, Poulantzas is preoccupied with the development of a theory of class that, while not departing from the essential tenets of Marxist and especially Marxian theory, can account for the manifest changes in contemporary class structure. The problem he considers is an inherited theory of class within Marxist tradition that is at best imprecise and at worst unable to explain contemporary divisions within the bourgeoisie, or the class position of what Poulantzas describes as the "new petty bourgeoisie."[15] Given a principal threefold division of society into bourgeois, petty bourgeois, and working class, he asks: who is to be assigned to which class among the myriad categories of managers, supervisors, service workers, and state bureaucrats? Poulantzas' *Les Classes sociales dans le capitalisme d'aujourd'hui* falls into three main parts, concerning the concept of class; contemporary fractions within the bourgeoisie; and the class boundaries of the new petty bourgeoisie or, from the other side of the boundary, of the working class.

Poulantzas distinguishes between structural class determination and class position. Structural class determination depends on one's objective position in a social structure dominated by a particular set of relations of production. Class position, however, can vary according to the will of different class fractions to identify themselves with other classes.[16] A highly paid sector of the working class is and remains a fraction of that class according to structural determination, but this does not prevent it from aligning itself with other classes on particular issues and thus taking up a different class position. Alternatively, office workers, who, according to Poulantzas, belong to the petty bourgeoisie rather than to the working class, may identify themselves with the proletariat. This is just the sort of distinction that would enrage an empiricist, but it comes down to saying that people can belong to one class and identify with another, a factor that can be of significance in political action and the formation of class alliances.

It is thus important to decide which categories of workers or non-workers are to be structurally assigned to which classes, or put another way, to decide what the criteria are for structural class determination. This is a question that is especially difficult to answer in the case of managers who, in the form of top management, are assigned to a ruling class on the basis of close personal connections with the owners of capital and influential decision-makers (Miliband), and yet are used as evidence that we no longer live in a capitalist society since industry is now run by professional managers rather than capitalists (Dahrendorf). Poulantzas seeks to clarify the structural class position of managers by looking not at the social origins or affiliations of the managers themselves but at the function of management within the global opposition of labour and capital.[17] Just as Marx portrays the capitalist and the worker as the personifications of capital and labour rather than as individuals, so Poulantzas depersonalizes managers and seeks to resolve the question of their structural class determination by looking at what they personify rather than who they are. For Poulantzas, top management personifies one aspect of capital, in that it is the function of capital in the capitalist mode of production to control the process of production. As controllers they therefore represent capital or personify one of its aspects just as bankers or shareholders personify another. They are thus structurally and objectively members of the bourgeoisie even if they do not possess any capital. Those in subordinate management positions, however, in so far as they are controlled rather than in control, are assignable to the petty bourgeoisie.

Similarly, the question of the existence or non-existence of a national bourgeoisie in France, as opposed to a foreign bourgeoisie and its local representatives – a "comprador" bourgeoisie – is resolved by looking at the underlying economic realities. Foreign, and particularly American investment in France has become so all-pervasive that it is no longer possible to distinguish between those sectors of industry that remain under "national" control and those under "foreign" control.[18] One has to distinguish between legal ownership and economic control. Legally a company can be in the hands of nationals, but even a minority shareholding on the part of a multinational company can put economic control into the hands of that company, particularly since monopoly capital now to all intents and purposes dictates the terms on which non-monopoly capital is suffered to continue in existence. Poulantzas, therefore, abandons the distinction between "national" and "comprador" bourgeoisie and replaces them with "internal" bourgeoisie.[19] The definition of class boundaries and of boundaries within classes is thus resolved by looking at economic control and, in the case of the bourgeoisie, at the positions of the different fractions in relation to international monopoly capital.

If the internal and external boundaries of the bourgeoisie are relatively straightforward, those of the petty bourgeoisie in relation to the other two classes are less clear. In order to demarcate the new petty bourgeoisie from the working class, Poulantzas elaborates a distinction between "productive" and "unproductive" labour.[20] This distinction is based on a narrow reading of Marx whereby it is claimed that Marx restricts "productive" labour to the production of material goods and the creation of surplus value, which is realized by the capitalist in selling those goods on the market.[21] This definition excludes all service workers who do not produce value in the form of material commodities, and limits the working class to a fairly narrow set of workers within manufacturing industry. In certain advanced capitalist societies, where an increasingly large proportion of all employment is in services rather than in production (so defined), this has the effect of reducing the working class to a minority of all workers.

A further element that serves to establish the different structural class determination of the petty bourgeoisie and working class is the distinction between manual and intellectual labour. This distinction does not, however, refer to the different tasks themselves and the extent to which they are performed manually or intellectually but rather to the separation of the working class from the intellectual control of production. If capitalist relations of production involve the separation of the direct producer from the material means of production, they also involve the separation of the same producer from the intellectual control and orientation of the process of production, which is consigned to an army of technicians and supervisors. Where the workers' productive activity is not reduced to a mechanical function, the extent to which they retain intellectual control over the activity is restricted and is anyway determined by the production process as a whole and by those who determine that process. The knowledge that has always accompanied production has been separated out from the process of production itself and been consigned as a guarded secret to draughtsmen, technicians, and office staff.[22] This *secret du savoir* (which is also a central feature of Weberian bureaucracy, although Poulantzas does not refer to Weber in this context)[23] is shared out among the various ranks of the petty bourgeoisie, who, of course, have a vested interest in keeping the secret.

The working class is thus distinguished by Poulantzas from the petty bourgeoisie at three levels: at the economic level, on the basis of productivity as against non-productivity;[24] at the ideological level, in that it is excluded from the *secret du savoir*; and at the political level, in that it is subject to supervision rather than being in the position to supervise others. There remains, however, a certain lack of clarity in this grand scheme for the splitting up of the mass of workers in contemporary capitalist societies into their structurally determined class positions. As Erik Olin Wright points out, the bringing together of the two "petty bourgeoisies," the traditional and the new, within the same classification is curious.[25] It cannot be on economic grounds, since the self-employed, small employers, and artisans who constitute the traditional petty bourgeoisie have little to do with the non-productive and exploited service workers of the new. And if it is on ideological grounds – for example, that they share a common subjective class position with respect to the other two classes – it would seem that we are no longer in the realm of the structural determination of class and that the ideological has replaced the economic as the determinant level. Apart from this, Poulantzas assigns some workers involved in the distribution of manufactured goods – transport workers, for example – to the working class, and not others, and makes the revealing distinction between the traditional kind of employee in retail establishments who is well-dressed and customer-oriented and the new hypermarket employee who marks up prices and empties boxes. The former is petty bourgeois and the latter is, increasingly, working class.[26] We seem to be approaching a Dahrendorfian situation where an employee who stops filling shelves to operate the cash register and then returns to marking up prices changes from one class to another and back again.

Poulantzas' whole approach to class is an attempt to define and refine the concept of class such that we can confidently assign any category of worker or functionary or investor to their appropriate structurally determined class position. Contemporary class structure, according to Poulantzas, is awkward and complex and cannot be satisfactorily accounted for by the traditionally ill-defined concepts of class within Marxist theory. He therefore attempts to bring class up to date. At the same time it is fundamental to much of Marxist theory, from the *Communist Manifesto* onwards, that class is not merely a theoretical construct imposed on society but rather part of the reality of social structure, a structure that itself consists of opposed classes in struggle. Poulantzas would not consider that he is refining concepts that are then to be brought to bear on reality and in terms of which that reality is in some sense arranged or organized, but rather that he is attempting to unearth the determining principles of structures that exist and whose determining principles are waiting to be unearthed. Erik Olin Wright, however, maintains that what Poulantzas has succeeded in unearthing is not what is there to be unearthed.

Wright is concerned with maintaining the importance of economics for class, and suspects that in certain cases – that of the "new" and "traditional" petty bourgeoisie, for example – Poulantzas allows ideology to hold sway over economy as a determining factor.[27] His principal quarrel with Poulantzas is over the question of what is or is not productive labour and with Poulantzas' narrow demarcation of the working class on the basis of his definition. But he also rejects Poulantzas' attempt to include the bulk of all workers and non-workers within the boundaries of one or other of the three classes, which leads to the assignment of some managers to the bourgeoisie and some to the petty bourgeoisie and to the splitting up of different categories of workers into one or other of the two subordinate classes, irrespective of the fact that they may all be forced to sell their labour-power to capital. For Wright, the reality of class is not so easily reduceable to a set of watertight compartments. His approach has two main purposes: to retain but redefine the distinction between productive and unproductive labour as the criterion for belonging or not belonging to the working class, and to produce a theory of class that can better account for certain apparently contradictory class positions.

Wright denies that Marx limits the definition of productive labour to the production of material goods. He draws attention to a passage where Marx suggests that there is little difference between a school and a sausage factory, in that the teacher and the sausage-machine operator both spend their working lives for the benefit of their employers.[28] Wright sees no reason for not seeing the provision of services, where those services are marketed as commodities, as equally productive of surplus value for capital as any other form of productive labour. He therefore redefines productivity in a broader and more traditional sense. But given the determinant role of economics for deciding who belongs to the working class and who does not, Wright emphasizes that ideology can also have a role in determining class boundaries, in that class solidarity among different kinds of employees against capital can play an important part in the consolidation of class. However, these criteria are still insufficient for determining which categories are to be assigned to which classes, except in the most general terms. Wright elaborates a series of characteristics that can serve to define class affiliation and, more importantly, the contradictory affiliation of those who fall in between the three major classes. These characteristics are threefold: control over the means of production, control over the labour of others, and control over the process of production.[29]

According to these characteristics the bourgeoisie and the working class are at opposite poles since the bourgeoisie retains ultimate control over all three while the production worker has control over none, except in a very limited sense over the process of production. By contrast, the petty bourgeoisie – which Wright defines in the traditional sense of small-scale employers, the self-employed, and artisans – have control over the means of production and the process of production but do not have control over or exploit the labour of others, except to a limited extent in the case of the small-scale employer. Once small-scale employers increase the number of their employees above a certain level, however, they come to fall outside the boundaries of the petty bourgeoisie and find themselves on the edges of the bourgeoisie proper.[30]

This intermediate class position is central to Wright's theory and is described by him as a "contradictory class location," since any individual in such a position has a foot in both camps while belonging to neither.[31] Such a position is also to be found between the bourgeoisie and the proletariat and the latter and the petty bourgeoisie. Top management, inasmuch as it implies substantial shareholding and capital ownership, can be included within the bourgeoisie, but all other grades of manager, technician, and supervisor find themselves in the contradictory class location between bourgeoisie and proletariat, inasmuch as they control labour and the process of production to varying degrees but do not have any ultimate economic control over the means of production themselves. Teachers and certain intermediate categories of artisan, who retain some control over their work process but have no control over the means of production nor over the labour of others, fall between proletariat and petty bourgeoisie, except for university professors with large research grants who can employ and control research assistants, in which case they find themselves between the petty bourgeoisie and the bourgeoisie. According, therefore, to how one rates on the three criteria of affiliation, one will find oneself in one of the three main classes or in one of the three contradictory class locations.

Poulantzas and Wright both set out with the same objective, to clarify the contemporary boundaries of class such that one would be in a better position to know who were one's allies, or potential allies, and who were one's enemies in the construction of socialism. In Poulantzas' scheme, which lies towards the abstractionist end of our axis in that it has at least a coherent existence in the abstract, whatever the difficulty of its being brought to bear on class as a phenomenon, the impression remains that the contradictions of experience have been sacrificed to neatness and theoretical clarity, and also – following Wright – that the possibilities of any broad working-class alliance are compromised by the narrowness of the definition of the working class. As Wright points out, such definitions are not simply of academic interest but are of immediate significance for political action.[32] Wright's own approach and suggested resolutions come closer to what I have referred to as a middle way between an empiricism snowed under by contradiction and detail and a theoretical abstractionism that would dearly like to reduce class to a simple threefold opposition. It is a middle way in the sense that it proceeds on the assumption that theoretical clarity is the prerequisite for understanding the world, since we can only understand the world in and through theory, but at the same time that theory has to be able to account for the world as experienced.

Underlying these various essays in empiricism and abstractionism is the characterization made by Pierre-Philippe Rey of the different tendencies in Marxist theory according to the direct experience, or otherwise, of class struggle.[33] For him, the strength of *Capital* lies in Marx's and Engels' involvement in political action, Engels' experience of working-class conditions in Manchester, and Marx's extensive reading and grasp of theory. Since Marx, Marxist theory has tended to lose contact with working-class experience. An intellectual stratum has arrogated to itself the monopoly of knowing what that experience consists in, and persists in denying that the working class itself can ever come to a sufficient understanding of its own class position on the basis of that experience. The frustration with theory expressed by Thompson and Miliband can be understood as a reaction against what Rey describes as the "bourgeoisification" of Marxist theory, while the efforts of Wright to devise a theory that can sufficiently account for the realities of class can be seen as an attempt to reconsummate the marriage of theory and experience that underlies the first volume of *Capital*.

CHAPTER SIX

Class Replaced:
Ethnicity in
Non-Marxist Theory

If class lies at the heart of the Marxist theory of society while being largely peripheral in the core areas of non-Marxist theory – with certain exceptions – ethnicity presents us with much the same picture, but in reverse. For mainstream Marxism, as we shall see in a subsequent chapter, the question of ethnic identity is relatively uninteresting alongside the phenomena that are held to be characteristic of different social systems and generative of the different types of social inequality that exist in those systems. There is a distinction to be made between the way in which people interpret the existence of differentiated social groups and the reasons why those groups exist in the first place, the latter not having anything necessarily to do with people's interpretations. Ethnicity, being one form of such interpretation, is therefore by definition – from a traditional Marxist perspective – an unreliable key to the processes that we observe.

Non-Marxist theory has a different set of focuses. In the Weberian-Parsonian tradition, what is considered to be interesting and problematic is not so much the way in which social inequalities have been generated and maintained in different societies but rather the way in which the values and principles on the basis of which social systems and collectivities oper-ate are articulated through individual action. The key moment for that tradition is not so much the creation of exchange value within the process of production but rather the translation of social values into action. It is that moment of individual decision, generalized across a society, that leads to the maintenance or the transformation of collectively held values.

Given that focus, it is not surprising that ethnicity occupies a central position in much of non-Marxist theory, since, on any definition, it con-cerns the way in which individuals identify themselves collectively and act in terms of those identities. Indeed it comes so close to what is considered to be of primary interest in non-Marxist tradition that the polarization between Marxist and non-Marxist perspectives on society can come to be seen as one between class and ethnicity as the two mutually exclusive core explanatory concepts.

If class as one of the core concepts for Marxists and all those operating in the Marxian tradition generates much argument, ethnicity is equally perplexing for non-Marxists. Daniel Bell in discussing the different kinds of ties that can be held to underlie the existence of communal groups – race, colour, and language, for instance – comes to ethnicity as a confusing concept that is used in a variety of ways. All the same, he considers it to be a term that is "too pervasive to escape" as a "common designation for a culturally defined 'communal group'" and concludes that "by and large, it will have to serve."[1] Before looking at some of the different approaches to ethnicity within non-Marxist theory, I shall briefly return to Weber, who, in many ways, found ethnicity to be as confusing and inescapable as Bell was to do some fifty years later.

In *Economy and Society* Weber poses the problem of ethnicity for theory, which comes down to its very universality. According to Weber, "wherever social interaction in rational form is not very widespread, almost every process of association, even one which is purely rational in make-up, attracts a spreading consciousness of community which takes the form of personal brotherhood based on an 'ethnic' communal belief-system."[2] This would equally apply to any association at a later period that was not based on systematic rules. That belief can be constructed around whatever conspicuous differences the believers choose that can be used to distinguish them from those outside the association. Such differences, if they had not happened to have been picked up to symbolize shared ethnicity, might be of little apparent importance – Weber gives the example of Greek women using perfumed oil and Scythian women butter on their hair.[3] Equally, they might relate to major differences of language, religion, or custom, but that does not mean that where such differences exist there are necessarily distinct ethnic groups whose boundaries coincide with apparent boundaries.

The underlying point is that the differences that have importance as distinguishing marks (or simply as reinforcing group solidarity and identity) can be real enough, although they can equally relate, for instance, to "fictional" descent from a common ancestor, but it is not these real and apparent differences that give rise to the differentiation in the first place. The reason for the association's existence always lies elsewhere – for example, at the level of economic action or self-protection. So it is the fact of association that is the given, whatever the reason for its coming into existence, and ethnicity follows from that fact. Any sociological study has to look at the different elements around which ethnicity can be constructed – including language, religion, descent, physical characteristics, and shared customs – all of which constitute fields of study in themselves.[4] But it also has to be aware of the underlying nature of the association that requires or gives rise to the belief in the first place and therefore of the nature of associations in general.

In his discussion of the forms of economic action, Weber attaches importance to the universal tendency towards monopolistic closure in certain kinds of economic association – that is, the tendency to restrict to a limited circle of members the benefits and privileges to which the association gives rise. It is in light of this tendency that one can frequently explain the genesis of the ethnic group, any cultural trait being acceptable as the basis for such exclusivity.[5] The ethnic group is comparable to the "status group," since by belonging to it – on the basis of ascription rather than achievement – one shares in what Weber describes as the "ethnic honour" of the group, although in this case the group in question is not by definition related to social stratification, as in the case of the status group.[6]

Ethnicity is thus a form of labelling. Weber maintains that all forms of association require conspicuous markers that can serve to differentiate members from non-members in order to exclude non-members from the benefits of membership and, perhaps more importantly, to provide a basis for group solidarity at the level of manifest appearances rather than (or as well as) at that of the economic or other interests that brought the group into existence in the first place.[7] Where it succeeds in creating or reinforcing such solidarity, belief in shared ethnicity, for all its being secondary to initial group formation, can come to be of primary importance for the consolidation or the continuity of the group's existence. In another part of *Economy and Society* Weber suggests that shared customs and usages can give rise to feelings of ethnic "identity," which can in turn "contribute to the creation of community."[8] So ethnicity, once unleashed, can come to be a force in its own right.

Beyond this, Weber does not attempt to elaborate a theory of ethnicity, and indeed suggests that a thoroughgoing sociological analysis would have to start by abandoning the term, since it deceptively gives the impression of the existence of a uniform phenomenon, whereas in fact it covers a wide range of disparate phenomena.[9] Ethnicity has, however, remained too central to be abandoned. Parsons, for instance, echoes both Weber and Bell when he states that ethnicity is "an extraordinarily elusive concept and very difficult to define in any precise way,"[10] and yet there is no getting away from it. In the following subsections I look at some of the ways in which non-Marxist theorists have attempted to produce definitive conceptualizations.

One of the main dividing lines between different non-Marxist theories of ethnicity is the division between ethnicity as a content in its own right and ethnicity as something that flows from the contact between groups that define themselves and each other as "ethnic."[11] The common-sense, classical notion of ethnicity holds that ethnicity is a content. Our ethnicity as Liverpool Irish, French, Ukrainian, or English Canadians, or New York Italians is everything that we are: our ancestry, language, area of residence, values, appearance, hair colour, religion, eating habits, and marriage ceremonies. It is pointless to try to separate out any one of those elements as being the core area of our ethnicity. They make up an indivisible whole. There are a number of ways in which that indivisible whole has been understood, but the two principal ones can be described in terms of the natural and the cultural, both of which have long traditions behind them. In the first case, ethnicity and ethnic solidarity are seen as the expression of natural, biological, or genetic factors. In other words, it is in our nature as human beings to act in ways that lead to the formation of ethnic groups. In the second case, ethnicity comes close to being identified with "culture" in its broad sense as the totality of the life-ways and life-styles of a particular people.

Van den Berghe's *The Ethnic Phenomenon* is a good example of the naturalization of ethnicity. He sets out from the assumption that the "underlying driving force" of ethnic sentiments is "ultimately the blunt, purposeless natural selection of genes that are reproductively successful."[12] Ethnic groups exist because of the natural propensity of individuals to act nepotistically. The more genes one shares with a given individual, the more one is naturally disposed to act in that individual's interests, since in enhancing his or her reproductive success one is by the same token enhancing the reproductive success of one's own genes. This is the genetic pull that underlies co-operation within the family, among kinsmen, and ultimately within ethnic groups based on common descent.

The key to ethnicity is thus not so much social as biological. And the pattern of that biological key is one of genetic self-interest: "The fundamental postulate of the model is that organisms, consciously or not, tend to behave in individually 'selfish' ways, i.e. in fitness-maximising ways."[13] The parallel with classical micro-economics is a conscious and explicit one.[14] Just as, in the tradition of micro-economics going back to Jevons and beyond, the individual is considered to be constantly evaluating the utility of spending additional money on something in a context where all social action is determined by the maximization of utility, so, in the context of co-operation and group affiliation, individuals are equally involved in cost-benefit analysis. In the latter case, however, the benefit is calculated in terms of the maximization of genetic reproductive success rather than some more nebulous factor such as pleasure versus pain, which is approximately the way in which Bentham defined utility.[15] It follows that individuals do not necessarily act in the interests of their kinsmen or fellow ethnic-group members rather than in those of their neighbours. The proportion of genes that one shares with one's kin decreases with the distance of the relationship. The calculus of fitness-maximization therefore may well require us to co-operate with close non-related neighbours rather than with distant kinsmen (who are distant both in terms of residence and kinship), inasmuch as one's own genetic reproductive success is more enhanced by co-operating with the former than with the latter.

There are thus two factors that bear on the process of deciding what is or is not a desirable association: "Degree of biological relatedness is one of the two main terms predicting co-operation or conflict. The other is the cost-benefit ratio of the transactions between actors."[16] The calculus is a precise one. Van den Berghe suggests that if a full sister gets twice as much out of the beneficent action of her full brother as the cost of the effort that he puts into it, then it becomes worthwhile for the brother in genetic fitness-maximizing terms to undertake the action, given that full siblings share half their genes. As the distance between relatives increases, the benefit accruing has to be proportionately greater.[17] Ethnic solidarity is therefore the translation of inescapable natural laws into terms of social organization. The ethnic group is as natural as the kin-group or the family. By the same token, socialism is doomed to failure since it presupposes the possibility of people acting unselfishly.[18]

In presenting ethnicity as a special form of sociality "irreducible to any other,"[19] and, more particularly, irreducible to class, Van den Berghe is explicitly applying the lessons of socio-biology to ethnicity.[20] But beyond that he is also within the tradition that seeks to naturalize social phenomena. Van den Berghe does not seek to naturalize social inequality in the same way as others working within the tradition have done, that is, with the evident intention of justifying it. He does attempt, however, to reduce social situations that are marked by inequality to natural rather than social causes. The logic of the argument is similar to that of E.O. Wilson when he forecasts the impossibility of the liberation of women, given our genetic inheritance.[21] Van den Berghe operationalizes his theory of ethnicity with reference to apartheid. Apartheid is not explicable in terms of some economic system but in those of the maximization of the reproductive success of South African whites. Ultimately the issue is the whites' "right of survival on South African soil."[22] This is not intended to be a defensive position, simply an explanatory one, but as in the case of Wilson on feminism, social issues are reduced to genetic determinism in such a way that there seems ultimately no point in anyone's attempting to do anything about them.

Van den Berghe, by making nature the key by which all social phenomena are to be explained, places himself outside the mainstream sociological tradition. As Sahlins has been at pains to point out, culture as the way in which human societies respond to the environments in which they find themselves is not reduceable to nature.[23] It was Durkheim who most clearly articulated the starting-point of the alternative position, although he was working in a tradition that goes back to Rousseau and beyond. For Durkheim, far from being reduceable to the natural, the social represents the triumph of human beings acting in many cases against nature. Egalitarianism, for example, operates expressly against natural inequalities of strength, as do all forms of social democracy and the redistribution of wealth.[24] Inasmuch as society, for Durkheim, represents the triumph over rather than the subordination to nature, it is more appropriate to look for social than for natural patterns of causality. The more customary and the properly sociological approach to ethnicity seeks to understand it in precisely such social terms.

Opposed to the understanding of ethnicity as natural and primordial is the view that takes it as being equivalent to the whole collective identity of a particular ethnic group, with its infinite number of component parts. This approach can also be situated within a particular current in the sociological tradition. It goes back at least to Tylor, writing in 1871, who considered that "just as the catalogue of all the species of plants and animals of a district represents its Flora and Fauna, so the list of all the items of the general life of a people represents that whole which we call its culture."[25] The idea is therefore to "classify and arrange" all known cultures in a "probable order of evolution,"[26] given that the pre-eminent aim of nineteenth-century social science was to set up an evolutionary trajectory with nineteenth-century industrial society at its foremost and uppermost end. Social anthropology thus set out to collect cultures with the intention of classifying them. Ultimate purposes have changed, at least officially, *en cours de route*, leading in one direction to a school of anthropologists referred to derisively by Leach as "butterfly collectors," culture-collection for them having become an end in itself.[27] However, the original intention has been important for establishing the idea that a culture is what a people is, and if what a people is is also held to be its ethnicity, then culture and ethnicity can come to blend imperceptibly into each other. Barth, in *Ethnic Groups and Boundaries*, refers to this all-embracing approach to ethnicity as one that treats the ethnic group as an "island to itself."[28] As an example of just such an island, I take an article by Dahya on Pakistani ethnicity in industrial cities in Britain.[29]

Dahya's basic assumption is that Pakistani ethnicity is what Pakistanis *are*. When they arrive in Britain as immigrants, their ethnicity comes under threat from a British ethnicity that includes everything from fish and chips to non-arranged marriages. Within the immigrant community, according to Dahya, there are those who attempt to maintain Pakistani ethnicity against the onslaught of English schooling and customs either for their own material or community interests or in the interests of tradition or belief.

Traders, for example, benefit directly from the maintenance of such ethnicity inasmuch as they enjoy a monopoly in the provision of consumer goods imported from Pakistan, or in the retailing of food, clothing, and ornaments that play a part in ethnic identity. Providers of services to the community also have a vested interest in ethnicity-maintenance since their privileged position depends on their retaining the custom of their Pakistani clientèle and thereby protecting themselves from the competition of professional groups in the broader society. The monopoly of these groups is threatened by the erosion of Pakistani ethnicity in the second generation, and they are strongly represented on all bodies that aim to protect and promote traditional styles of life.

Dahya goes on to argue that the housing preferences of newly arrived Pakistani immigrants can only be properly understood against the background of their ethnicity. Property ownership (however small the amount of land or the dwelling might be) is the great desideratum in rural Pakistan, and it is understandable that immigrants to Britain, who tend, almost without exception, to come from smallholding families, seek to buy houses rather than to rent them. Rex and Moore's study of Sparkbrook, by contrast, is built round the notion that Pakistani immigrants tend to be forced into buying old, decaying properties as a result of racial discrimination. Councils actively discriminate against them in the allocation of council houses, building societies refuse to lend to them for the purchase of better-quality housing, and private owners will not let to them.[30] Dahya rejects this argument on the basis of Pakistani preferences that are built into Pakistani ethnicity. They want to own rather than to rent, partly for the reasons suggested above and partly in order to remit as much money as possible to their families, who, in the early 1960s, were for the most part still in Pakistan. Indeed, they rarely had the choice, in that they remained under the authority of the head of their extended family. They were also predisposed to open their houses to as many of their relatives and acquaintances as possible on the grounds of hospitality and community self-help.[31]

What Rex and Moore see as overcrowding and slum conditions are therefore – according to Dahya – the continuation, in Britain, of the laws of hospitality and the residential practices that exist in rural Pakistan. Solid stone, brick, or cement houses are also the exception rather than the rule in their villages of origin, and few of them have the amenities that even the more dilapidated housing in Britain has – electricity, gas, water, and drains, for example. Rex and Moore condemn the living standards of Pakistani immigrants in Britain through British eyes and blame them on British racial prejudice, whereas Dahya explains them as a result of choices in line with ethnicity-based preferences. He does not deny that such immigrants are constrained to buy the least expensive housing on the market by their own financial circumstances, nor that they are subject to racial discrimination, but emphasizes that such housing is generally close to their place of work and, whereas it allows for the development of what outsiders might call a ghetto, to insiders it constitutes a protective environment and one in which ethnicity can be maintained. For Dahya, therefore, Pakistani ethnicity in Britain is what distinguishes the Pakistani community from the surrounding society. It is not so much a boundary phenomenon between the two groups as the totality of their separate identities as groups.

Abner Cohen's approach to ethnicity is somewhat similar. He begins with the following broad definition: "An ethnic group can be operationally defined as a collectivity of people who (a) share some patterns of normative behaviour and (b) form part of a larger population, interacting with people from other collectivities within the framework of a social system. The term ethnicity refers to the degree of conformity by members of the collectivity to the shared norms in the course of social interaction."[32] For Cohen, the fact that the collectivity in question should form part of a larger population is important. If it does not, but represents rather an entity in itself divorced from other collectivities, we are dealing with nationality rather than ethnicity.

As an example of such an ethnic group Cohen chooses the City of London business and financial elite. His point is that any form of association can be organized on either formal or informal lines, or, more usually, a combination of the two. By formal organization, Cohen understands Weberian bureaucratic rationality, with its implied efficiency in achieving group goals. Informal organization concerns the whole panoply of ritualized and symbolic behaviour that can grow up around an association and can contribute to the maintenance of group identity and cohesion. These various forms of behaviour constitute norms to which members of the association are required to conform in order to be considered members and to enjoy the fruits of membership. Where an association is only informally organized (that is, is not formally constituted as an association), it is precisely these informal patterns of organization that create the cohesion that otherwise might be created in formal terms. An employers' confederation with offices, researchers, office staff, and membership would thus be an example of formal organization, where the organization can ensure continuity and cohesion irrespective of any informal organization that may exist alongside it. The City elite, by contrast, has no formal existence as an association, but it exists none the less, is seen to exist, and sees itself as existing. What is more, the conduct of business and financial deals in the City depends heavily on a shared system of norms that allows for mutual trust and provides the basis for the purely word-of-mouth agreement and understanding that underlie a large proportion of business transactions. This evokes the notion of Miliband's ruling elite,[33] except that here it is a relatively small group of businessmen and bankers who speak with the same accent, have their clothes made by the same tailors, went to the same schools, take the same newspapers, go to the same concerts, and marry each other's sisters. There grows up an informal organizational network in which individual members can recognize each other by their cufflinks, their turns of phrase, or their shoes and that comes to provide the basis for what Cohen describes as an "ethnic" group. This definition is slightly more nuanced than Dahya's in that it refers by definition to groups within groups, but it still treats the totality of a shared life-style as constituting ethnic identity.

This approach to ethnicity not only has connections with classical cultural anthropology but also with mainstream non-Marxist sociology, inasmuch as that sociology has been primarily concerned with values, or, as Therborn suggests, with the nature of the ideological consensus that underlies and permits the existence of social systems.[34] The constellation of values that characterizes a given society or subgroup within that society is merely another way of approaching its culture. One can approach it classically in terms of "all the items of the general life of a people" (Tylor), but one can also approach it at the level of the values and shared ideas that lead a people to behave and produce in a certain way. The idea of ethnicity is thus well suited to the study of systems of ideas that are characteristic of particular ethnic or national groups. Schneider's study of American kinship would be a case in point.[35] Technically speaking, *being* American is not normally considered a question of ethnicity, given that American society is itself supposed to be composed of ethnic groups, but there is a point at which it comes to be difficult to maintain a distinction between concepts when what they refer to is essentially the same phenomenon but at different social levels.

These are all examples of ethnicity or ethnicity-related factors understood as constituting a closed system, whether or not that closed system is explicable in terms of nature or, as in the case of Cohen's business elite, in terms of function or monopolistic closure. They differ from Weber's position in that for Weber the ethnic group is not constituted out of its culture but rather uses culture – among other things – to define and allow itself to exist as an identifiable group. Cohen's position is close to Weber's, but there remains a distinction made by Weber between culture and ethnicity that is to some extent blurred in both Dahya's and Cohen's argument.

For Dahya, culture would seem to be interchangeable with ethnicity as a way of referring to the totality of practices and beliefs that make up Pakistani identity in Britain, and Cohen presents what one might consider to be the shared culture of the City elite as being constitutive of – or simply being – their shared ethnicity. Weber and Parsons, by contrast, see culture as one of the ways in which ethnicity can be symbolized. This viewpoint is further developed by Fredrik Barth, who distinguishes between ethnicity and culture by remarking that the same ethnic group can undergo cultural change over time. It is therefore incorrect to say that it is shared culture that is constitutive of ethnic identity; ethnicity is rather a feature of social process and interaction between groups.[36]

One could take, as an example of Barth's argument, the case of Scottish Highland ethnicity, which was, at one stage in history, considered to be intimately bound up with the clan system. With the demise of that system, the same ethnic category could still be identified on the basis of the survival of Scottish Gaelic, but with the language itself in decline through the nineteenth century and the emergence of a new form of protected subsistence land-use (crofting), the same ethnic group came to be defined in terms of land-use ("the Highland crofter," "the crofting areas of Scotland"). Presumably with the demise of that system, some other feature will take its place as in some way distinctive of Highland ethnicity, even if it is merely that of geographical location in a remote and distinctive area. In other words, Highland ethnicity is simply that. This would suggest that ethnicity is not reduceable to culture, inasmuch as culture cannot relate to an untransformed physical environment, whereas ethnicity can. Ethnicity can equally use the untransformed physical characteristics of human beings as markers that are also dissociable from culture. In other words, ethnicity can use cultural features as labels, but it can equally well use anything else that comes to hand.

Parsons comes closer to articulating the Weberian position. Whatever the reason for the survival of ethnic groups in American society, they use cultural factors – such as eating habits – as symbols that stand for the existence of the group but do not necessarily have any central role in the maintenance of the group's existence.[37] We are in the presence, therefore, not so much of the survival of ethnic identities that pre-dated immigration into the United States as of the manipulation of some aspects of those identities to symbolize group identities in the new situation. The question then becomes what ethnic groups really consist of, if what is normally taken to be their ethnicity – that is, for example, *being* Italian – emerges on closer scrutiny to be a sort of "empty symbolism."[38] Parsons' position on ethnicity is ultimately unclear. America is held up as the type of the "ethnically pluralistic national societal community,"[39] and yet Parsons interprets Schneider's reference to the empty ethnic symbol as meaning that "the symbolization of ethnic identification is primarily focused on style of life distinctiveness within the larger framework of much more nearly uniform American social structure. This social structure is differentiated by class, by region and by type of community, for example, metropolitan contrasted with small town, but not very greatly on an ethnic basis."[40]

We thus move from the ethnic group as an island in which everything that is distinct and unique about it constitutes its ethnicity to the ethnic group as a functional entity whose actual distinctness from other surrounding groups comes to be increasingly vestigial. This leads to the notion of ethnicity as a boundary phenomenon. That is, ethnicity does not, or should not (in that we are free to define ethnicity in any way we want) refer to group identity in isolation but rather to groups in contact with other groups.

For Wallman and Barth ethnicity is a feature of contact between groups.[41] Just as in a Marxist analysis of class the existence of one class presupposes the existence of another, so in this approach to ethnicity the existence of an ethnic group presupposes the existence of another such group or groups. Wallman approaches the question of "racial" or "ethnic" divisions in Britain (having decided that there is no really sound basis for distinguishing between the two)[42] not so much as relating to differences of substance or differences in cultural practice and life-style (as in Dahya's study) but as boundary phenomena. For social or economic reasons that have nothing to do with ethnicity, there exist bounded groups within British society that consider themselves to be groups and are considered as such by outsiders, and certain characteristics of these groups are chosen to mark the boundaries between them. Every boundary has two sides to it, and the way it is defined on one side may be different from the way it is defined on the other, each group selecting what it wants as the differentiating feature.

Wallman looks at three kinds of ethnic process to illustrate what she means: boundary formation, boundary shift, and boundary dissonance. The process of boundary formation is illustrated in the description of the creation of a housing-action area in South London. By a stroke of the planner's pen, a certain area of substandard housing is designated for special treatment, grant aid, and renovation. This administrative act creates a distinction between the insiders who live within and therefore belong to the area and the outsiders who do not, in that the insiders develop a sense of belongingness and group identity that did not exist before. The purely haphazard boundedness of the housing area is thus translated into an "ethnic" community boundary.[43]

This example demonstrates the way in which ethnic boundaries flow from social conditions and have nothing necessarily to do with pre-existing cultural or other differences. Any such differences may, however, then be brought into play as boundary markers in so far as they coincide with social boundaries. If, for example, the majority of those living in the area have some form of distinct cultural homogeneity, and there is therefore some congruence between the imposed boundary and that homogeneous group, then the one can come to be identified with the other, and the stigma of living in a substandard housing area can come to be attached to belonging to the ethnic group that is identified with it. This is a point that Ulf Hannerz also makes concerning ethnicity and class in the United States. Traditionally there has been such a high level of congruence between the two that the one can come to be identified with the other, such that the socially mobile ethnic-group member may have difficulty shaking off the class stigma that attaches to the group. In terms of boundaries this means that if the majority of all first-generation Italian immigrants to the United States are classifiable as working class, then in a given city where the bulk of the working class is composed of such immigrants, being *Italian* can come to be associated with being *working class*.[44]

The phenomenon of boundary shift, as described by Wallman, is also relevant to this process. It can arise from the bundling together into the same ethnic category of groups who consider themselves to be ethnically distinct.[45] In Britain this has been the lot of those "Asian" immigrants who come from different parts of the Indian subcontinent, are frequently of different religious affiliations, speak different languages, and have different cultural practices. On the socio-economic basis of their occupying the same position in British class structure, they have been grouped together under the label "Asian" by dominant opinion in the "host" society. This external ethnic labelling and boundary construction (society being henceforth divisible into Asians and non-Asians) has had the effect of reducing the significance of the boundaries within the group classified as Asian and increasing that of the boundary that separates them from the "native" British. Boundary formation from without can thus produce boundary shift within. Something of the same process is described by Hannerz in relation to the Jewish immigrants of long standing in the United States and the more recent impoverished Jewish immigrants from Eastern Europe. In spite of the socio-economic gulf that lay between the two groups, their being bundled together in the same category by dominant WASP opinion (on religious grounds) has led to the existence of a solidarity that did not exist before.[46]

Boundary imposition can therefore give rise to boundary shift. The third of Wallman's boundary processes relates to dissonance as the opposite of congruence.[47] In fact the two tend to coexist, inasmuch as there is always a minority that falls within the boundaries of, for example, an "Italian" working class in various parts of North American cities without itself being Italian. The dissonance is resolved by their being labelled "Italian." Wallman's example concerns rich members of the black community in a society where "richness" is normally associated with "whiteness." Here the dissonance is resolved by seeing rich blacks as "whites."

There are thus two principal sets of opposition within the different non-Marxist approaches to the theory of ethnicity. There is an opposition between those who ascribe to ethnicity a natural, biological basis and those who see it as arising from social factors, and there is an opposition between those who conceptualize ethnicity as a content in itself and those who see it as a phenomenon arising out of the contact between groups. These different theoretical approaches, however, share a concern with the role played by ethnicity in actual or potential social conflict. This concern has been well articulated by Daniel Bell.

For Bell, ethnicity has come to replace class as the central factor in the consolidation of groups for strategic purposes.[48] He considers that the period when economic factors and relationships were at the heart of social structure in complex societies, and when it made sense to talk of class confrontation within the realm of production as the feature of central structural importance, has now given way to a period where political factors have come to be more important than economic ones. Industrial disputes are now decided more at the level of political negotiation than in straight subordination to market forces. It follows that class is not as important as it once was, although it is possible that it might re-emerge in the context of a new economic crisis. The enduring significance of ethnicity in America Bell considers a result of the fact that ethnicity as a form of group affiliation is ideally suited to the political arena, since it is both expressive and instrumental.[49] The significance of ethnicity thus flows from the kinds of changes that are taking place in society, as a result of which ethnicity has come to replace class as the focus for group identity and action.

CHAPTER SEVEN

The Players and the Masks: Marxist Approaches to Ethnicity

I have placed the various approaches to class in contemporary Marxism on an axis running from empiricist to abstractionist, according to whether the primary concern is the experience of class or its conceptualization.[1] There is, however, no disagreement within Marxism as to the reality of class as a phenomenon. In the *Communist Manifesto* Marx and Engels state that "the theoretical tenets of the Communists are not based in any way on ideas [or] on principles invented or discovered by some social reformer or other. They are just general expressions of the actual relations in an existing class struggle, a continuing historical movement that is taking place before our very eyes."[2] The idea that class is not a construct placed upon the world but a reality that exists in it resurfaces frequently in Marxist theory. Poulantzas, for example, condemns the notion of social class as a model, since it suggests that there is a reality that exists external to class, the latter being just one way in which that reality can be divided up.[3] For Poulantzas, the richness of reality is not something that exists apart from class but is class itself. This is scarcely surprising, since Marxism is based on the premise that classes exist and that existing class struggle underlies the replacement in history of one mode of production by another. To call into question the reality of class is therefore also to call into question a basic premise of Marxism.

In the case of ethnicity the situation is different. Ethnicity is an analytical construct that can help us to understand certain phenomena in the world but is not a reality in the same sense as class. Class is not a construct that helps us to understand but is what is there to be understood. Beyond this, however, ethnicity is marginal to traditional Marxist theory inasmuch as that theory is built around class struggle and relations of production. The ethnic or national affiliation of the agents involved in this class struggle may intrude upon it in one form or another but are of only incidental significance. The important factor is ownership of and separation from the means of production, not which ethnic groups may or may not be represented among one or other of the two classes. At best such ethnicity may be of passing interest in a given historical situation, but it is neither the central interest nor the lasting one.

Again the *Communist Manifesto* establishes the marginal significance of ethnicity for Marxism. In a series of well-known passages Marx and Engels answer the accusation that communists seek to abolish nationality and the homeland. They describe the bourgeoisie, with its development of the world market, as already breaking down national boundaries. Although the proletariat will have to take power within the nation-state, it will be one of a different order from that of the bourgeois nation-state and one whose boundaries will eventually disappear with the end of the exploitation of man by man and nation by nation.[4] These are, of course, the sweeping pronouncements that one expects of a manifesto, but none the less they show the slight significance attributed by Marx and Engels to questions of nationhood and nationality. Such distinctions are of decreasing relevance and importance in a world where increasingly the same classes confront each other everywhere, regardless of national boundaries.

This sets the tone for the treatment of ethnicity and nationality within the Marxist tradition as peripheral to the global struggle between bourgeoisie and proletariat. That struggle ends up bringing all other struggles and oppositions into alignment with itself. Nationality is the hollow shell in which class struggle is localized, whereas ethnicity is the mask that conceals class identity. Both have to be taken into account, but only in order that the shell might be broken and the mask torn aside. I begin by looking at certain approaches to ethnicity within Marxism that illustrate this traditional understanding. Subsequently I turn to the questions that have been raised concerning it, notably by Saul and Nairn, and to the theoretical perspective on ethnicity put forward by Rousseau, in which it ceases to be considered just a shell or a mask but can have a role in the determination of class. I finally consider a context in which ethnicity completes its displacement from the periphery to the centre, for a particular brand of Marxism, in the form of racism. This approach to Marxist approaches to ethnicity could be described as looking first at ethnicity the mask, second at ethnicity the role, and third at ethnicity and the players themselves.

According to Marxist tradition, ethnicity is the mask behind which actors conceal their class position both from each other and from themselves. This process of concealment recalls the fetishization of relations of production, in which the exchange-value of two products ceases to be seen as the equivalent of the work that went into their production and comes to be seen as inherent in the products themselves (so many oranges being "worth" so many apples). The concealment becomes complete when the oranges are simply considered to be "worth" so much money. Money, therefore, comes to be the mask that hides relative values in terms of labour. The reality of production relations is hidden behind the "face value" of money. So it is with the outward marks and tokens of ethnicity that serve to mask underlying relations of production and exploitation.

One example of this approach to ethnicity is Micheline Labelle's *Idéologie de couleur et classes sociales en Haïti*.[5] In the area of Port-au-Prince there is a bourgeoisie, a petty bourgeoisie, and an industrial proletariat, while in the country areas there are three main categories of peasantry that can be ranked in relation to each other on a scale running from moderate wealth at one end to poverty at the other. In general, these class distinctions coincide with differences of colour, with paler skin at the bourgeois and petty bourgeois end of the spectrum as a result of greater intermarriage with Europeans. It is thus a simple step to "explain" the differences between classes in terms of biological differences rather than relations of production, and this is what Labelle describes as the *"idéologie de couleur"* or *"idéologie coloriste"* in Haïti.[6] In other words, the poverty and hard physical labour of the poorer peasantry is associated with their blackness, and this association is made not only by the bourgeois and petty bourgeois but by the poor peasants themselves. Equally, the intermediate position of the petty bourgeoisie is "explained" by their mixed composition in terms of colour, while the wealth of the bourgeoisie is attributed to their "whiteness." There is a further characteristic of colourist mystification: not only is wealth and power attributed to whiteness, but whiteness is attributed to wealth and power in so far as wealthy blacks in certain contexts can be referred to as "whites."[7] This is the process associated by Wallman with "boundary dissonance,"[8] that is, where the exception to a rule is incorporated within a general classificatory scheme by a form of fiction.

The conclusion of the study is thus that the relationships among classes in Haïti are mystified as relationships among groups stratified on the basis of colour, differences of colour being not only associated with different strata but considered in some way to "explain" those differences. The class identity of the actors and the nature of their roles in the process of production are concealed behind the mask of ethnicity, or rather, the mask becomes their identity. This mystification serves to maintain the exploitative position of the bourgeoisie and the exploited condition of the poorer peasants and the urban proletariat, inasmuch as it is considered to be in the nature of things that those with lighter skin should be bourgeois and those with darker skin proletarians.

The notion of the functionality of ethnicity for capitalism lies at the heart of the traditional Marxist approach. It is central, for example, to Marxist analyses of the effects of immigration on class relations and class consciousness in Europe and North America. It has always been the effect of migration to bring into close contact groups that previously had little or nothing to do with each other and therefore exhibit significant differences of language and custom. The problems for mutual comprehension and communication thus created become acute with that particular long-distance form of labour migration that came into existence with the industrialization of Europe and North America, the development of resource extraction in South and East Africa, and the end of slavery in Central America and the Caribbean. In the last two cases tens of thousands of indentured labourers were exported from the Indian subcontinent in the latter half of the nineteenth century to work on the Caribbean sugar plantations and on railway building in Africa.[9]

In the early years of industrialization in Europe, the wildly fluctuating but none the less steadily increasing needs of capital for labour power were satisfied by drawing off the surplus population from the rural hinterland or, in the case of England, from densely populated rural Ireland, maintained in a state of non-industrialization, with the exception of Belfast, by the Act of Union of 1800.[10] Such relatively localized migration brought together groups with different dialects, religious affiliations, and, in the case of Irish immigrants to Britain, broader ethnic identities and traditional hostilities. The incoming immigrant groups were also forced to accept whatever work they could find at whatever wages that were on offer. There thus emerged a congruence between their position within the working class and their identity as a group distinct from that amalgam of internal migrants and natives of the industrial towns that then constituted the English working class.

The dividing lines within the working class were thus drawn both along lines of skill and pay levels, and along those of religion and broader ethnic identity. The hostility between groups was fuelled by the fear on the part of the native or established working class that their conditions of work would deteriorate with the readiness of the new arrivals to work under any conditions, a fear that in many cases was justified.[11] The underlying reasons, therefore, for intergroup hostility were economic, and incidental to those causal factors were the various distinctions of religious affiliation and ethnic identity. Because of the congruence between the two, the incidental ethnic division came to be symbolic of the underlying economic one, and a convenient way of identifying the threat posed by each side as perceived by the other. Needless to say, this caused both sides to displace on to each other what should have been their conjoined hostility against the exploiting class. The established working class attempted to maintain its relatively privileged position by excluding immigrant labour from its preserves and the latter reacted against that exclusion. Attention was thus displaced from the underlying economic causes of the hostility on to the superficial attributes of the groups involved, and, as in the case of colourist ideology in Haïti, those superficial attributes, from being purely incidental, became first emblematic and finally an integral part of intra-working-class conflict. In the context of inter-ethnic hostility within the nineteenth-century English working class, Marx noted in 1870 that the native English worker "feels himself a member of the ruling nation and so turns himself into a tool of the aristocrats and capitalists of his country *against Ireland*, thus strengthening their domination *over himself*. He cherishes religious, social and national prejudices against the Irish worker. His attitude toward him is much the same as that of the 'poor whites' to the 'niggers' in the former slave states of the USA. The Irishman pays him back with interest in his own money. He sees in the English worker at once the accomplice and the stupid tool of the *English domination in Ireland*."[12]

The displacement of hostility away from the dominant class and on to working-class rivals is a familiar effect of the long-, and even short-, distance labour migration that has come to be commonplace where capitalism creates surplus population in some sectors (agriculture, for example) and a demand for labour-power in others (manufacturing industry). Whereas in the nineteenth century the need for labour-power could be largely satisfied from the various rural hinterlands of the industrializing powers, accelerating production in the post–second World War period and competition for labour-power, together with declining birth rates, have created a situation where even Canada has been forced to modify its whitist immigration policy in order to maintain its labour supply.[13]

Over and above the internal demand for labour associated with the economic boom period of the 1950s and 1960s, there has been the demand for a work-force that has no choice but to work at minimum and even sub-minimum wages in sectors where competition from outside the capitalist industrial heartland – in areas where wages and costs are lower – has forced down profit levels. The only way profit levels can be maintained in, for example, the Canadian garment industry or some of the core sectors of British textiles and manufacturing is by reducing wage costs and fixed capital investment in new machinery. Thus the familiar situation of the immigrant worker: low wage levels, antiquated machinery, poor working conditions, and long hours, and this need only be for the maintenance of existing profit levels, not their increase. The bulk of such enterprises are caught in a descending spiral that only a protectionist economic policy can stop, and immigrant labour – preferably illegal, since illegal immigrants are less likely to protest – is the ideal accompaniment to the antiquated machinery that is forced to extend its working life beyond the point at which, all things being equal, it has ceased to be competitive.

This is the background to the contemporary Marxist approach to ethnicity and the working class in the old industrial heartlands, and in areas immediately peripheral to those heartlands. Ethnic consciousness is seen as an incidental effect of long-distance labour migration, one that comes to play a central role in maintaining divisions in the working-class and displacing working class hostility from its natural enemy – the owners of the means of production – on to those who are seen to be class rivals. It is thus functional for capital, and entrepreneurs in the sectors affected are invariably suspected of playing on linguistic and other differences to maintain a divided and preferably ill-informed and non-unionized workforce.[14] The role of ethnicity can only be understood in terms of class struggle, and attempts to explain it that do not take that struggle into account are missing the point.[15] If one limits oneself to the superficial differences of colour, language, or custom in order to explain inequality, one is in danger of becoming as mystified as those who explain their own social position in terms of such variables. The real issue is relations of production, and a proper approach to ethnicity has two aspects. First, in analysis, we need to see through the masks of ethnicity themselves to the roles and actors that are concealed behind them, and second, in a program of political action (and most Marxist analyses have action as their goal) we need to expose the division of the working class on the basis of ethnicity for what it is: a form of self-deception that can only be of benefit to capital.

Such studies tend to concentrate on the experience of immigrant workers, notably women, in the worst-paid sectors of the economy, and their isolation behind the barriers of linguistic and cultural difference at work and at home.[16] They emphasize the need for the native working class to be demystified concerning the role of immigrant labour in the economy. Attention needs to be drawn to the fact that immigrant labour creates a demand for goods and services and occupies low-paid positions in manufacturing and elsewhere that have been rejected by native labour. It is only such demystification that can lead to working-class solidarity and an end to racism. This is the traditional Marxist approach to ethnicity in industrial capitalist societies where ethnic differentiation and inter-ethnic conflict are seen as side-effects of labour migration, but side-effects that are none the less causes of mystification. Ethnicity is not, therefore, dismissed or ignored, but is rather viewed as an element of secondary interest and importance that conceals what is really determinant, a minor player who succeeds in upstaging the main characters.

While it is important to present the conditions of existence of an oppressed ethnic minority and to explain how the divisions created on the basis of ethnicity contribute to the maintenance of the domination of capital over a divided working class, it is still necessary to give ethnicity as a concept a place within theory that goes beyond any function it may have, and to face up to the nature of ethnicity as a way of forging unity and solidarity that has, on many occasions in the past, proved more effective than class. Edna Bonacich adresses the first of these inadequacies in her theory of the split labour-market.[17] She explicitly rejects traditional Marxist explanation, which, she writes, "takes as given that almost everything serves the interest of the capitalist class. Thus the key theoretical question becomes: In what way does this phenomenon serve these interests? The question is parallel to the functionalist question: How does this phenomenon preserve the social system? In both cases, if one can show how it serves these interests (either of capitalism or of the social system), the phenomenon is felt to be 'explained.'"[18]

What she proposes as an alternative is a theory relating to the development of a split working class under capitalism, partly as a result of colonialism, but principally as a consequence of the struggles of organized labour within capitalist society. One part of the working class succeeds in becoming relatively better off in terms of wages and conditions; the other – consisting largely of women and immigrant workers – constitutes a cheap labour force. The latter necessarily represent a threat to the former, and in so far as the internal class division coincides with differences of "race," ethnicity, or sex, intraclass hostility can come to be expressed in terms of racism or sexism. Class division, however, remains the basic determinant.[19]

While writing off the more traditional approach, split-labour-market theory resembles it in treating ethnicity or race as the mask that has to be stripped off in order to discover the "real" relations underneath. It differs only in that capital is no longer considered to be in some way the instigator of the process that leads to the mystification in the first place. But inasmuch as the more traditional approach sees the process of masking as having its origin within a *system* of oppression rather than in the *will* of a dominant class within that system – which is the case in the examples given above – the differences between split-labour-market theory and traditional Marxist theory would seem to be minimal.

The problem underlying these different approaches remains a theoretical one. It is, in other words, insufficient to approach a phenomenon such as ethnicity simply at the empirical level of conditions of existence and function, and problematic to treat it merely as a form of mystification of production relations that will disappear with a correct understanding of those relations. Such is the basis for a reassessment of ethnicity, and beyond ethnicity, of nationalism, for a school of Marxism that has found the traditional approach inadequate.

John Saul's article "The Dialectic of Class and Tribe" brings together some of these preoccupations, as does the work of Rey, Laclau, and Nairn.[20] The principal butt of Saul's article is not so much that form of Marxism that writes off ethnicity as mystification but rather non-Marxist approaches to urban Africa in which a class analysis is dismissed in favour of one in terms of tribalism. Saul echoes Mafeje's sentiments in "The Ideology of Tribalism,"[21] in which tribalism is accepted with reservations as a way of defining a certain kind of pre-urban social organization but is dismissed as being misleading and irrelevant in the context of urban migration.

Mafeje's main point is that in any city in the world the inhabitants are divided on the grounds of religion, language, origin, and a host of other factors, as they are in urban Africa. Why then is the phenomenon described as tribalism in Africa and not elsewhere? Although it may draw on pre-urban tribal divisions, among other things, it is not itself an example of tribalism and should not be described as such, but is rather the result of new urban conditions and can only be understood in the light of them. Saul would agree with this inasmuch as urban ethnicity in Africa is distinct from tribalism and therefore cannot adequately be explained in the light of tribalism. At the same time he draws on Rey's essay on the articulation of modes of production to explain certain characteristics of urban ethnicity in Africa with reference to prevailing modes of production.

Rey distinguishes three phases in the implantation of the capitalist mode of production in a social formation where it has not come into existence as an indigenous development, as was the case in western Europe.[22] In the first case it is present alongside existing modes of production inasmuch as it develops trading links and to some extent exploits natural resources but does not otherwise interfere with the existing modes of production. This phase does not presuppose the existence of a labour force separated from the means of production, and therefore of its own reproduction, but simply the presence of foreign capital on the periphery. In the second phase capital intrudes more directly into existing modes of production and fundamentally alters their character but without entirely displacing them. This is the stage that has been reached in the majority of economies outside the industrial heartlands; it is particularly marked in Africa by the familiar forms of labour migration in which the migrants are brought up within their home areas and return there at the termination of employment or on retirement. The labour migrant retains a foot in both camps, and capital is relieved of much of the financial burden of reproducing and maintaining the labour power it needs when it is not actually in employment. The third phase in Rey's scheme is the total penetration of the capitalist mode of production into all sectors of production and the disappearance of all pre-existing modes in their subordination to capital. However, this phase has only been reached in one or two of the most industrialized countries.

Saul draws attention to Rey's second phase and the relationship that it proposes between urban industrial capitalism and the various modes of production in the non-industrial hinterland that are accompanied by tribal forms of social organization.[23] Migrant workers in such a phase have structural class determination and class position – in Poulantzas' terms[24] – in urban society but also retain their tribal affiliation and status, which is reactivated on return to the home area. This is the real dialectic between class and tribe that exists in the experience of the individual worker. Such extra-urban affiliations can also serve as the basis for the building up of political followings by would-be powerful individuals in the urban bourgeoisie or petty bourgeoisie, as well as the familiar relationships of patronage that accompany all immigration. Saul, therefore, suggests that class and tribal relations (properly so called) can coexist within the experience of the individual worker and that the latter are not simply a form of mystification, although they can provide the basis for non-class alignments in urban communities.

However, the question is not simply one of the articulation of modes of production and the "reality" of class and tribal relations in experience but of the "appeal" of ethnicity or of nationalism in the forging of political unity across class lines but within ethnic and national boundaries. For Nairn, the great failure of Marxism has been its inability to come to terms with, or even understand, nationalism.[25] This is the more regrettable since any attempt to organize political action on the grounds of class awareness runs headlong into questions of ethnic and national identity. Nairn attributes the contemporary development of nationalism first to imperialism. Non-industrialized countries, or their ruling classes, were duped into believing that they would gradually come to share in the fruits and riches of industrialization and "Western" or "Northern" consumerism with the spread of capitalism. The reality of imperialism, however, was to demonstrate that, far from being included within the brotherhood of industrialized nations, peripheral economies were to be brutally maintained in the status of poor relations, and more than that, poor relations who contributed more than their fair share to the family budget and yet were to be permanently barred from taking their place at the table. The only way open to nations thus excluded, and as a reaction to such exclusion, was either to create a form of national solidarity or to fall apart at the seams along internal ethnic and geographical divisions. This has led to the "acceptable" and "unacceptable" nationalisms of, for example, Latin America and Asia, their acceptability depending on the viewer's location along the political spectrum.

A nationalism on a different scale came into existence in Europe and in Asia in the 1930s, but for reasons that are not unlike those that led to the formation of nationalist movements elsewhere. Germany, Italy, and Japan were all, in different ways, within or on the edge of the industrial heartlands and yet were threatened with relegation to an inferior league in markets dominated by foreign capital. Nationalism in the form of fascism was, and is, the same reactive phenomenon as nationalism everywhere, which, according to Nairn, all contain the seeds of both the good and the bad. Nationalism is not in itself a gateway through which all social formations *necessarily* pass on their way to capitalist or socialist development, as some have suggested, but it is none the less a gateway, and one over which is placed the two-faced image of Janus. On the one hand, Janus looks back to a past, mythical if necessary, and on the other, towards a future in the name of which the nation is summoned. Nairn's point is that, once passed, the gateway of nationalism does not allow a return passage, since nationalism unleashes forces that take on a life of their own independent of the will of those who conjure them up. Marxism is therefore at its peril in not recognizing nationalism for the power that it is.

Laclau makes something of the same point, in a more restrained way, in his explanation of the rise of fascism in Germany in the 1930s.[26] In any social formation, appeals to the masses can be made either on grounds of class or on those of the power bloc against the people. The bourgeoisie frequently succeeds in imposing its own class perspective on society and thereby plunges the subordinate classes into a state of false consciousness. The "people" can also be appealed to, however, on the grounds of populism or democracy against an abusive power bloc that may well consist of an outmoded class that is still hanging on to the reigns of power. The working class and petty bourgeoisie in Germany were, according to Laclau, open to being appealed to on this latter basis, and were effectively and successfully so appealed to by fascism. It was the strategic error of Marxism that it failed to do the same but rather waited fatalistically in the wings for the collapse of the capitalist system from its own internal contradictions.

The point of Nairn, Laclau, and Saul is that Marxists, in dismissing ethnicity and nationalism, can end up not only mystifying themselves as much as they hold others to be mystified but, from the point of view of political action at any given historical conjuncture, put themselves in a weak strategic position. This is illustrated by Saul in relation to the Mozambique Liberation Front (FRELIMO).[27] The FRELIMO began by attempting to forge national unity by suppressing the many ethnic and linguistic differences within the population, but they were ultimately forced to accept those differences and to emphasize instead the normality of ethnic diversity and the need for diverse ethnic groups to come together in unity without compromising their separate identities.[28] Of the many strands in the thinking of Saul, Laclau, Nairn, and others, therefore the principal one is the need for Marxists to face up to the reality of ethnicity. They all approach the problem at the empirical level, particularly Saul in his discussion of Mozambique. The question of the role played by ethnicity in class formation, however, has also been given a theoretical formulation by Jérôme Rousseau, drawing on Shivji's work in Tanzania.[29]

Rousseau starts out from Shivji's distinction – within the framework of Tanzanian class structure – between the metropolitan bourgeoisie, the commercial bourgeoisie, and the petty bourgeoisie. The metropolitan bourgeoisie is European and generally non-resident. The commercial bourgeoisie is Asian and includes all those social categories in which Asians find themselves: landowners, businessmen, professionals, functionaries, managers of foreign-owned companies, and so on down to small tradesmen, artisans, and manual workers. The petty bourgeoisie is African and includes intellectuals, functionaries, merchants, farmers, soldiers, bureaucrats, and salaried staff in general. Rousseau finds this to be an unacceptable classification since many of the same categories are found in both the bourgeoisie and petty bourgeoisie and cannot be considered to belong to distinct classes on the grounds of relations of production. At the same time, he recognizes that the ethnic distinction between Africans and Asians in Tanzania is an important one and one that is constitutive of the identity of two opposed groups with contradictory interests. Rousseau has already defined class as existing in any social formation where there is between identifiable groups such an opposition of interests ultimately determined by economic considerations. In the case of Tanzania, Asians and Africans would on the basis of this definition constitute two different classes, definable in terms of relations of production and of ethnicity. Rousseau considers that in terms of relations of production there are two parallel and distinct bourgeoisies, distinguished from each other on the basis of ethnicity, an Asian and an African.

This is, according to him, the only description of Tanzanian class structure that can properly fit the reality of that structure. It has important implications for the role of ethnicity as a determinant of class. Rousseau's view of what is or is not determinant is similar to that of Poulantzas. He considers there to be three determinant levels, the economic, the political, and the ideological, with the economic level remaining ultimately determinant. In the Tanzanian example the class position of the Asian and African bourgeoisies is determined by each of these three levels, and ethnicity, located at the level of ideology, has a role in determining that position. Ethnicity is thus brought within a Marxist theoretical framework of class determination. Rousseau suggests the working combination of this broad, generally applicable definition of ethnicity (in line with Marxist theory) and a close analysis of the specific role of ethnicity in any given social formation.

All these approaches represent attempts to tame the beast of ethnicity and bring it within the fold of Marxist theory and practice in a domesticated state before it breaks down the fences and tramples on the carefully constructed conceptualizations from which it has been excluded. The question is whether such theories leave us in a more satisfactory state of *understanding* ethnicity than we were in when we started out. They provide a functionalist understanding that, within the capitalist mode of production, ethnicity can have the function of maintaining the working class in a state of mystification and therefore of helping to maintain the sway of capital over labour; they provide a further explanation of the role of ethnicity and nationalism as a response to imperialism, or threatened economic subordination; and, at least in Rousseau's formulation, they incorporate ethnicity within a particular kind of Marxist theoretical framework. But there remains the impression that, in spite of the usefulness of these approaches, there is still an important aspect of ethnicity that remains defiant and untamed. They are principally concerned with the role that ethnicity plays as a response to imperialism, a means of forging national unity, a binding force among urban migrants, a mainstay in the maintenance of capitalist relations of production, or as one factor determining class position. We have moved from ethnicity the mask to ethnicity the role, but we are still at the level of structures and functions, at the level of the play, and need to move closer to the players behind the roles.

Althusser maintains that in order to understand *Capital*, or the nature of capitalist exploitation, one has to have had experience of that exploitation as a member of an exploited class.[30] This in itself suggests that for all the talk of the mystification of the working class, the only group in society that can really be said to be mystified is the petty bourgeoisie (and perhaps some members of the bourgeoisie, when they allow themselves to be carried away by their own rhetoric), and no one more so than the intellectuals who claim to be in a state of demystification. If one extends Althusser's notion to ethnicity, one could also maintain that ethnicity can only really be understood by those who are or have been oppressed on the grounds of their ethnicity. I consider this possibility in the light of one approach within Marxism in which ethnicity plays a central role. This approach is centered on racism. It is not a question of those instances where racism is deplored from the outside by those who have not been its victims, but rather of certain texts in which those who have known oppression on the grounds of their ethnicity set that experience within a Marxist understanding of its causes.

Racism in Sivanandan's "Alien Gods," for example, is not a question of mystification, nor even of the role that it plays in the maintenance of one system or another, but of the irrationality and inhumanity of the attitudes of one group, definable in terms of ethnicity, towards another.[31] For Sivanandan such attitudes have their roots in the relationship between colonizer and colonized, in which the former, in turning the latter into an appendage of a system of production and capital formation that has its centre elsewhere, destroys the independent identity of the colonized.

According to Sivanandan, the dilemma faced by black intellectuals who exist in a no man's land between the colony that they have left behind and the metropolitan mother country that refuses to accept them is the need to find a language in which they can begin to recreate an identity that can be something other than the debased identity that has been suffered to exist under colonialism. The problem is that the only language available is that of the colonizer and the only literature in which the individual has been steeped is the colonizer's literature, and both this language and this literature are themselves part of and constitutive of an identity from which the black intellectual is excluded and that in many cases has constituted itself in opposition to a blackness and an imagined savagery that were necessary to bolster up the white supremacist delusions of the Elizabethans or the Victorians.

If the colonizer has constructed a self-image that defines itself in opposition to a conjured-up barbarism, the colonized is caught in a bewildering cross-fire of contradictory self-images. Franz Fanon relates how the Martiniquais intellectuals are brought up to think of themselves as white, francophone, and French (distinguishing themselves, for example, from the "black" Sénégalais), but that when they travel to France and the metropolitan university, they discover that they are neither white nor French, being continually and brutally excluded from white French society.[32] The longer they stay in France, the more complete the exclusion and the destruction of the self-image, but at the same time the more impossible it becomes to return to Martinique, particularly since returned *diplomés* are viewed by family and acquaintances as the embodiment of the very image that for the *diplomés* themselves has been destroyed. This crisis of identity is parallel to that described by Sivanandan, who concludes that the only way to the forging of a new identity is to seize the language of the oppressor and to remould and reform it such that it becomes the vehicle for the expression of black experience and the means to a recreation of black identity.[33]

The problem of ethnicity is thus posed by Sivanandan in terms of the imprisonment of the colonized in a debased self-image that is continually reinforced by racism and from which the only escape is by forcibly appropriating the tools that have hitherto been in the hands of the oppressor. Fanon, by contrast, poses the problem in terms of a false consciousness that comes to be brutally flawed by the realization of its own falseness. Sivanandan also relates the question of racism to that of working-class solidarity. The only positive outcome he can envisage is that those who are racially oppressed will come to understand the economic roots of that oppression under capitalism; further, that it is only a historical accident that the oppressors are white. At the same time, the white working class needs to be brought to an understanding of the racial oppression to which it has been party and that has taken the concrete form of the relegation of blacks to the worst jobs, the underclass, the subproletariat.

The principal goal of this approach is to force Marxists to an awareness of the oppression on the grounds of race that exists as a concrete reality alongside exploitative class relations. It is clear, though, from the works of Sivanandan and Fanon, that such oppression can never really be understood by those who are never likely to be in the position of experiencing it but, on the contrary, are on the side of the beneficiaries, however much they might attempt to put themselves in the position of the oppressed. Such exercises are similar to the attempts to comprehend and communicate working-class experience by those who have never had any. Indeed, Sivanandan goes so far as to say that at least the black intellectual has the advantage over the white in that he necessarily has a direct experience of oppression, whereas the white intellectual's sympathy with the oppressed – considered inevitable by Sartre – can only be on the basis of intellect and not of experience.[34]

Such approaches to racism, based on the experience of oppression, bring us closer to an understanding of the reality of "race" or ethnicity. They help us to penetrate behind the mask and the role to the players themselves and the way in which relationships of oppression emerge in the distorted self-images that dominant classes construct for themselves and impose on those they dominate. Such self-images are an integral part of relationships of oppression. They serve as the basis for the continual reconstruction of those relationships in their own image. Perhaps we should say that we have penetrated behind the mask only to discover that the player was the mask.

PART TWO

Parts of a Whole: Identity and Inequality

CHAPTER EIGHT

With or Without Class?
The Problem of
Pre-industrial Society

The question of whether or not classes exist in pre-industrial society depends, naturally enough, on how one defines class. According to the Weberian definition, there are classes in such societies, given the existence of a market and different categories of people who have different capacities to command goods and services on the market according to their possession or lack of property, or their occupying some commercial or professional position. Without such market relationships there are no classes. Equally, according to Marx's definition, where there exists a category of persons who appropriate the surplus produced by others without themselves being producers, there exist two opposed classes. Or one could follow Dahrendorf and find classes wherever there exist imperatively co-ordinated associations, which could easily amount to all known and imaginable societies. It is clear, therefore, that any question we might ask concerning the existence or non-existence of class has to specify its terms carefully, since we are otherwise liable to be arguing in circles or at cross purposes. Nor should we lose sight of the interests that underlie the putting forward of one definition rather than another, and our opting for one of those definitions.

Against the background of these cautionary remarks I turn to the question of the existence of class in non-market-dominated societies. In this case the question is not entirely meaningless since it has been proposed (by Sahlins) that it is inappropriate to think in terms of class *on any definition* in relation to such societies.[1] Sahlins' study relates to a series of Polynesian island societies as they are held to have existed before European intrusion. The basic organizing principle in these societies is kinship. They are differentiated into those with a marked degree of stratification, with, for example, three distinct "status levels" (in Sahlins' term), and those where stratification is barely existent and yet not sufficiently absent for such societies to be termed wholly egalitarian.[2]

The more highly stratified of these island communities has a complex form of kinship organization that is described as a "ramage" system. This means that all individuals have their place on a vast genealogical tree. The tree consists of a central senior lineage that runs down through the line of eldest sons, and a number of branches (or ramages) that start with the younger sons at the point where the system is conceived to begin. This system is necessarily subject to change through the rising power of a junior lineage, but Sahlins holds that in such cases, while secular power goes into the hands of the rising lineage chief, the senior lineage retains its hold over the traditional aspects of chiefdom. In the less stratified islands kinship organization is much less complex and more localized, with only the immediate descent lines from, for example, a common grandfather being carefully remembered.

The reasons for these two distinct forms of kinship organization are related by Sahlins to questions of resource use and the possibilities and constraints operating at the level of the natural environment. In the more stratified ramage-type system, where the whole society is "placed" in terms of kinship, there is a tendency for scattered settlement and productive specialization, whether in fishing or the production of any one of a number of specific inland crops that might be favoured by a particular environment. The nature of the environment thus favours a particular kind of resource use, which itself leads to scattered specialization. This process, far from leading to a dismembered form of kinship organization, requires that the broadest possible links between groups be maintained, since producers, in order to obtain what they need, are obliged to maintain widespread exchange relationships.

Kinship connection in the form of the ramage system thus serves at one level as a framework in which exchange can take place. In the less stratified systems, by contrast, the constraints of the environment are such as to produce coastal village settlements with limited specialization, each family unit producing the bulk of its own needs. Contrary to what one might expect, this higher density of settlement is accompanied by a more limited kinship system, since there is no need to maintain exchange relationships with a number of specialist producers.

The pattern of kinship organization is thus directly related to the way in which production takes place. Alongside kinship, however, there is also the question of stratification, which both arises out of production and at the same time informs the process of production. The greater the surplus that can be produced beyond the needs of the individual producer, the greater the number of individual non-producers that can be supported, whether at the chiefly status level or in the form of craftsmen and other specialists. Those islands with the highest degree of stratification, therefore, are also those with the greatest productivity. However, these are not market economies, so producers do not meet on the market to exchange their produce, with all the possible uses and abuses of market exchange that are central to both Marxian and Weberian notions of class. Instead the produce is circulated: in purely reciprocal exchange between direct producers and within the framework of their kinship connection, and in the appropriation by higher status levels of the surplus that is produced beyond the needs of the direct producers. That surplus is consumed by the individuals and their families at the higher status levels, and is distributed to the various craftsmen and specialists who are employed by those individuals. Anything that is left over is stored up for redistribution to the direct producers on festive occasions.

It is this last function of appropriation by the higher status levels, consisting of the chiefs and stewards, that is taken by Sahlins to characterize the role of those levels in society. It is not just a case of appropriation as such, but of redistribution. The chiefs store up produce for redistribution at times of need or festivity. This is their primary function and the rationale behind their being permitted to appropriate the surplus produced by those who are, according to the official ideology at least, their kinsmen. Towards the less stratified end of the spectrum of island societies such functions of redistribution and supervision, associated on occasion with arbitrary personal power, are much less pronounced. In the case of the Tikopia as studied by Firth, for example, they are almost vestigial, although the "chief" retains some authority as a production organizer and mediator.[3]

For Sahlins, therefore, these are not class but "kin" societies, and such stratification as exists is only within the all-encompassing framework of kinship. He is clear in his rejection of class: "In contrast to the social classes of market-dominated societies, status differences in kinship societies do not, as a rule, depend on differences in private wealth. Status inequalities in primitive societies are not accompanied by entrepreneurial enterprise and the complete separation of producers from the factors of production. Social relations of mastery and subordination are here not correlates of economic relations of owner and labourer. Modern sociological definitions of class which stress occupational standing, class antagonisms, differences of interest, and the like are not applicable to societies of the primitive order. To maintain a distinction, therefore, between what are really different phenomena, categories of rank in kin societies will be designated 'status levels' and the term 'social classes' will be reserved for the social strata of market-dominated societies."[4]

In suggesting that "class" should only be used of market-dominated societies, Sahlins is in effect espousing the Weberian definition of class and rejecting the Marxian, but he appears to reject the latter for reasons that have little to do with Marx's use of the term. The "complete separation of producers from the factors of production," for example, is not the *sine qua non* of class relationships for Marx but only the process that accompanies and makes possible the development of capitalist relations of production and the coming into existence of the opposed classes of bourgeoisie and proletariat. And it is only in the context of those relations of production that the distinction between owners and labourers comes to be of full significance.

Classes for Marx exist wherever one identifiable category of persons in a society appropriates the surplus produced by another and uses that surplus to ensure its own subsistence without itself necessarily being involved in production.[5] However that relationship may be disguised, or however that surplus may be extracted, the basic relationship is one between two opposed classes with opposed interests. Set against such opposition is a form of primitive communism in which any surplus that is produced is communally appropriated. In certain kinds of lineage-based societies one can speak of the non-presence of class in Marxian terms inasmuch as no one category in that society appropriates surplus at the expense of another, leaving aside the universal element of communal appropriation for the support of the young, old, or incapable. In the societies described by Sahlins, however, this is not the case, since there is clearly appropriation of surplus by a chiefly class and by an intermediate class of stewards, however it may be dressed up in terms of kinship or justified in those of periodical redistribution. Such redistribution has its own logic in a society where wealth cannot be stored for long periods, and is a key element in the mystification of what are, in Marxian terms, relationships of class.

This discussion of Sahlins' work constitutes an illustration of the problems involved in the use of the concept of class in relation to pre-industrial societies. When Sahlins suggests that modern sociological definitions of class, including the Marxian definition, are inapplicable to non-market-dominated societies, he is really advancing a Weberian definition of class. And if one objects, one is likely to be doing so on the basis of a different definition. In other words, the argument has never really been joined since each side is arguing from different premises. The point is not whether there were or were not classes in Polynesian societies but rather that according to Marx there would have been (in some of them), and according to Weber there would not have been (in any of them), for the simple reason that class means something different in each case.

At issue is the adequacy of the correspondence between the way that a society is conceived to operate and the way it actually does. From a Marxian point of view, Sahlins' conceptualization is inadequate or incomplete in that it leaves out a major determining factor in social organization.[6] In accepting "native" explanations for the existence of status levels at their face value and in claiming that the kinship system constitutes the underlying logic of the system as a whole, Sahlins simply reproduces the dominant ideology promulgated by the chiefly class. Yet he believes that to produce a conceptualized system in which classes play the principal role is equally to produce a system that does not correspond to the reality, the reality being marked rather by a form of vertical cohesion and functionality of the different levels according to the organizing principle of kinship and within the constraints laid down by the environment.

The question of adequacy is equally central to the different interpretations imposed on Fredrik Barth's Swat Pathan material by Barth himself and by Talal Asad.[7] Here a question that has been lurking in the background in the discussion of Sahlins' study comes into the open, that of the relative importance of, on the one hand, individual choice and action in the determination of social structure – at the heart of Weberian and subsequent structural functionalist approaches to society – and, on the other, the role of social structure itself, and particularly class structure, in determining such individual choices and actions. Sahlins' stratified lineage-based societies are essentially functionally organized collectivities composed of individual kinspeople, with such constraints as may exist operating primarily at the level of the environment and only secondarily at that of social structure. Other writers have adopted even more individualistic approaches to such societies, choosing to view them as characterized by a form of primitive capitalism in which society as a whole is composed of fledgling capitalists and their entourages, and in which everything is brought down to a calculating individualism.[8] Ultimately such individualistic approaches require one to view all forms of association in terms of personal ties and personal choices, a tendency that is well exemplified in Weber's explanation of the development of the patrimonial state and of feudalism.[9]

For Weber, the development of social structures in which authority is in the hands of an individual ruler arises from a form of localized patriarchalism. The origin of such systems – which might take the form of the patrimonial state, where everything depends on the ruler's whim, or of feudalism, where the rights of the king are to some extent limited by those of the various strata beneath him – lies in the dominant position of the senior kinsman in a more or less extended family unit. In so far as that unit expands, with junior kinsmen establishing themselves over a wider area but still under the authority of the senior kinsman in the senior lineage, the patriarchal form of authority comes to be (in Weber's terms) patrimonial, based neither on rules nor on personal charisma but on tradition. At the centre of this conception is the idea of the household producing and catering for its own needs, and including within itself the various special skills necessary for its subsistence. This is the archetypal "budgetary unit" for Weber, that is, an economically oriented association that produces for its own subsistence rather than for profit or trade.[10]

As this productive unit expands, it can come to be the basis for the development of the patrimonial state, with the various areas of state responsibility coming to be vested in the different specialists within the ruling household. But all attachments within such a state remain centred on the person of the ruler, whose authority is based on tradition.[11]

This notion of patrimonialism can serve as the vehicle for the conceptualization of social structure as consisting either of a series of parallel and competing vertically integrated patrimonial associations or of a unitary pyramid-type structure in which every member of society is to some extent under the authority and despotic control of the chief, as in Sahlins' highly stratified island societies. It fits particularly well with an individualistic view in which all individuals are considered to act on the basis of their own choices and enter into personal relationships with powerful patrimonial figures. Society comes to be seen as the vertically integrated unit of the household writ large.

Barth's approach to Swat Pathan society is an example of such a viewpoint. This society consists of a group of Pukhtun landowners who control the land by right of conquest, having taken over the region in question in the seventeenth century, and the non-Pukhtun majority who are subject to their domination. The Pukhtuns are divided into a majority of small landowners who work the land themselves and a minority of large landowners who do not. Each of the large landowners keeps a men's house, and those who choose to be part of an individual landowner's following demonstrate it by spending as much time as possible therein, most of the day and night if they do not work and all night if they do. The men's houses are constructed in easily defensible positions, and the social distance that separates the various groups that frequent them is carefully respected in sleeping and eating arrangements.

The key to the building up of a following is control over land, which is let out on a share-cropping basis to tenants. The landowner takes between three-quarters and four-fifths of the produce, which is used partly for his own subsistence and partly for redistribution in the form of hospitality in the men's house. The acceptance of this hospitality on the part of those who choose to belong to the men's house puts them under obligation to the landowner and constitutes the basis for their serving as a fighting unit under his control. No one is obliged to belong to a men's house, however, although anyone who does belong to one is obliged not to belong to any other. Being a tenant of a Pukhtun does not in itself involve a relationship of political allegiance, while being a house tenant does, with the heads of the locally dominant Pukhtun lineages controlling the various wards into which the villages are divided. However, the house tenant is still not obliged to belong to the men's house of the owner, and Barth gives the example of an individual working the land of one Pukhtun, living in a house belonging to another, and visiting the men's house of a third.

The large Pukhtun landowners are at the head of both productive units and the body of those who belong to their men's houses, and are bound to them by their redistribution of the surplus exacted from their tenants. The amassing and control of land is thus assured by one kind of vertically integrated Pukhtun-dominated association and the use of land in production by another, with in many cases the implements and seed used by the tenants being supplied by the landlord himself and the implements being maintained by craftsmen employed by the landlord and paid for from a share of the produce.

The operative units in society are thus Pukhtun-dominated, patrimonial-type associations, and the heads of the various men's houses compete with each other for followers and clients, the more so since the outcome of disputes tends to be decided by the numerical strength of the different power blocs. The leaders of the power blocs of declining importance are involved in a descending spiral of increasing redistribution to retain a hold on the diminishing membership of the men's house, a process that requires the selling-off of land and the further reduction of their resource base. The leaders of rising power blocs are caught in a different kind of spiral. In order to meet the increasing demands of their followers, they have to increase the amount of land under their control, which generally means encroaching on the land of their weaker patrilineal kinsmen. But the more such weaker lineage segments are dispossessed of their land and their leaders killed or forced into exile, the greater the number of individuals who are bound to seek vengeance on the person who is amassing the land. There is, therefore, an ever greater likelihood of that person's being killed and of the land that he controls being split up among the members of his lineage. Large concentrations of land are also under the constant threat of being broken up simply by the fission of unwieldy power blocs.

The political landscape in Swat – up until the fairly recent past and the development of a more centralized administration[12] – was thus composed of opposed power blocs dominated by Pukhtuns struggling to amass and control land. Each area included a number of such blocs, which maintained alliances with other blocs outside the area. Underlying this factionalism was a Pukhtun code of behaviour, which called for extravagant bravery and the immediate seeking of vengeance when circumstances required. Indeed, the ability of an individual to build up and maintain a following depended in large part on the extent to which his behaviour was held to be in conformity with the heroic code.

The key element for Barth in this continual ebbing and flowing in the power of individual Pukhtuns is that of choice.[13] Swat society is composed of a mass of calculating individuals who choose, according to their own best advantage, the tenancy agreement or the men's house that best suits their interests. The ebbing in the following of a given Pukhtun reflects the collective decision of his followers that better protection and greater profit

– in the form of access to redistributed produce – can be had elsewhere. Barth admits that given the shortage of land, the abundance of population, and the need for protection, the actual freedom of choice open to would-be tenants is limited; none the less, they choose, and it is through such choices that the central features of Swat social structure – production units under the control of the Pukhtun landlord, Pukhtun-dominated power blocs organized around the men's houses – come into existence. Social structures are thus explained on the basis of the rational calculation of the individuals of which they are composed.

Asad proposes a different way of viewing the society, based on the existence of class in its Marxian sense.[14] Rather than placing a construction on Swat society that splits it up into vertical units, he considers it preferable to look at the class positions of the various categories involved and the constraints that those positions put on them. In a Marxian class analysis the emphasis is not on the individual Pukhtun as the focal point of a Weberian patrimonial association – the leader and his followers – but rather on the individual Pukhtun as the member of a class of landlords who are both aware of themselves and organize themselves as a class in opposition to the non-Pukhtun majority. Ownership or control of land is restricted to Pukhtuns and to a lesser extent to a "caste" of "Saints" who acquire land from Pukhtuns as recompense for their peacemaking efforts and frequently to provide a buffer between the donor and his Pukhtun rivals. Judicial power and authority is also restricted to Pukhtuns, who alone are allowed to speak in the assemblies that are called together for the resolution of disputes. So the Pukhtuns, in spite of their rivalry and factionalism, constitute a dominant class that lives off the surplus produced by agricultural tenants and uses that surplus to maintain the followings that help to assure the maintenance of Pukhtun dominance.

The mass of tenants and labourers also constitute a class whose interests are opposed to those of the Pukhtun landlords. They are characterizable as a class in that they do not themselves control land. They are separated from the means of their own reproduction and only have access to those means on the terms that are laid down by the landlords, which include the giving up of four-fifths of what is produced to the landlords. Barth makes individual choice the operative principle on which social organization is based, but for Asad, the landless class has no real freedom of choice. It is obliged to enter into tenancy agreements in order to survive, and given the pressure of population, the individual has little choice which agreement and which landlord he will choose. So the contractual agreement between lord and tenant is both in appearance a free contract between individuals and yet one in which one party lays down the terms of the agreement and the other party has no option but to accept them. The nature of the choices that are open to the landless majority, therefore, are wholly determined by their class position, and to present choice as the operative principle is to ignore the factors that determine those choices in the first place.

According to Asad it is only the conceptualization of Swat society on the lines of class that can expose the reality of that society.[15] He does not deny the existence of power blocs but sees them as being primarily of ideological significance, as a way of deflecting and inhibiting the development of class awareness among the landless by imposing vertically integrated structures of allegiance. They also create the very need that, for the purposes of the non-Pukhtuns, they are there to fulfil – the provision of security. The struggle between power blocs for the control of land threatens the security of the tenantry and obliges them to seek the protection, and support, of those very power blocs. The vertical organization of society into rival blocs and factions is thus a complex masking of the deeper and more threatening (for the Pukhtuns) horizontal division between classes. Barth presents us with the mask but not the underlying reality. Asad concludes his reconsideration of Barth's analysis by deploring the unwillingness of the students of other such societies, and notably anthropologists, to think in terms of class. Again, such disputes come down to the question of adequacy. For Asad, Barth's description of Swat society is inadequate as an account of the structural constraints that determine the kinds of choices that are made, which is not to deny that people choose. Barth, for his part, admits the existence of such constraints but considers them to be of secondary importance to the choices themselves and the patterns of allegiance that arise as a result of them.[16]

Whether or not there were classes in a given social formation depends on the definition of class that one chooses to adopt. But it is not just a question of how one characterizes a reality the essential features of which are not in dispute. Sahlins' choice of a Weberian rather than a Marxian definition of class means that Polynesian society is portrayed differently from what it otherwise might be. Stratification is seen as being in some way a rational adaptive response to the environment, and the role of the chiefly status level as being primarily redistributive. A Marxian approach suggests that there is a universal and inevitable tendency to class formation wherever productivity levels and social organization permit. Once such opposed classes come into existence, that opposition colours all other forms of opposition and organization. Inasmuch as classes are held to exist in Polynesian society – from a Marxian perspective – then that society is only understandable in the light of class opposition. The same is true of the Swat Pathans. Given the existence of the two opposed classes of Pukhtun landlords and landless non-Pukhtuns, any explanation that fails to take that opposition into account ignores the single most fundamental feature of Swat society. It is in this sense that a Marxian class perspective cannot easily coexist with any other: it cannot recognize the validity of an approach to society that fails to take the reality of class struggle into account. The reason is clear in the case of Asad's criticism of Barth. From a Marxian point of view class is determinant of individual choices and actions.

This sortie into the field of understanding pre-industrial society with or without class serves to re-emphasize that Marx's approach to class is of a different order from those of Weber, Parsons, et al. The latters' definitions may or may not be useful ways of *describing* society, depending on what one wants to find out, or of *classifying* groups within society according to their economic or occupational situations, but for Marx class opposition underlies the structures and alignments we may see, and any attempt to understand those structures without taking it into consideration can only remain superficial.

Before looking more closely at the choice that we are obliged to make among these various definitions, I turn to certain questions raised by E.P. Thompson about what one really means by class in relation to pre-capitalist society. There is, first, Marx's classic distinction in the *Eighteenth Brumaire* concerning the French peasantry, who constitute a class by virtue of their finding themselves in common economic conditions and in conflict with other classes on the basis of those conditions, but who do not constitute a class in that they have no national political organization, no corporate unity or self-awareness beyond the purely local level.[17] This distinction is at the heart of the traditional Marxist approach to class and is also adopted by Dahrendorf, for example, where he speaks of "latent" and "manifest" class interest.[18] The idea is that in a limited sense a class can be said to exist without the members of that class themselves being aware of it, but it only comes to exist in the fullest sense of the word with the self-awareness of the class as a class. This is the approach adopted by E.P. Thompson, whose "making" of the English working class is the forging of its self-consciousness as a class in the early nineteenth century, leading to collective political action in its own class interests.[19] What existed before, therefore, was not "class" in the full sense but rather the potentiality for class.

There is a further problem according to Thompson, which is that the notion of class as a way of characterizing opposed categories within a society only came into its own with the Industrial Revolution and its progeny – the industrial bourgeoisie and proletariat. It was only at this stage in history that such opposed categories began to think of themselves as classes, and it is only at this stage that one can speak of class consciousness existing.[20] To speak of class or class-consciousness in relation to pre-capitalist or pre-industrial societies carries a different set of implications, since classes as such did not exist in those societies. What did exist were opposed interest groups that can be labelled classes on the basis of a definition of class that derives from nineteenth-century experience. It is not merely a distinction between classes that exist without being aware of their classness and those that exist and have achieved that self-awareness, but rather one between class in the full sense of the word (existing as a class, aware of itself as a class, and organizing itself as a class) and a collectivity or interest group that we may or may not choose to describe as a class. In the first case, such classes can only be said to exist subsequent to the development of industrial capitalism; in the second, we are free to find classes in any society we choose, but they can only remain a construction that we place on that society.

This is essentially Thompson's point in relation to class.[21] From the Industrial Revolution onwards class is "present" in the evidence, in that groups organize themselves as classes as well as being the conceptual tool with which the historian attempts to understand society. Prior to that revolution groups organized and thought of themselves on other lines, and we have to be more careful in understanding those struggles as struggles between classes. At the same time the study of ancient and feudal societies has demonstrated that no other concept can adequately account for the reality of struggle within those societies.

Thompson is also opposed to the static theoretical formulations within Marxism in which any historical period is characterized by a dominant mode of production, itself reduceable to specific relations of production between definable classes. This makes a mockery of the complexity of different historical periods, in which there are no hard and fast lines of division; it also reduces the experience of class to something that necessarily accompanies and defines a given mode of production. The neatness and precision of theory fail to do justice to the complexity of class as it is lived, and rather reduce history to a set of empty definitions. Class is held to be something that exists automatically by virtue of the existence of a given mode of production, whereas for Thompson the existence of class in the full historical sense only arises as the consequence of class struggle, with class consciousness coming into being in the course of that struggle.[22]

For Thompson eighteenth-century English society is not automatically divisible into opposed classes in the way that certain schools of thought within Marxism might suggest. Instead there are the various interest groups and factions that make up the gentry on the one hand and the mass of the poor on the other, ever ready to object vociferously at the perceived erosion of what they took to be their traditional rights. Thompson sees society as having been a "field of force," with the gentry at one pole and the plebs at the other, and with intermediate categories aligning themselves with one pole or the other depending on their respective interests.[23] The relationship between gentry and plebs is one of reciprocity, in terms of which the poor are given leeway to riot, protest, burn, and huzzah in defence of their interests at least until the 1790s. On the one hand there are the vertical relationships of patronage that link place-seekers and place-bestowers, and the broader cultural hegemony of a paternalistic gentry that was accepted by the poor, but only at a price, and on the other the traditional culture of the poor themselves, from which the working-class identity of the nineteenth century was to emerge. Eighteenth-century society cannot, therefore, be characterized simply in terms of vertical relation-ships nor of straightforward class opposition but only in terms of the combination of vertical and horizontal alignments that were to begin to crystallize in the 1790s along the lines of what would become nineteenth-century class divisions.

Thompson's approach introduces a set of nuances into our understand-ing of class. We need to avoid a form of mechanical class reductionism that reduces history to a sequence of simplified class oppositions. We need also to distinguish between class in the fullest sense of the word and class as a way of explaining underlying structural determination. Asad's analysis of Swat society would be an example of the latter, in that the objective relationship of different categories to the means of production (that is, land, seed, and implements) is considered to underlie and define whatever forms of association that emerge. By contrast, Hamza Alavi's study of a Punjabi village describes a society in which the vertical factionalism that was to be found in Swat Pathan society coexists to an increasing extent with explicit class consciousness and class organization among a dispossessed tenantry forced to work as wage-labourers on the consolidated estates.[24] In this latter context it is clear that class in the fullest Thompsonian sense of the word has come into existence – that is, what in Swat society is the latent potentiality for class has here led to the emergence of class. This, how-ever, does not imply that class is not a reality underlying Swat social struc-ture but simply shows up the different ways in which the concept of class (within a Marxian framework) can be applied to different kinds of society. We end up distinguishing between class as the underlying structural opposition between groups that informs and determines whatever associ-ations and alignments may emerge at the surface of social structure, and class as the emergence of that underlying opposition into the light of day in the form of explicit political class organization.

In looking at the different kinds of theoretical construction that have been placed on class, or perhaps more accurately, in which the concept of class is used to characterize a particular aspect of the reality that the theory-constructor chooses to see, I have continually made a distinction between Marxist and non-Marxist approaches. The reason, as I have already suggested, is that according to the Marxian understanding of class, class struggle is the key to all social structures that are not characterizable as strictly egalitarian or primitively communist. In non-Marxist approaches to class, class follows from some aspect of social organization, while in a Marxist approach social organization follows from class. We have the choice of using class as a key to understanding society or as a secondary form of classification, a way of arranging people in groups whose *raison d'être* is not so much class struggle as occupational and family status, market opportunities, or membership in a chess club. Which approach we choose necessarily depends on what we want to find out about society, what we want to do with that information once we have extracted it, and, ultimately, who we are in the first place.

But the choice can also be brought down to arguments that stand apart from our interests as such and relate rather to the level of explanation that different approaches can offer. It is in this sense that we can ask whether Sahlins' Weberian approach to class (or the lack of it) gives us a sufficient understanding of Polynesian society, that is, an understanding that adequately accounts for the evident inequalities in individual Polynesian societies. We can also ask how adequately Barth's analysis on the basis of individual freedom of choice explains the reality of Swat Pathan society. In both these cases the suspicion remains that an important level of explanation has been omitted, that of the determination of the actions and choices open to individuals according to the positions they occupy in relation to the means of subsistence (that is, free access to or separation from), and their rights or otherwise to dispose freely of the fruit of their own productive activity. It is not that such rights can exist apart from the political alignments of the broader society but rather that those alignments cannot be understood separately from the overall class relations of which they are a part.

CHAPTER NINE

In Search of Identity: Ethnicity and the "Boundaries" of Social Anthropology

In looking at non-Marxist theories of ethnicity, I identified two opposed conceptualizations: ethnicity as embodying the totality of a group's identity, irrespective of whether that group was or was not in contact with other groups; and ethnicity as a boundary phenomenon between groups, a set of markers by which one group differentiates itself from another.[1] This latter conceptualization of ethnicity was already described by Weber, who considered ethnic labels to be used by groups for, among other reasons, monopolistic closure.[2] For Weber any apparent difference is suitable material for the ethnic labelling of one group by another, or, more importantly, for self-labelling, defining the set of markers that can exclude non-members of a group from the benefits of membership. Underlying both non-Marxist and Marxist approaches was also the question of functionality: the functionality of ethnicity for the maintenance of group solidarity and identity on the one hand (relative to other groups) and for the maintenance of an exploitative system of production on the other.

We need to move closer to a characterization of ethnicity that goes beyond function and can allow us to juxtapose class and ethnicity in the way that Nairn, Saul, Laclau, and others have suggested rather than simply seeing it as the mask or the mystification of class relationships. In this chapter I look at some approaches to ethnicity in the practice of social anthropology, building particularly on the notion of ethnicity as identity. Initially I consider the role of boundaries in the constitution of the object of social anthropology or the process of ethnography itself, the attempt to reduce the complexity of what is observed to a set of coherent identities that are then reproduced in the form of a text. Subsequently, I consider the position of social anthropologists themselves on the boundary between "cultures."

In the establishment of the identities of the objects of study, which for social anthropologists tend to be groups that are ultimately definable as groups through the very identities that are imposed on them, one has to distinguish between the way in which the fundamental identity of the group is established with respect to the boundary that separates the observer from the observed, and the way in which the group itself is held to construct its identity on the basis of various internal and external boundaries. Needless to say, both these cases involve constructions placed on different kinds of material by the ethnographer, although the boundary that separates the ethnographer from those written about may only be more or less explicitly recognized.

It is central to linguistic theory that identity is only conceivable in terms of opposition. Whether one thinks of the particular range of sounds that are used in a given language to construct semantic units or the range of semantic units itself that constitutes the basic vocabulary, in each case the identity of the phonemes or the identity of the semantic units is established by their being opposed to or differentiated from all other sounds or units within the closed system of the language.[3] In other words, identity is not something essential to the phoneme or the semantic unit itself but only exists in opposition. It is equally central to the practice of social anthropology that groups are identified and are held to identify themselves in relation to other groups, while subgroups are identified in opposition to other subgroups within the group.

In *Tristes tropiques*, for example, Lévis-Strauss "identifies" the Bororo both in relation to his own identity but also, more specifically, by presenting the set of oppositions that exists within the Bororo community and is present both at the level of the spatial arrangement of the village (into two separate divisions) and at that of the Bororo's conceptualization of themselves.[4] The Bororo are identified by virtue and in terms of their own dichotomous self-image and practice, in which the males of one half marry the females of the other and cross over the boundary to reside with their wife's family on marriage, and in which all ceremonial and productive activities are organized along dichotomous lines, with, for example, the men and women of one moiety taking charge of the funeral ceremonies following the death of a member of the other.

Bororo self-conception is thus intimately linked to the notion of boundary. There is, for example, the boundary that separates them from non-Bororo or from Bororo residing in other villages, and that which separates the living from the dead. This latter boundary is one that is evoked in the dances that accompany funeral rites and one that the village sorcerer or spirit medium finds himself straddling, he being half present in village life and practice as a villager but also half possessed by spirits and therefore on the other side of the boundary. There are also the internal boundaries that divide one half of the village from the other, the men from the women, and – for reasons that remained obscure to Lévi-Strauss – those born upstream from those born downstream. Initially the system in which Bororo identity is constructed is thus defined both at the conceptual and at the physical level, and subsequently the various units of which that system is composed – which might be individuals, or houses, or the moieties themselves – are presented.

There are several ways in which the construction of Bororo identity can be understood within the framework of Lévi-Strauss's text. There is, for example, the way in which the Bororo represent themselves to themselves, the way in which Lévi-Strauss succeeds in representing them to himself, and the way in which we – as readers of the text – succeed in grasping and remembering that representation. These three processes of representation are all dependent on opposition and the conceptualization of boundaries. The Bororo conceive of themselves through opposition, and we are only able to conceive of them by using the same set of oppositions. This suggests that the process of identification or of constructing identities is itself a process of opposition and therefore of the construction of boundaries. All ethnography as a process of identifying specific human groups, is thus built explicitly or implicitly around the notion of opposition. I now turn to three cases where the question of opposition is explicitly addressed: one where the boundaries conceptualized are in a sense absolute; one where the notion of boundary is itself called into question but is none the less central to the analysis; and one where boundary is dispensed with as a way of conceptualizing a multi-ethnic society other than as constituting the outer limits of the system itself.

In the first case, John Galaty, in an article on the Maasai, is concerned with the identity of Maasai pastoralists in relation to neighbouring groups of hunters.[5] Even though such groups are marginal to the Maasai, in that they do not compete for access to the same resources or otherwise directly intrude on Maasai pastoralism, they are none the less central to the way in which the Maasai conceive of themselves. Maasai self-conception is framed in terms of the differences that exist between their own practices and those of the hunters. Being a Maasai is as much a question of *not being* a hunter and slaughterer of animals as it is of *being* a pastoralist. Their own pacific, milk-producing pastoralism is opposed to the violent meat-producing activities of the hunters, the Maasai carefully tending their own animals and the hunters wantonly killing theirs. This opposition – from the Maasai point of view – is also reduced to one of purity versus pollution, in which the slaughtering of animals and the shedding of blood is seen as a polluting activity unsuitable to Maasai.

For Galaty, therefore, Maasai identity is constituted both at the level of the practical differences in productive activity that distinguish them from neighbouring hunters and at the symbolic level, in that various aspects of those activities are opposed to each other as symbolizing the domain of the pure, peaceful Maasai in contrast to that of the polluted, belligerent hunters. The constitution of identity thus operates at both the conceptual and the practical level, much as the dichotomous self-image of the Bororo for Lévi-Strauss is matched by the divided plan of the Bororo village.

Leach, in *Political Systems of Highland Burma*, is also preoccupied with questions of identity and of boundaries.[6] He is concerned to undermine the traditional approach within social anthropology that sets out from the premise of the bounded group and then proceeds to reconstruct the bounded identity of that group in the form of a text. As examples of such boundedness outside time and within space he cites Firth's work on the Tikopia and Evans-Pritchard's study of the Nuer.[7] In the latter case the elegance of Evans-Pritchard's work is directly linked to the limitations of the construction that he imposes on Nuer society. For Leach the reality of social structure is more fluid, confused, and changing than such monographs would suggest. In the Kachin Hills area of Burma with which he is concerned, he considers the boundaries between groups – by which they identify themselves and by which they are identified – to be both constantly shifting, inasmuch as groups cross from one side to the other, and yet stable, in that the structural changes in society are still understood in terms of the same set of oppositions. In spite of constant change and flux, therefore, there remains a certain boundary stability.

The stable correspondence that exists among the Bororo and the Maasai between the actual social organization of the community and the conceptualization that the community has of that organization is matched among the Kachin hill tribes by a different kind of correspondence. Kachin social organization is conceptualized as being based on both egalitarian and aristocratic principles in a process of slow, cyclical change in which an aristocratic hierarchy develops up to the point of egalitarian rebellion, at which point the process starts over again. The Kachin identify themselves not only in terms of this fluctuating internal opposition between the principles of equality and hierarchy, but also by imagining a more global opposition between themselves and a nearby valley-dwelling people called the Shan.[8] The Shan, who are frequently raided by the Kachin, and protected by those same Kachin – at a price – are organized on more permanently aristocratic lines. It is these two sets of boundaries – the shifting internal boundary between egalitarianism and hierarchy and the more permanent external boundary between the Kachin and the Shan – that are central not only to the way in which the Kachin construct their own identity but to the way in which that identity is reconstructed by the ethnographer.

In a study of Guyanese society by Lee Drummond, the very notion of boundaries is called into question as a way of conceptualizing that society.[9] In terms of origins Guyana is a mixture of East Asians, Amerindians, Africans, Portuguese, and English. But in practice the boundaries between these groups are fluid and confused enough that it is impossible to define one or other of the groups as in some sense an ethnic or cultural island distinct from the rest. Drummond suggests that instead of resorting to the standard linguistic model that uses the self-contained and coherent system of a given language to understand the cultural group as a bounded entity, it is more productive in societies such as Guyana to use a model based on Creole.

Creole is used throughout Guyanese society but varies widely in the form that it takes in different social contexts and among different groups. It corresponds as a system to the cultural continuum in which distinct culturally or ethnically definable groups exist but only inasmuch as they are identifiable on one or other point of the continuum along which all groups tend subtly to blend into each other. Although there are no boundaries in any hard and fast sense in Guyanese society, identity is still established through opposition, but a form of opposition that exists within a continuum. The nature of that opposition is continually changing according to context, which might be – in Drummond's description – the marriage of a Hindu groom to a Christian bride at which the members of the groom's family refuse to attend the Catholic mission ceremony and the groom's brothers take great exception to the dancing that accompanies the reception. Group identity established through opposition and boundary demarcation is thus continually present, but the boundaries crop up in different forms, at different times, and in different places.

Thus, whether a society is marked by a kaleidoscopic set of oppositions that take on different forms in different contexts (as in the case of Guyana) or by oppositions that are more stable and defined, opposition itself remains central to the construction of identity. This reinforces the idea that boundaries and opposition across boundaries are essential to ethnographic practice. Before turning to the question of how social anthropologists inhabit the boundary area between their own society and that under study – much like the Bororo village sorcerer on the boundary between the living and the dead – I look further at the boundary as constitutive of the ethnographic object, in order to get closer to the construction of identity as the object of social anthropology.

Rosemary Harris's monograph *Prejudice and Tolerance in Ulster* is a portrait of an Ulster border community.[10] The community is reconstructed in the monograph, and therefore identified, in terms of opposition and boundaries. There is, for example, the opposition between those who live in the local village and those who live in the rural hinterland that surrounds it; between the relatively wealthy valley farmers, who have changed over from labour-intensive flax cultivation to livestock breeding following the Second World War, and the poorer mountain farmers working the infertile soils on the edge of the upland peat bogs; between Catholic and Protestant, with the Catholics themselves divided into villagers and poor mountain farmers (with one or two wealthier Catholic farmers in the valley) and Protestants divided into villagers, poor mountain farmers, and wealthy valley farmers. Finally, there is the boundary between the Republic of Ireland and the North – imposed by the British government in the 1920s – which not only defines the community as a "border" community but constitutes a dividing line within the community that underlies the opposition between Catholic and Protestant, with the former constrained to accept the border as a political reality and the latter determined to maintain it.

Alongside these fundamental oppositions there are others that provide further co-ordinates by which people place themselves, or can be placed by the observer, on a mental map of the community. For any individual there are "kin" and "non-kin." Since there are few Catholic-Protestant marriages and since, where such marriages do take place, one or other of the partners tends to cut existing ties with his or her own kin, kinship ties tend to be maintained only with one's co-religionists. And since in the mountain areas kinsmen tend to co-operate only with kinsmen, Catholics and Protestants do not generally co-operate with each other unless the remoteness of kinsmen combined with the proximity of a neighbour belonging to the opposite denomination gives rise to such co-operation.[11]

At a variety of other levels identity is also constructed through opposition. Among Protestants, Presbyterians are opposed to Episcopalians, and both are opposed to Methodists and Baptists, who have made heavy inroads into their congregations. Protestants are also divided into skilled and unskilled labourers, tradesmen, professionals, poor mountain farmers, and wealthy valley or infield farmers. All these groups come together within the egalitarian framework of the Orange Order around the common interest of anti-Catholicism, although it is an egalitarianism that is not always congenial to the wealthier or higher-status Protestants.[12]

Underlying all these boundaries between and within groups is the sexual division of labour. In the lowland areas women keep and breed poultry and use the income to provide for the household budget. The men work the land and use the income to maintain and renew equipment and purchase livestock and feed. The wives of the wealthier Protestant farmers are to a large extent housebound, and express – according to Harris – more prejudiced opinions about the "other side," – the Catholics – having less contact with that other side than have their husbands.[13] There are thus a variety of ways in which individuals can place themselves with respect to others and be placed in a mapping of the community, but the Protestant-Catholic opposition underlies all others, with separate schools, shops, sports, clubs, and dance halls.

The process of identification within and of the community thus comes down to the perception of boundaries. Those boundaries run between households; between lowland and hill farmers; between one community of hill farmers isolated at the head of a valley road and another community over the hill; between wealthy Protestant yeoman farmers and unskilled Protestant labourers; between Presbyterians and Episcopalians; and, at the most fundamental level, between the mass of Catholics concentrated in the poor upland farms and the wealthier Protestant farmers and villagers. To identify the community in the form of an ethnography is to describe the set of principal oppositions by which the members of the community identify themselves, and the bulk of the field-work that underlies the study consists of questioning individuals in order to unearth the significant boundaries across which opposition is conceptualized. The process is akin to the learning of a language, in which a range of semantic units all occupying spaces within a single system have to be identified through their opposition to each other – except that in the case of a community, it is the units themselves, the members of the community, who construct their own identity on the basis of a particular set of oppositions.

The role of the boundary in the constitution of the identity of the ethnic group – whether for the members of the group themselves or for the observer – is also a central preoccupation in the different case-studies relating to southern Norway, the Sudan, the Rift Valley of Ethiopia and elsewhere, included in *Ethnic Groups and Boundaries*, edited by Fredrik Barth.[14]

In Blom's Norwegian case-study included in this collection,[15] the evident boundaries that exist between highland and lowland farmers in one part of southern Norway come under consideration precisely because they are *not* associated with distinct ethnic identities, in spite of the fact that the differences between the two areas and the kind of farming that is undertaken in each of them have led to differences in social structure and cultural adaptation. While highland and lowland farmers identify themselves in opposition to each other, those opposed identities are set within an overarching identity that includes both groups and is constructed on the basis of common origin, common language, and, in spite of local differences, common culture. The maintenance of such an overarching identity has an economic explanation: lowland farmers bring their cattle up to the highlands in the summer to be looked after by the highlanders and to benefit from the rich mountain pasture. Just as kinship in Polynesia is presented by Sahlins as the framework in which exchange relationships can take place,[16] so in southern Norway the same function is assured by an overarching identity that includes both highland and lowland farmers.

Haaland's study of the Fur and Baggara in western Sudan relates to a boundary that is both ethnic and permeable at the same time.[17] The Fur are sedentary hoe-cultivators and the Baggara nomadic pastoralists.

Although the two peoples come into frequent contact, they are distinct in language, culture, and social organization. Wealth among the Fur is measured in terms of the quantity of cattle that individuals manage to accumulate, but at a certain level of accumulation they are no longer able to go on increasing their herds by remaining hoe-cultivators. They have the choice, therefore, either to stay as they are and be content with a limit on the number of cattle that can be supported or to join the Baggara as nomadic pastoralists and thus allow their cattle to go on increasing.

This latter choice is one that Fur frequently make, even though it entails changes in lifestyle and language. It also means a change in the division of labour within the family, since among the Baggara the family is a co-operating unit, whereas among the Fur, husbands' and wives' activities are kept separate. What is more, those Fur who have recently crossed over the boundary between the two groups are judged by their Fur kinsmen in terms of behaviour that the Fur would normally expect of the Baggara. The Baggara are noted for their hospitality, and visiting Fur are critical of their newly nomadic kinsmen if they fail to live up to the same standards. The wealthier and more ambitious among the Fur thus tend to become Baggara. A considerable number of Baggara themselves, however, abandon the nomadic life altogether and migrate to the towns. Haaland suggests that were it not for the replenishment of the Baggara by the incorporation of Fur recruits, they would probably be diminishing in number. The boundary between the Fur and the Baggara is thus a well-defined ethnic boundary, and yet it permits a continual cross-flow in one direction. That cross-flow, however, not only does not call into question the existence of the boundary itself but even reinforces it, inasmuch as the Fur who cross over take on the characteristics of the Baggara.

Such a permeable ethnic boundary is to be distinguished from the relatively impermeable, where there is congruence between ethnicity and social inequality. *Ethnic Groups and Boundaries* includes two examples: one concerns the relationship between Lapps and Norwegians in northern Norway[18] and the other that between *Ladinos* and American Indians in Mexico.[19] In the Norwegian example, the irony of the situation is that the Norwegianization of the Lapps is actively encouraged by Norwegians, although the stigma that is attached to Lapp identity by the Norwegians is so strong that there is in practice little chance of the Lapps' being accepted as Norwegians.

Eidheim, in his study of the area, distinguishes between the two private domains in which Lapps encounter Lapps and Norwegians Norwegians, and the public domain in which the two groups come into uneasy contact with each other. The latter domain is characterized by a feature that is often part of the relationship between a superordinate and a subordinate ethnic group, where linguistic difference is part of that ethnic differentiation: the speaking of the subordinate group's language is largely confined to the private domain, while the language of the dominant group holds sway in the public. Inasmuch as the intention on the part of the dominant group is to eradicate the subordinate group's ethnic identity (without necessarily eradicating their subordination), the first priority is to eliminate the signs of that identity from any situation in which the two groups come into contact with each other. This is particularly the case in the maintenance of a language that is by its very nature incomprehensible to the dominant group and therefore liable to be considered subversive.

The second example of a relatively impermeable ethnic boundary concerns an American Indian pueblo and the inhabitants of a neighbouring town in Mexico. Here the Indians are not encouraged to abandon their culture and identity by the relatively wealthy and dominant *Ladino* town-dwellers. On the contrary, the boundaries are rigidly maintained. Among the Lapps and Norwegians there was equally rigid boundary maintenance, in spite of the fact that Norwegianization and therefore unidirectional boundary-crossing was supposedly encouraged. In practice the Lapps were obliged to abandon their own culture without having any right of access to that of the dominant group. In the Mexican example, the only Indians who succeed in becoming absorbed into the *Ladino* community are, ironically, not those who accumulate sufficient wealth (since the strict egalitarianism among the Indians would prevent it) but rather those widows and their children who are forced to leave the pueblo and live in the town. The Mexican and northern Norwegian examples thus provide illustrations of relatively impermeable ethnic boundaries that are associated with relationships of social inequality.

The final two cases that I look at from *Ethnic Groups and Boundaries* are not so much concerned with the specific interaction between two groups as with the set of oppositions that exist between a geographically localized group and surrounding groups and that emphasize and reinforce different aspects of that group's identity. In the case of the Pathans in the northwest frontier area of Pakistan – with whom we have already come into contact in Swat – Barth associates the maintenance of Pathan identity with the survival of certain core institutions, notably hospitality, the deliberative council, and the seclusion of the domestic domain.[20] The fate of these core institutions is different on different frontiers of the Pathan area. In the east there is a continual cross-flow into the Punjab, resulting in the loss of Pathan identity. There is thus a relatively stable but permeable boundary between Pathans and non-Pathans, with unidirectional outflow from the Pathan side. In the north, in Swat, the Pathans or Pukhtuns constitute a dominant landlord class and maintain their core institutions. In this area, Barth suggests, even the landless classes will eventually come to be considered – and to consider themselves – Pathans. In the west the dominant Pathan group in Afghan politics has abandoned its Pathan identity and become Persian in language and culture to differentiate itself from other Pathans, while in the south the boundary between the Pathans and the Baluch is gradually moving northwards without there necessarily being any movement of population. As a result of warfare, Pathan lineages tend to "cross over" to the centrally organized Baluch, but being unable to maintain their core institutions and particularly the council or *jirga*, they gradually lose their Pathan identity and come to be considered Baluch. On each of the frontiers, therefore, there is a particular kind of boundary between Pathans and non-Pathans that is characterized by Barth in terms of core institutions, although it is clear that the maintenance or loss of those institutions is only the result of underlying social pressures.

In Knutsson's study of the Arsi in the Rift valley of Ethiopia the emphasis is more on the various forms of productive activity that differentiate the Arsi from their neighbours and determine to some extent the kind of boundaries that exist.[21] The Arsi had been transhumant pastoralists, spending part of the year on the lakeshore and part of the year in the mountain pastures. At a certain time they were ousted from those mountain pastures by Amhara highland farmers – a dominant group throughout this area of Ethiopia – and were subsequently forced to lead an impoverished existence on the edge of Lake Zwai. With respect to the Amhara, who are orthodox Christians, the Arsi play up their Islamic faith as an ethnic marker. With respect to their other neighbours, ethnic differentiation is in one case the framework within which exchange takes place (lakeshore sorghum and millet farmers exchanging with island fishermen and weavers) and in the other signifies the lack of any exchange or contact.

In all these examples, ranging from Lévi-Strauss's drawing out of the opposition between the two halves of the Bororo village to Harris's construction of the identity of an Ulster border community or Haaland's opposition of the Fur and the Baggara across a boundary that none the less permits unidirectional cross-flow, we have been concerned with identities, which can, in some cases, and for reasons that are not always clear, be labelled "ethnic." The fundamental principle has been that identity is only constituted or constructed through opposition, in that a group identifies itself by setting up a series of oppositions between itself and other groups. There is thus a superficial resemblance between the concept of the ethnic group and the Marxian concept of class, in that the latter is equally indissociable from opposition. While the opposed interests that serve to define Marxian classes are based on a different kind of opposition from that which sets ethnic groups into opposition with each other, none the less, where there is congruence between class and ethnicity, it is a congruence based on the coming together of two forms of opposition. The ethnographic reconstruction of identity, however, has a further aspect that serves to define the ethnographic project and is directly related to identity and ethnicity, which is that of the role and position of ethnographers themselves, poised, as I have suggested above, like the Bororo sorcerer, between two worlds.

If there were one way in which one might sum up the history of social anthropology, it would presumably relate to the morbid fascination of a rapidly changing industrial civilization with the construction of its own identity through the contemplation of whatever societies can be found that are as different as possible from itself and therefore susceptible of providing the greatest number of perceived oppositions. If individuals and groups know themselves by differentiating themselves from others, or by setting up a series of oppositions that can signify such differences, the problem of a dynamic, expanding industrial civilization, inestimably more powerful than any other civilization with which it comes into contact and sweeping all such other civilizations into its own global system of resource extraction and transformation, is to find the opposite that can serve to establish its own identity. The difficulty is that there are few, if any, peoples who have not already been corrupted, decimated, or evangelized by the very civilization that seeks to find its flawless mirror image (understood as the reverse of itself), and a flawed mirror image is almost as bad as no image at all. Identity as the object of social anthropology – that is, the reconstruction of the identities of suitably remote peoples in the form of ethnography – is the serving up of a series of would-be images of itself to a civilization marked by a crisis of identity, just as capitalism might attempt to "know" itself by coming to an understanding of the modes of production that preceded it. Underlying the construction of the identity of those under observation is the construction of the observer's own identity, which, if we follow Goldmann's suggestion that individuals are indissociable from their class background,[22] is nothing other than the construction of a particular class identity that has its *raison d'être* in the context of a particular social formation. In a sense, the identity of the entire social formation that has spawned the observer in question is implicated in the confrontation between observer and observed – if one can really claim that social anthropologists have ever observed more than they have been observed.

In Harris's study of the Ulster border community, the primary issue, and one referred to by Harris,[23] is the oppositions that arise from her being a Protestant Englishwoman: the Catholic interviewees are opposed to her on the grounds of her Protestantism, and the Protestant interviewees are opposed to her on the grounds of her Englishness. The subject-matter of the book is determined both by who she is and by the kind of guarded information that her mainly Protestant female informants are prepared to give her about the community, which is itself determined by their perception of who she is. The Englishman or woman abroad is, first, English and abroad, and the various peoples who have been dominated, deported, and expropriated in the recent colonial and imperial past do not normally allow them to forget it. The subject of *Prejudice and Tolerance in Ulster* by an Englishwoman and on Ireland is, therefore, at a primary level, the English in Ireland. But to a greater or lesser extent one could say the same about any ethnography where the ethnographer travels to the edge of his or her own world and looks over it. That process is nowhere better represented than in *Tristes tropiques*.

Lévi-Strauss set out with the intention of discovering among the vestiges of the Indian peoples of the Amazon basin human society reduced to its simplest form, as Rousseau had conceived of it without being certain whether it had ever in fact existed. Lévi-Strauss writes:

I had gone to the end of the world looking for what Rousseau calls "the almost imperceptible changes at the very beginning." Behind the veil of the too learned laws of the Caduveo and the Bororo, I had continued my search for a state which – again according to Rousseau – "does not exist anymore, which may not have existed at all, which will probably never exist, and yet concerning which it is necessary to have an accurate idea in order to come to a sound judgment of our present state." I was more fortunate than he in that I believed that I had discovered it in the form of a society that was itself in its death throes, but concerning which it was no use my speculating whether it was or was not a left-over: traditional or degenerate, it none the less presented me with one of the most impoverished forms of social and political organization that it is possible to imagine. I did not need to turn to the particular sequence of historical events that had kept it in – or, more probably, brought it back to – this elementary state. All I had to do was to observe and reflect upon the sociological experiment that was taking place before my eyes. But it was the society that revealed itself. I had searched for a society reduced to its simplest possible form. Nambikwara society turned out to be in such a reduced state that all I discovered were the men of which it was composed.[24]

Lévi-Strauss's journey to the end of the world is thus rewarded by his stumbling across a form of society reduced to its simplest Rousseauesque state. The end of the world – from a eurocentric point of view – is, however, also the end of the world that he sets out to discover: when he finally succeeds in tracking down the legendary and ultra-primitive Tupi-Kawahib, they are already at one day's journey from their village and on their way to abandoning their way of life altogether by assimilating themselves to an outpost of civilization in the form of the trading station. Lévi-Strauss, like so many folklore collectors, anthropologists, and students of dying languages before and after him, is at hand to note down the final agonies of a people that had, incidentally, been destroyed by European civilization but that was nevertheless, and in its very moment of extinction, to be of service in the construction of that civilization's identity.

The subject of *Tristes tropiques*, and of all more conventional ethnographies, is an ethnicity that is constructed on the basis of what are, in Lévi-Strauss's examples, the destructive and consuming opposition between the British and India in India and the genocidal opposition between colonists and Amerindians in Latin America. India and Latin America are set up as two polar opposites, with social and historical complexity and over-population on the one hand and archetypal simplicity of social structure and low population density on the other.[25] Where *Tristes tropiques* goes beyond conventional ethnography, however, is in taking for its very subject the construction of identity and the nature of the process by which European civilization first invented savagery and then set out to discover it – as a way of coming to understand itself.

CHAPTER TEN

Coming into the Open: Capitalism and the Emergence of Class

The distinguishing feature of capitalist relations of production, as opposed to all forms of productive organization that precede them, is that they involve the emergence of class in the full Marxian sense of two self-conscious and politically organized opposed classes, with various other classes struggling to hang on to their privileges or being forced into alignment with one or other of the two main classes. A principal interest of E.P. Thompson, for example, is to understand the process whereby the underlying pre-capitalist class structures of the eighteenth century, which coexist with a variety of vertical alignments, patron-client relationships, and what he describes as "gentry-plebs" reciprocity, emerge in the first half of the nineteenth century in the form of fully polarized class opposition in the Marxian sense.[1] This transition between class as a determinant but submerged feature of social structure and class as an open political opposition, or between class struggle as deflected and concealed in pre-capitalist social formations and coming into the open with capitalist relations of production, is the principal subject of this chapter. Before looking more closely at Marx's approach to that transition and at a series of examples in which class in the full Marxian sense can be seen to emerge, I juxtapose certain aspects of Weber's theory of class and class consciousness alongside Marx's two-fold understanding of class in the *Eighteenth Brumaire*: that individuals can make up a class by virtue of the fact that they share certain economic conditions that serve to place them in hostile opposition to other classes; but that in so far as they have only local connections and no broader sense of community or political organization, they cannot really be said to constitute a class.[2]

Weber's definition of class corresponds to some extent to Marx's first understanding in that it does not imply any self-awareness as a class on the part of the categories so classified. This is indeed one of the bases for Weber's distinction between classes and status groups, in that the latter are aware of themselves as groups and recognized as such.[3] Class, in contrast, is simply a way of classifying different categories of agent in society. However, self-awareness of class position on the part of those who make up a class, and *as* a class, is not excluded by Weber, but it differs in certain subtle ways from Marxian class awareness. It can arise, for example, where a negatively privileged property class comes to realize that its poor life-chances result both from the inequitable distribution of property and from a particular economic order that causes such inequitable distribution, rather than being in some way fixed and immutable.[4] It is then that – for Weber – negatively privileged classes can create more rational forms of association that can come to be the basis for class struggle and replace the more irrational and *ad hoc* forms of protest and action that normally characterize such classes. Class struggle thus arises at particular historical periods and under particular conditions and can have certain effects within those periods and under those conditions, but it remains essentially localized, arising out of the realization on the part of a negatively privileged class of the fact of negative privilege.

Marx and Weber are sufficiently close to each other to be confusing, and yet their conceptions of the role of class struggle and of class awareness are fundamentally different. For Weber class – as a situation – can give rise to class awareness, which can give rise to class struggle, which may, in certain circumstances, have the result of changing the existing situation. For Marx class struggle, as a relation between structurally opposed classes (in the primary sense), can give rise to class awareness, which in turn can give rise to class in the full sense: structurally opposed, self-aware, and politically organized. In looking at the emergence of fully developed class structures in the Marxian sense, therefore, one has to keep Weber's alternative scheme in mind, the real question being whether open and visible class struggle is better conceptualized as an isolated event arising out of perceived inequalities in class situation and against a normal background of acceptance of that situation or as a moment at which the generalized struggle between classes that underlies and informs social structure comes into the open.

The present chapter is concerned with a period of transition between one kind of social organization and another, during which the nature of the opposition between classes is itself changing. In Swat society, whereas classes may exist (in the primary structural sense), fully developed classes are not present.[5] Certain reasons for this state of affairs are advanced by both Barth and Asad. The principal reason for the lack of development of class consciousness and class organization among the non-Pukhtun sharecropping tenants is presumably the same as that which inhibited such a development among the nineteenth-century French peasantry – that is, they are parcelled out across the countryside in small groups and villages.

The exigencies of producing to survive, and particularly of producing in order that the landlord class might survive – not to mention the army of craftsmen and specialists – tie the mass of the population to the land and their own localities. More widespread visiting, communication, and contact can only be the lot of the trader or the privilege of a leisured class that is freed from the necessity of being directly involved in production.

There are a host of class-divided societies in which class in the full Marxian sense is impossible for the producing as opposed to the non-producing class. In Swat, full class association was possible for the Pukhtun landlords since they had the leisure, the contacts, and the organizational structures that permitted such association. But it was never possible for the non-Pukhtun class of producers. Any class-divided society, therefore, that is based on localized peasant or handicraft production, with an aristocracy of non-producers assuring its own subsistence by appropriating the surplus produced by others, is bound to be blocked at the stage of some possibility of full class organization for the aristocracy but no such possibility for the producers.

Apart from the problems of localization and compartmentalization – which can run to the coexistence of a shared aristocratic dialect throughout a given area with mutual incomprehensibility among the scattered groups of localized peasant producers – there is also the question of coercive force. It is evidently in the interests of an aristocracy to prevent the realization of negative privilege on the part of an exploited class, for such realization, in Weber's terms, can lead to open class conflict. In one sense this is ensured by the various barriers already mentioned, but these can be insufficient to prevent the rapid development of occasional peasant class consciousness, as the quickly spreading food riots in the eighteenth-century French countryside demonstrate.[6] Any system that involves the maintenance of a class of non-producers by a class of producers is bound to be based on some form of institutionalized coercion. In Swat, for example, coercion plays its part in preventing the development of horizontal class alliances among the non-Pukhtuns. The general climate of insecurity created by the opposed, vertically integrated power blocs obliges small tenants to seek the protection of, and therefore ally themselves with, one of those blocs. And that opposes them to neighbours who, for one reason or another, enter into different alliances. In the event of inter-bloc warfare, such neighbours find themselves on different sides.[7]

These are two of the barriers in the way of the development of full class consciousness and action on the part of a negatively privileged, or oppressed, majority. Such class organization can only come into existence where social compartmentalization and isolation have been overcome and where the coercive apparatus controlled by the dominant class has been neutralized, or at least successfully confronted with some form of equiva-

lent force. Both these eventualities can, ironically, accompany the development of capitalist relations of production. The irony is that such relations
represent a highly developed and efficient way of extracting the maximum
of surplus value for the benefit of a class that has successfully appropriated the means of production, but at the same time they create possibilities for class association on the part of the producers, possibilities that have
never previously existed to the same extent. Producers under capitalism,
unlike share-cropping tenants, for example, do not produce in isolation.
On the contrary, the tendency has been to bring workers out of their rural
solitude and concentrate them in factories and the towns that spring up
around them. This concentration not only represents the end of the isolation of the individual producer, and therefore the beginning of the possibility of class association, but also the potential basis for the development
of a counter-force in society that can confront the coercive apparatuses
that have traditionally been in the hands of the dominant classes.

This is not to say that the dominant classes within a capitalist system
necessarily forgo their attempts to break up and isolate producers – and
the individual corporation can be as vertically integrated as any Pukhtun
power bloc – nor that the coercive apparatus is not continually adapted
to cope better with the changing threat posed by organized labour. All
such attempts and adaptations, however, gain a certain piquancy from the
fact that the system itself creates the circumstances that favour working-
class consciousness and organization, which consciousness and organization it then has to expend great efforts in neutralizing. The cup of surplus
value for the capitalist is thus poisoned by the very possibilities of working-
class association that capitalism brings into being. This, of course, is Marx's
and Engels' point in the *Communist Manifesto* – capitalism creates the class
that will eventually lead to its own downfall – and is also the more general
preoccupation of Marx throughout *Capital*. In this context I now turn to
a set of examples in which the issues of full class formation and capitalist
relations of production can be considered.

Alavi's study of a village in West Punjab gives some idea of the way
in which class opposition can emerge from within social structure.[8]
Productive and political organization as it has developed in this area of
the Punjab – in the wake of the settlement made possible by irrigation works
in the earlier part of this century – in some ways resembles that in Swat.
In both cases there is a class of large landlords, an intermediate class of
independent smallholders, and a class that is obliged to enter into share-
cropping agreements, in Swat in order to gain access to land and in the
Punjab to supplement the little that can be produced from their own holdings. Equally in both cases the largest landlords tend to become the leaders
of political factions to one or other of which the share-cropping tenants
are obliged to belong. As has been seen in Swat, any possibilities of horizon-

tal class association among direct producers are more or less pre-empted by such vertical alignments. In Alavi's Punjabi village, however, economic change is serving to undermine such patterns of allegiance.

It has become apparent to the large landowners that greater profits are to be made by consolidating their land into larger units, by mechanization, and by hiring wage-labour. The bulk of the share-cropping tenantry have thus been removed from the parcels of land that they traditionally held on the large estates as tenants and have been reduced to their own holdings, the latter being large enough to provide for some of their subsistence needs but small enough to oblige them to work as wage-labourers for the large landowners. This has the effect of bringing together the former share-cropping tenants as wage-labourers on the large estates and thus creates the possibility for a greater awareness of their common class interests, in opposition to those of the large landowners and employers. Inasmuch as successful strike action has already taken place (on the part of women cotton-pickers), there is present an element of full class association and consciousness. The strike in question, however, was localized in a particular village, the members of which all belong to the same lineage, and is thus indicative only of localized class consciousness combined with some degree of lineage solidarity.

Here, therefore, is an example of existing lineage solidarity serving alongside wage-labour as one basis for class solidarity and class-based political action. Alavi also suggests that such corporate action on the part of the direct producers is facilitated by their having less to lose than had been the case under share-cropping tenancy, although this presumes that employers have sufficient difficulty hiring wage-labour for them to be unable to penalize striking workers. The study thus concerns a transitional stage in production and political organization, with the gradual undermining of vertical patterns of allegiance and dependency and their replacement by the first stirrings of full class consciousness on the part of direct producers. It is an example that takes us one step beyond the form of social organization that is present in Swat, with its hidden class structure.

I now turn to a case history of class formation that took place over a wider area and a more extended time period.[9] It is also one in which kinship as the apparent basis for social organization (as in Sahlins' Polynesia)[10] gives way to class. A given area of land in the Scottish Highlands, at least up until the end of the first half of the eighteenth century, was held in the first instance from the feudal superior (in the case of Badenoch, for example, the Duke of Gordon). The area was subdivided into baronies, which in turn were subdivided into the various farms of which they were composed. Such farms were let out to individuals (tacksmen) for rent and for a given period of years. They in turn let out part or all of the land so rented to tenants, who subsequently let part of it – and generally the worst part – to subtenants. Beneath the subtenants were the various cottars and landless classes. By the mid-eighteenth century, the land was held in return for a combination of money-rent, food-renders, the provision of cartloads of peat, and customary labour services. The money element might be commuted back into additional services or rent in kind where the tenants were incapable of paying or where the person from whom they held the land so decided. The provision of such rents and services also coexisted with the obligation of providing military services where they should be required.

There was thus a hierarchy of tenure running down from dukedom through baronies – of which the holders had heritable jurisdiction over those who in turn held land from them – to tacksmen, tenants, and sub-tenants. The farms could also be held by tenants' handing over a down payment, which was then returned in full at the termination of the contract – a form of interest-free loan in place of rent – as well as by life-renting, where, for example, the widow of a clan chief was given a farm and the revenue that accrued from that farm for as long as she lived. After three generations of continuous possession, all such tenants and subtenants acquired the right of ancient possession and therefore the right to remain on the land.[11]

Alongside this hierarchical pattern of tenure existed the clan system, based on agnatic patrilineages in which sons and daughters were considered to belong to their father's clan. In practice, in any given area the proprietor in feu (who held directly from the feudal superior), the tacksmen, life-renters, and more substantial tenants all belonged to the same clan. Smaller tenants, subtenants, and the landless classes tended to belong to subordinate clans. If one powerful clan exercised hegemony over a wide area that included many local clans and their chiefs, such local clans tended to take on the dominant clan name and ultimately might lose their own clan identity. The history of the Highlands is one of clans moving into given areas and gradually consolidating their hold over the farms within those areas. That process of consolidation took place by force of arms, by finding tacksmen and larger tenants from among fellow clansmen, by establishing the right of ancient possession and defending it, and by careful clan endogamy, aimed at ensuring that the right of ancient possession thus established remained within the clan. At the same time there was some limited exogamy with respect to the various sub-clans that might constitute the smaller tenants and subtenants within a given dominant clan's area, largely consisting of the giving of women by the dominant clan to the subordinate one, which had the effect of reinforcing the ties between the two groups without at the same time giving any additional rights over land to the subordinate clan.[12]

Traditional Highland society was thus hierarchically structured on the basis of rights to land, with any given tenant's right being more or less protected through the right of ancient possession and by virtue of that individual's being born into a clan that had acquired such rights. At each level of tenure there was a slightly different relationship between the tenant or the individual who rented the land and the process of production. A considerable proportion of the subtenant's productive activity, for example, necessarily went to provide the rents and services to the tenant from whom he held, and that tenant, according to MacPherson, might be more than able to pay the rents and services to the tacksman from whom he held simply from what he received from his own subtenants.[13] He might thus be able to hold his much larger unit of land for nothing, his own produce being for his household's subsistence and profit. But even where he could not use the rents and services of his subtenants to hold his land for nothing, a much smaller proportion of his overall productive activity would go towards paying the tacksman or superior tenant from whom he held than in the case of subtenants.

The tacksmen themselves either let out all the land that they held from the proprietor in feu and subsisted and paid their rents without being involved in production at all, or let part of it and worked the rest. The larger part if not all their income thus derived from the productive activity of others. At the highest level the proprietor in feu presumably lived wholly off the revenue from tacksmen, would generally be the chief of the clan within the given area, and would call on the manpower of all his various tenants and subtenants for military purposes. There was thus a semi-feudal system of tenure, in which the surplus labour of the lower strata was appropriated to a greater or lesser extent by the higher – while the lower none the less had some security of tenure – and in which the system itself was bound together by clan affiliation.

This pattern of tenure and clan allegiance was politically unacceptable in the broader eighteenth-century context, particularly given the Jacobite loyalties of the clans, and was thrown into disarray after the defeat of the 1745 rebellion. But it was also increasingly unacceptable in the light of eighteenth-century economic theory and practice.[14] Adam Smith, towards the end of the century, published his *Wealth of Nations*. The wealth to which he refers does not consist in the accumulation of coinage or precious metals but in the goods produced from a given area of land or from the use of a given quantity of capital in production.[15] In order to increase the wealth of nations, therefore, it is necessary to increase productivity and not just the accumulation of precious metals.

The traditional parcelling out of land in the Highlands coexisted with a fairly high rate of productivity in global terms, but the goods so produced were largely consumed on the spot by the producers. The surplus was raked off for consumption by tacksmen and clan chiefs (and increasingly in the eighteenth century such chiefs were developing expensive tastes and spending more time in Edinburgh and London than among their clansmen).[16] With the development of capitalist manufactures and capitalist agriculture (employing wage-labour) in the south, it was increasingly desirable that the Highlands should be "improved," that the land should be cleared of the bulk of its population, and that rather than having their land farmed by managers, the proprietors (that is, the clan chiefs) should let it out to capitalist tenant farmers, who would be more motivated to maximize productivity.

This process was expected to have several results. It would greatly increase the profits to the clan chief from a given area of land; increase productivity per head of those involved in agricultural production and permit a greater amount of what was produced to be sent for sale in the rapidly growing manufacturing centres; create greater prosperity among those left in the Highlands and therefore an improved market for urban manufactured goods; and above all result in a large influx of dispossessed tenants and subtenants into the manufacturing centres, which would increase the amount of labour available to capital and also expand the market for the agricultural products from the very land of which those tenants had been dispossessed.[17]

From the point of view of clan chiefs anxious to increase their income and thereby maintain the style of life to which they had become accustomed, from that of would-be capitalist tenant farmers, and from that of the urban-based manufacturing interests, this was the ideal solution. The problem was to get rid of the population already densely established on the land as cottars, landless labourers, subtenants, and tenants, in the last two cases clinging on to their holdings by right of clanship and ancient possession. The answer came in the form of the Clearances, which really consisted in the unilateral declaration of private property on the part of the clan chiefs, or at least, the denial of the tenurial rights of their fellow clansmen and tenantry, which amounts to the same thing.[18] This process of evicting the tenantry and forcing them to establish themselves on the barren west coast of Scotland, or in Glasgow, or in the colonies, accelerated in the early years of the nineteenth century – and throughout this period the civil and military power was ever ready to come to the aid of the evictors – when the price of processed seaweed (kelp) rose steeply as a result of the Napoleonic war and the consequent difficulty of obtaining imports. It was now more than ever in the interests of the proprietors to evict their tenants and replace them with capitalist tenant sheep-farmers, while the evicted tenants themselves could be set to work at the kelp. This, therefore, was a period in which the bulk of the Highland tenantry was evicted from its lands and resettled in relatively barren coastal and island townships. Each family – and there is a striking parallel with Alavi's Punjabi village – was given just enough land not to be able to survive, so they were forced to work at the kelp, which was then bought by the proprietors at price levels that were barely sufficient to provide for the producers' subsistence.[19]

By displacing their tenants, and in the process flying in the face of clan solidarity and traditional rights of tenure, the proprietors and clan chiefs succeeded in reaping much larger profits from the clan lands and also from the displaced clansmen and women forced to work as wage-labourers in the kelp industry. This brought into being the "crofting" system, in which the units of land are either too small or barely adequate to ensure the subsistence of those working them, who therefore have to work as wage-labourers, or part-time fishermen, or seek government assistance in order to survive.

Throughout the nineteenth century the lot of the crofters fluctuated with the sudden drop in prices in the kelp market, the loss of the potato crop and resultant famine, further evictions by the landlords to create sporting estates and sheep farms, and forced emigration. By the end of the century some security of tenure and resettlement of lands from which they had been removed was guaranteed to crofters by legislation resulting from the findings of the Crofters' Commission of 1884. The commission had been appointed after the Highland Land War of the 1880s, when famine and rising rents forced the crofting population into revolt.[20] From that time on, crofters have remained in a state of marginalized subsistence production and dependence on central government.

For our present purposes, what is important in this brief survey of Scottish Highland and Island history in the eighteenth and nineteenth centuries is the transition from a pre-capitalist mode of production in which class structure was buried in clan structure (but where class was none the less present as a determining feature) to straightforward capitalist relations. The very individuals or descendants of those individuals who formerly confronted each other as clan chiefs and clansmen within a framework of reciprocal rights and duties now confronted each other as landowner and proletariat, while in the areas from which the tenantry had been evicted a new class of capitalist tenant farmers had come into being.

This process did not in itself produce classes in the full Marxian sense, although here again class consciousness and political organization on the landlord side developed well in advance of any such organization on the part of the crofter working class. However, the sustained evictions and rent increases, combined with the lack of security of tenure, the fact that landlords and their agents occupied all the official posts of command in Highland society and therefore were able to call on the civil police and the military to enforce their will, and against the background of famine, disease, and forced emigration, eventually gave rise to crofter and cottar class consciousness and political action in the Land War, which itself gave rise to protective legislation. Hunter's study of the crofting system further emphasizes that the coming into being of such class consciousness was assisted by the spread of the Free Presbyterian church in the Western Highlands, which helped to create the framework in which class organization could take place.[21] The fiery public meetings that marked the early stages of the religious movement were the forerunners of the political activism of the later period.

It is frequently pointed out that whereas capitalism had a slow and painful birth in the European heartland from the Middle Ages onwards, elsewhere it has been suddenly imposed, either by economic pressure or by force, or by both. The latter was the case in the Scottish Highlands, where economic and political pressure destroyed a hierarchically organized and semi-feudal clan system and replaced it with the triumvirate of the landlord, capitalist tenant farmer, and marginalized crofter/wage-labourer. As a result of this transition the clans were destroyed, but class came out into the open.

Alavi's Punjabi village and events in the Scottish Highlands demonstrate different ways in which a pre-capitalist mode of production is gradually or suddenly transformed into one in which capitalist relations become predominant. In the Scottish case in particular one finds certain elements that tend to be characteristic of such transformation wherever it takes place. There is, for example, the separation of the direct producers from the means of production (and of their reproduction), which goes hand in hand with the conversion of land from a system of tenure in which right of possession or use is by virtue of kinship into one in which land becomes private property. Land, in other words, becomes a commodity that can be bought, sold, or leased rather than the basis for subsistence production by right of ancient possession, whether that production coexists or not with the extraction of surplus by a non-productive class. However, that separation itself is not productive of capitalist relations of production. In Swat, for example, non-Pukhtuns were separated from the land by virtue of conquest, and in order to have access to it they were obliged to enter into agreements with the Pukhtun landlords on terms laid down by them, but this does not imply capitalist relations of production. Those require that the possession of the means of production (whether in the form of land or equipment) be in the hands of the capitalist and that the capitalist subsequently purchase the labour power that he needs for a given period of time, which labour is then put to work with the means of production at his disposal. Capitalist relations in agriculture therefore require the capitalist farmer either to buy or rent a farm and then hire wage-labour to work it, he himself retaining ultimate control over the labour process and the means of production.

Separation is thus one stage in the development of capitalist relations of production, or a prerequisite for that development, in that there has to be a work-force available to capital that has no alternative source of subsistence. Separation, however, will only lead to capitalist production given the presence of available capital. According to Pierre-Philippe Rey, capitalism first requires the existence of a labour force that has been separated from the means of its own reproduction.[22] In the French Congo in the late 1920s and early 1930s, direct producers were taken forcibly off the land and put to work on the construction of a railway line. At the conclusion of the project those who had survived no longer had the option of returning to the land they had left and were obliged to seek wage employment. It was, therefore, simply a question of bringing international finance capital and labour together in order to create the conditions of existence of a capitalist mode of production. A similar series of events takes place in the Scottish example. It is first necessary to remove the bulk of the population from the land by force or otherwise. This has the effect of "freeing" the land as a commodity that can then be let or sold to a capitalist farmer and "freeing" the labour-power that originally worked it and now has to seek wage-employment. In Scotland the wage-labour thus "freed" was then brought together with capital either in the coastal settlements or the lowland industrial conurbations and put to work. Or, inasmuch as there was no work for it to be put to, it was disposed of by emigration to the colonies, or even *en route* to the colonies, since there was a high mortality rate on the vessels then carrying emigrants across the North Atlantic.[23]

This process of separation and combination (with all that it implies for the possibilities of full class association) is universal to the development of capitalist relations of production. For Marx, the history of the English Middle Ages is the history of the brutal separation of the producers from the land, or the land from the producers. From the fifteenth century onwards, the enclosure, by the great feudal lords, of arable land for the creation of sheep-walks amounted to the privatization of large tracts of land that had previously been held in common for tillage and grazing. Subsequently, with the development of capitalist manufacturing in the eighteenth and nineteenth centuries, the artisans and handloom weavers, among others, were also separated from the ownership of their tools and equipment and forced into wage-labour.[24]

Lenin describes one way in which separation and subsequent combination comes about.[25] Among the lace-makers in a given region there are those who specialize in taking the goods produced to the market and thereby gain marketing expertise, which makes them increasingly indispensable to the producers. The position they come to occupy enables them to enrich themselves at the expense of the producers by paying the producers less than they receive for their produce. The capital thus accumulated not only allows them to lend money to the lace-makers and thereby to place the latter in their debt, but also leads to the situation where they pay in part or in whole in raw materials for the finished products.[26] This, as Lenin points out, is close to a form of industrial capitalism. All that is required is for the capitalist merchant to set up premises in which the lace-makers are brought together and in which equipment and raw materials are provided by the capitalist, and capitalist manufacture in the strict sense has come into being.

The cornering of handicraft manufacturers and artisans by merchant capital is as typical of the development of capitalist manufactures as is forced separation from the land in the case of agriculture. In the first instance the producers are separated from the market; in the second from their traditional suppliers of raw materials; and in the third from their own premises and equipment. Merchant capital installs itself upstream and downstream of the process of production before moving in on that process itself, but only where that is the most profitable option. To return to the Scottish example, Hunter describes the way in which the crofter-fishermen were provided with boats and equipment by the fish-curers in Castlebay and Stornoway, who then bought the fish that they caught.[27] The fishermen came to be permanently in debt to the curers, although the latter ensured that they still made sufficient money to keep fishing. The curers were not interested in moving any closer to the actual process of fishing, it being more profitable to leave it in the hands of nominally independent (although indebted) crews.

The upstream and downstream presence of merchant capital is an omnipresent factor in the emergence of capitalist relations of production. Rey cites research on French agriculture in the 1970s to show that capitalist agriculture does not simply "replace" an existing peasantry.[28] Suppliers and marketers install themselves alongside the peasant producer, who, in being forced to mechanize and increase the size of his holding to remain competitive, comes to be increasingly in debt to the financial interests that allow for his expansion. As in the case of the Hebridean fish-curers, the large corporations that hem the agricultural producer in on all sides are reluctant to move in on the process of production itself. As long as it remains more profitable to leave production in the hands of a nominally independent producer, the otherwise vertically integrated food-distribution and -retailing corporations will continue to do so.

Another instance in which subsistence producers are hemmed in and that can lead to the development of capitalist agriculture is that involving usurers' capital. Darling, in his study of indebtedness among the Punjab peasantry, describes the process whereby those with marginal or even quite large holdings had to borrow in the bad years and pay off their debts in the good.[29] Following the introduction of the *Pax Britannica* in 1849 (and

Darling was writing before it had come to an end), the old system under which lenders had to remain answerable to the community for their actions and were therefore obliged to be moderate in their demands gave way to the protection of the usurer by the law. The marginal peasant producers quickly succumbed to the high rates of interest demanded by the money-lenders, such that in good years they were unable to rid themselves of the debts accumulated in bad, and indeed faced a future in which they stood no chance of freeing themselves from debt.[30] The usurer then tended to take all that they produced, leaving only so much as allowed them to survive and continue producing. This in itself is not a capitalist relation of production, although it is a relation of production based on usurer's capital, since the producers remain in physical possession of the land, being obliged merely to forfeit the bulk of their production to the usurer. Usurers can, however, also be themselves agriculturalists and can take advantage of the situation to remove the debtor from the land and add it to their own, taking a further step on the road to being capitalist farmers and employers of wage-labour.

These are some of the ways in which accumulated capital can be brought to bear on independent subsistence production or production for exchange and give rise to capitalist relations of production, with all that that implies for the development of explicit class association. They all imply the intrusion of capital in or around the process of production and the gradual leverage of the producers away from the means of their own reproduction, such that they can only have access to them on capital's terms. There are thus two fundamental requisites for the development of full-blown capitalist relations of production: the existence of "free" (that is, separated) labour, and the existence of accumulated capital. But capital once accumulated (whether by merchants or money-lenders) has ways of bringing about the situation in which labour is forced to sell itself on capital's terms.

Class consciousness leading to political organization (and class in the full Marxian sense) was thus made possible by the development of capitalist relations of production. It was for this reason that Lenin welcomed the development of capitalism in Russia as the means whereby the isolation and "narrowness" of rural life could be overcome and replaced by a socialized, mobile, and intelligent work-force that would inevitably become conscious of itself as a class opposed to agricultural and industrial capital, from which consciousness the political action necessary for the overthrow of the capitalist class and of capitalism would develop.[31] Socialism, therefore, could never arise from localized rural peasant production (in spite of the dreams of utopian Morrissite socialists and in spite of the hopes that were later to be engendered by the Chinese revolution) but could only result from the development of full working-class consciousness under capitalism.

CHAPTER ELEVEN

Ethnicity's Revenge: Labour Migration and Racism in Industrial Societies

In the last two chapters I have looked at the construction of identity through opposition as one aspect of what is understood by ethnicity, and at the coming into existence of class in the full Marxian sense, along with the development of capitalist relations of production. With reference to the Scottish Highlands, this latter process was characterized as one of class structure replacing clan structure, or rather, as the coming into the open, in the form of conflict between a crofter working class and the classes of landlords and capitalist tenant farmers, of an underlying class structure that, in its more feudal guise, had previously been "seen" in terms of clan relationships. This development could be described as class replacing ethnicity as the explicit organizing principle on which alignments and allegiances are based. There is, however, nothing automatic about that replacement. Thompson amply demonstrates the long drawn-out beginnings of English working-class consciousness,[1] and equally political action by crofters in the Western Highlands was the result of decades of famine, deportation, rent increases, compulsory labour in order to "earn" famine relief, and lack of security of tenure, all stemming from the original unilateral denial of the ancient rights of possession by the clan chiefs.

If, in the Scottish Highlands, ethnicity gives way to class at the level of perceived identity, in the case of long-distance labour migration class can give way to ethnicity. It is ironic that the very process acclaimed by Lenin, one in which isolated peasantries and agricultural labourers are brought together by capital and can thus come to an awareness of their common class position and interests as an industrial working class,[2] can also give rise to the creation of new ethnic boundaries and divisions. The socialization of labour can work in the direction both of class formation and of ethnogenesis. Such ethnogenesis is comparable to that which takes place in the context of any migration where previously remote groups or peoples suddenly find themselves in contact with each other. The creation of new ethnic boundaries in such circumstances is an inevitable accompaniment of the continual construction and reconstruction of their respective identities.

In contemporary labour migration, however, there are further factors that complicate the situation. Such migrants do not find themselves juxtaposed to existing populations so much as incorporated alongside them within the same system of production. Ethnic boundaries may thus coincide with, cross cut, or be entirely contained within the various occupational and class boundaries that already exist in the society. There is, therefore, necessarily and immediately a conflict between ethnicity and class as vehicles for the construction of identity wherever the congruence of boundaries between the two does not lead to their both being vehicles at the same time and for the same group.

This is one aspect of the "problem" of ethnic minorities in industrial societies. In contemporary Britain, however, there is a further element that is brought to bear on the construction of class and ethnic identity, that of the legacy of colonialism, inasmuch as post–Second World War long-distance labour migration to Britain has brought the colonizer and the colonized into direct confrontation on the colonizer's home ground. For the present I look at the nature of the "problem," the various "solutions" that have been put forward, and the general significance of the question for class and ethnicity.

Whereas class in the form of group identity and political action tends to ebb and flow with historical circumstances and is never necessarily present (a point about which there is a certain convergence in Marxian and Weberian theory), ethnicity is not only omnipresent but is itself intimately bound up with identity. One could say that where different group identities exist, ethnicity exists. But class formation and ethnogenesis are also differentiable from each other in the sense that coming to a consciousness of class can be a long and difficult process and one that is liable to be thrown into reverse, while coming to a consciousness of oneself as a group in opposition to other groups (ethnicity) is the immediate consequence of contact between groups. Class consciousness, therefore, develops slowly and is always liable to be undermined by dominant discourse, intraclass divisions, and changing economic conditions. Ethnic consciousness, on the other hand, is invariably present, and is indeed implicit in consciousness itself.

The "problem" of ethnic differentiation and division thus springs into existence as a direct result of labour migration and in the context of class division. Where ethnic markers coincide with inter- and intraclass dividing lines, the resultant hostility between classes and class fractions can come to be seen as flowing from the relationships between ethnic groups. Ethnicity, therefore, becomes the "problem," and an entire industry of trouble-shooting social research is built up on premises similar to those of Myrdal, who, in *An American Dilemma*, arrives at the conclusion that if there were only a change in the "hearts and minds" of white Americans, the black "problem" would disappear.[3] This is akin to saying that famine in the Third World could be prevented if people could be persuaded to eat more. In both cases it is not changes in attitude that are required in themselves but changes in attitude that would lead to changes in inter- and intranational relations of production.

In post–Second World War Britain and particularly since the 1960s the "problem" has tended to carry an ethnic label, and numerous solutions, framed in ethnic terms, have been put forward. Before looking at those various exercises in social cosmetics, we must consider the nature of the problem that requires the label in the first place. In a previous chapter I looked at some of the economic pressures on old established industries in the industrial heartlands that lead them to seek a low-cost and malleable work-force in order to offset the effects on profitability of declining competitiveness.[4] Antiquated machinery and cost-efficient (in other words, dilapidated) installations combine with a non-unionized and often illegal immigrant work-force to maintain some form of marginal profitability. The process underlying this development is well described by Piore.[5]

The demand for labour has always followed a cyclical pattern under capitalism, according to the iron laws of competition and against the background of the various combinations of under-consumption and over-production and over-consumption and under-production that give rise to periods of crisis and boom respectively. Industrial capitalism requires a work-force that remains available for the periods of boom without having to be supported during the periods of crisis, an industrial reserve army that is always ready to be called up to the front. Given a non-unionized work-force and a large surplus population, there were no problems for capital, or are no problems where these conditions still apply. Where the bringing together of labour, however, leads to class consciousness and political action in the form of unionization, one of the first demands of organized labour is for a guarantee of continued employment. There thus comes into existence what Piore describes as a "dual labour-market."[6] On the one hand there is a permanently employed, unionized – or non-unionized, but none the less protected – work-force, and on the other a work-force in the more traditional sense, which can be taken on or dropped as circumstances require.

After the Second World War the older industrial nations were no longer able to guarantee sufficient labour-power to meet the demands of industry in the secondary sector of the labour-market, given the economic boom of the 1950s and 1960s. Various measures were taken to import labour from whatever sources were available but within the constraints of the different, more or less exclusive immigration policies of the countries concerned. The dual labour-market was thus consolidated, with largely native, male, unionized labour in the better-paid primary employment sector and women, adolescents, and immigrants brought in to make up the secondary sector. Several countries had from the beginning the policy of only temporarily admitting secondary-sector immigrant workers.

In Britain the various provisions of the Aliens Act, which had been successfully used during the two world wars to make life difficult for foreigners, were circumvented by bringing in British passport holders from the old dominions of the Empire.[7] Such immigrants were, during the early period, mainly single male target workers who came for short periods in order to earn as much money as possible with the intention of then returning home. Because the demand for such workers remained high, however – native workers being unwilling to return to the secondary employment sector – temporary target workers tended also to remain, with the added impetus in Britain of legislation in the 1960s that restricted their rights to bring in dependants. This impending legislation had the effect of bringing about the more permanent establishment of workers who otherwise would probably have remained on a temporary basis, as well as the immigration of their families to circumvent the effects of what was to be the Commonwealth Immigrants Act.[8] As Piore points out in relation to the United States, all "temporary" immigration is liable to become permanent where immigrants are not brought in for officially restricted periods.[9] This leads to an element of permanence in the secondary sector that is undesirable from the point of view of capital and more particularly of the state, which has to support such workers when they are not needed by capital. Piore suggests that in order to maintain the dual labour-market in the form best suited to industrial capitalism, secondary-sector immigrants should only be given temporary labour permits.

Piore thus provides an initial approach to the "problem" of ethnic minorities in industrial capitalist societies. Under industrial capitalism secondary-sector workers have to be dispensable or, ideally, disposable at those periods when they are no longer needed. Ideally for the system, internal migrant workers who give up subsistence production to go to work in the towns can be returned to their home areas; women who have been brought into the labour market can be sent home; adolescents can be temporarily enlisted in the armed services, put into abeyance for a year or two in higher education, or "supported" by their families while receiving minimal social-security payments from the state; and temporary labour immigrants can be refused work and residence-permit renewal. All these options give the various sectors of resource extraction and transformation the necessary flexibility to meet the cycle of boom and recession.

However, what was possible in the past, and what is still possible in many Third World countries, is less possible in advanced capitalist societies. In such societies the capitalist mode of production has largely penetrated into even the remotest corners of the economy. There is no longer a sub-sistence sector to which unwanted workers can be returned. The arrival of women in ever larger numbers on the labour-market since the Second World War has coincided with the growing acceptance of the fact that they have as much right to be there and to be paid at the same levels as men. Presumably the acceptance of that fact, and the legislation that accompa-nied it, simply reflected capital's need for additional labour-power, but it also means that capital is not as free to dispense with the services of unwanted women workers as it has been in the past. Leaving aside the question of school-leavers, who can only be kept out of the labour-market temporarily, there is in addition the problem faced by those countries – Britain and Canada, for example – that have tended to admit permanent rather than temporary labour migrants.

The upshot of Piore's argument is that such countries have acquired a secondary labour force that cannot be conveniently removed from the labour-market when circumstances require. He suggests temporary labour migration as the only solution for capital, and in the same vein would presumably also suggest the temporary admission of women to the labour-market. At a time of long-term recession such "solutions" are relatively academic, in that unemployment makes heavy inroads as much into the primary as into the secondary employment sector, but none the less they can illustrate one aspect of the "problem" of the labour migrant from the point of view of the system.

Permanent immigration of secondary-sector workers is thus, according to Piore, problematic for capitalism, but it can also be problematic for the labour migrant. The migrant does not come entirely of his or her own accord. Piore explains the mystery of why migrants come from certain specific areas rather than others by reminding us that they are in the first instance subject to a recruiting drive that selects those areas. However, once a channel of labour migration is opened from a given area, migrants continue to flow down it whether recruitment is maintained or not and unless legislation is introduced to shut it off.

Such migrants are therefore originally recruited for certain specific sectors of the labour market. In post–Second World War Britain, given the boom in production in the 1950s and 1960s, native male workers were moving out of the low-paid sectors in manufacturing and services. Employers sought to replace them by bringing women into the labour-market and hiring immigrant workers. Immigrants thus arrived with a niche in the system already prepared for them, generally at the lowest levels of pay, in the worst conditions, and at the most unsocial hours. They found themselves con-fined to precisely those sectors that native labour had refused: London

Transport; the night cleaning of offices and public buildings for large contract-cleaning companies at below minimum wages; furnace work in the foundaries; rag-sorting in textiles; portering in hospitals; and generally the lowest-paid positions in a variety of sectors.

Whatever resistance black workers in particular put up to the conditions in which they work and live, they have not always had the support of the trade unions, more concerned to protect existing differentials.[10] It is not so much a question of immigrant groups' taking over certain sectors and erecting protective ethnic barriers around them – so as to keep the advantages to themselves – but rather of their finding themselves confined to those sectors through no choice of their own. The ethnic barriers are erected by white native labour and as much if not more by the dominant classes in society that hire immigrant labour in the first place and stand to benefit most from the value that it creates.

What is true of employment prospects is also true of living conditions. Immigrant workers invariably end up in the worst housing in the more run-down parts of the larger cities. That situation can be explained (following Dahya)[11] on the basis of immigrant preferences: they will choose housing that is close to work; self-protective environments out of range of white native middle- and working-class hostility; low-standard bought housing rather than better-standard, or at least newer, rented housing. Immigrant settlement patterns can also be explained (following Rex and Moore)[12] with reference to the hostility and racism in the wider society, which discriminates against immigrants by refusing to lease, sell, or finance housing outside certain specific areas. Whatever explanation or combination of explanations one chooses to follow, the fact remains that immigrant workers end up in the worst housing in areas that the white working class has largely abandoned.

Here again, as in the case of employment prospects, black immigrants find themselves walled in by an ethnic barrier set up by white English society. In Weberian terms, one could say that the white English working class and petty bourgeoisie have created a form of monopolistic closure to prevent the immigrant from acceding to their privileges and thereby help to establish the very privileges they seek to protect, since for privileges to exist, somebody has to be excluded from them. I omit the ruling class from this process only because they have a set of ethnic barriers of their own that are of proved effectiveness as much against the native working and middle classes as against immigrant labour. Put another way, the native working and middle classes man the outer defences while the ruling class locks itself up in the keep.

The problem for black immigrants is thus their containment in the worst employment and housing sectors within a set of watertight ethnic barriers. If the problem is without issue for the first generation black immigrant in Britain, and at a time of relatively full employment, it is the more acute for those who are generally miscalled "second-generation immigrants."[13] The bitterness of the parents at the employment and living conditions they have been forced to accept is frequently translated into the hope that their children will not be subject to the same conditions. But those children are processed by an educational system that continues the ethnic and class containment that they already know from their home environment and that ends up condemning them to the same third-class status as their parents. And increasingly, continuing recession and the changing demands of capital remove the possibility of even third-class employment. The result is frustration and despair in the face of a system that not only refuses to accept black school-leavers as full and equal citizens by hemming them in with uncrossable ethnic barriers but also physically contains them within run-down areas in the inner cities under the close observation of the local – and sometimes not so local – constabulary. The repressed bitterness of the first generation becomes the open hostility of the second.

What is problematic for capital is thus also problematic for the immigrant worker, more particularly since certain elements in white British society are not content with the mere construction of ethnic barriers but insist on violence as a means of maintaining them. Life for black British workers and their families is not only difficult but dangerous, particularly given the re-emergence of fascism and the ambiguity in the reaction of the conservative establishment and the police to that re-emergence. The extreme right and certain of their more sober fellow-travellers on the right and centre-right have worked themselves into various states of racist hysteria that have come out at different times in the violence of the National Front and the not less portentous warnings of Enoch Powell. These attitudes are a curious mixture of xenophobia and delusions of ethnic superiority and become the more strident and alarmist the more Britain's actual position in the world declines into relative insignificance.

The extreme right chooses to consider the black sector of the British working class as in some way the "problem" on which everything can be blamed and whose removal would restore full employment and prosperity and contribute to the maintenance of a certain kind of white British ethnicity, just as it adopted similar attitudes towards the Jewish community in the east end of London in the 1930s. Whatever the nature of the "problem" so identified, however, it can be said that when the extreme right identifies a problem, it immediately becomes a problem for everyone else, and not least for the group identified as problematic.

For the left, the "problem" of ethnic minorities is precisely the containment of one sector of the working class behind the ethnic barriers erected by the other. The result of that containment is to split the trade-union movement into an increasingly frustrated black section and a self-protective white establishment, and to make any political action on the basis of working-class unity problematic. Essentially, the position on the left is that such divisions within the working class can only serve the interests of capital.

Alongside these various bearings on the "problem" of the ethnic minority is the position of the state itself as stabilizer of the system and guarantor of the continuation of the capitalist mode of production. To say that a permanently established labour force in the secondary employment sector is problematic for capital is really to say that it is problematic for the capitalist state, inasmuch as capital itself takes no responsibility for the maintenance of its own work-force beyond the point at which that work-force is capable of producing surplus value for capital. The state, in that it guarantees the subsistence of the unemployed (by taxing those who remain in employment), fills something of the same role as the subsistence agricultural sector in the early stages of capitalism. In the latter case the cost of the reproduction and formation of the labour-power required by capital is borne by the home community, which also maintains the migrant worker through unemployment, incapacitation, and old age. Thus one could say that capital only supports the worker under such a system when the worker is actually working for capital, but that would be to turn the capitalist mode of production upside-down, since it is in fact the worker who maintains the capitalist.

In advanced capitalist societies the state has precisely the same role in guaranteeing the reproduction, formation, and maintenance of labour-power for capital. The work-force not only reproduces itself by producing the value necessary to provide for its own subsistence, but it also reproduces and increases capital by producing surplus value, and guarantees the subsistence of those out of work and its own replacement in the form of a rising generation of workers by providing for state expenditure in the form of taxation.

The problems that we have been looking at come to be, sooner or later, problems for the state. When capital is unable to use the labour-power available to it, the state has to provide for it. When the anger of the black sector of the working class boils over into public protest, the state has to contain it. And when the same black sector of the working class lives under continual threat of right-wing violence, the state has to make some attempt to protect it. Such "protection" frequently consists in the police accompanying National Front marchers into minority areas for the ostensible reason of preventing violence, but creating the impression of a joint police – National Front operation, which the sympathy of some police officers for National Front goals does nothing to allay.[14] The "problem" of ethnic minorities – which is essentially the problem of capitalism on the one hand and British racism on the other – comes therefore to be a problem for the state as stabilizer of the system.

If it is true that any research project has to start by identifying the problem that it is attempting to answer, it is equally true that the existence of problems leads to the burgeoning of research projects. This is particularly so where the problem is identifiable as a problem for the state and where the bulk of all research monies is controlled by that same state. This has led to what the black left in Britain refers to derisively as the "race-relations industry." When this industry went into full production in the 1960s, it specialized in two kinds of products: a string of monographs in which concerned academics addressed the problem of race relations in all its different guises, and without generally going beyond those guises to the underlying relations of production and ingrained racism; and the formation and marketing of community-relations officers recruited from the ethnic minorities, whose job it was to be a form of lubricant between the heavy machinery of the state and the resistance of the black community. As far as the monographs are concerned, they invariably isolate one aspect of the "problem" and offer suggestions about the various ways in which the apparatus of local or central government might be adjusted to cope with it.

Rex and Moore, for example, in their study of Sparkbrook, come up with the notion of "housing class structure."[15] The problem is defined as being in large part caused by the confinement of immigrant workers to low-standard housing within specific areas. This serves to realize in spatial terms the very tendency to construct ethnic barriers around the immigrant community that lies at the heart of the problem. That process of barrier-construction is facilitated by the quality of the housing itself, which comes to be identified with the immigrants who occupy it: thus they are held responsible for a process of urban decay that in fact has its roots in structural changes in the broader society. There is thus a congruence between the closing off of the black sector of the working class within the lowest-paid sectors of industry, their being closed off in the lowest housing class, and their being shut in behind the barriers created by a racist belief-system. Rex and Moore conclude that if the barriers in any one of these areas can be destroyed, the existence of the others can be called into question. This again echoes Myrdal's approach in *An American Dilemma*, where it is suggested that improvement in one area – for example, middle-class opportunities or education – can have an effect in changing white attitudes in other areas.[16]

For Rex and Moore, one way to catalyse a change of attitude is to open up better-standard housing to ethnic minorities, particularly by ending discrimination in the allocation of council houses and mortgages. Underlying this suggestion, however (although in an unstated way), is the assimilationist view that the problem can be resolved by breaking up ethnic minority concentrations in low-standard housing and distributing the families around a variety of "better" neighbourhoods. As is suggested in Dahya's study, it is far from clear that immigrant workers would welcome such a change, given their need for community protection from violence.

Another example of the race-relations industry's output is Lambert's study of policing.[17] There is no sector of the race-relations problem that has obtained more funding or led to the setting up of more commissions of inquiry than police/ethnic-minority relations, the front line of interaction between the state and the minorities. Lambert sets out from the popular notion, and one that has often been put forward by the police themselves, that the black sector of the working class is more criminally inclined than the rest of the population. He concentrates on inner-city areas of Birmingham with high concentrations of immigrant workers. His first conclusion is that immigrant workers have no choice but to live in the "twilight" areas of the city, the very areas that tend to attract organized crime (or the executive branch thereof), prostitution, and other forms of non-respectable subsistence practices. There is, therefore, a distinction to be made between the fact that such areas have, on the one hand, high concentrations of immigrant workers and, on the other, higher than average crime rates. These two facts are not connected. Statistically Lambert demonstrates that charge rates for blacks tend to be either equivalent to or lower than those of the native white working class or Irish immigrant groups in the same areas, although there is some variety in arrest and charge rates depending on the nature of the offence in question.[18]

All such studies lead to two principal conclusions: popular attitudes that make the false connection between high crime rate and high immigrant concentration need to be changed, and the attitudes of the police towards the immigrant community need to be radically revised, along with the policing machinery. If in Rex's and Moore's study the ethnic-minority problem was viewed as in part a housing problem, in studies of police/ethnic-minority relations it comes to be seen as a problem of policing.

Nowhere has this been more the case than in the outbreaks of popular protest in Britain in 1981, which led to something approaching major conflagrations in Manchester, Liverpool, and London. Whereas there was some consensus over the existence of social causes underlying the outburst of anger on the part of the young black and, to a lesser extent, white unemployed, from the point of view of the Tory government those causes did not justify that outburst.[19] From the start the government's response was to ensure the restoration of public order before giving any attention to social causes, which effectively meant equipping the police with the tear-gas, water cannon, and armoured vans necessary to clear the streets. What changed the situation was a change in policing practice from a policy of defensive containment to one of aggressive dispersal.

Once the more critical confrontations had passed, the principal question to be asked by the establishment was not so much how social conditions should be changed to address the problems of the black community but how the policing machinery could be altered to prevent such outbreaks from recurring. The report of the official inquiry concentrates on this latter aspect, and the suggestions include increasing police awareness of and sensitivity to the special conditions obtaining in ethnic-minority areas, particularly through the recruitment of black policemen; bringing policemen back to a community-policing role built round personal contact and foot patrols; and increasing the police capacity to respond by improving their weaponry, crowd-control training, defensive equipment, and radio communications, and by introducing specially prepared mobile units that could be brought in within minutes of the first call for assistance.[20] Amid the multitude of explanations, accusations, and partisan exchanges that took place in Parliament, policing inexorably moved on to the centre of the stage.

Where the ethnic-minority "problem" surfaces in the form of collective action on the streets directed against the police, it comes to be interpreted as essentially a policing problem and one that can be resolved at the level of policing. Since the role of the state is not to change the terms on which certain sectors of the working class sell their labour to capital but simply to maintain the existing system in operation, it becomes comprehensible that the state would restrict itself to an operational response. Any problem has to be formulated so as to allow for its resolution, and the threat to public order is precisely such a formulation for the state, although it does not preclude various forms of tinkering with the system after order has been restored and the policing machinery revised.

The state, as a collection of apparatuses and rule-bound hierarchies, can only understand problems in certain ways, in that they have to be translated into the form of simplified binary language that the state bureaucracy is capable of processing. The ethnic-minority "problem" has proved to be one that has been difficult to translate as long as it seethed below the surface in untranslatable ways. But the moment repressed frustration changes to open confrontation, the state has a word for it – "riot" – and an answer – improved policing. That the state had a similar reaction to mass trade-union picketing at the time of the Industrial Relations Act under the Heath government, not to mention popular protest in Northern Ireland, is symptomatic of its neanderthaloid intelligence, which controls a vast and costly repressive apparatus always in need of victims to repress.

The state resolves the problem by reinforcing personnel-carrying vehicles and giving the police plastic bullets, which, among other things, are normally sufficient to keep people off the streets until the next election. The right, the liberal centre, and the left have more radical ideas concerning the resolution of the "problem." The right, and more especially the extreme right, goes for what Enoch Powell has described as the "voluntary repatriation of New Commonwealth immigrants,"[21] although it is not clear what repatriation means for the English-born children of first-generation immigrant workers. However, while waiting for that outcome, the right naturally encourages the state to clamp down on those who – other than themselves – disturb public order. The liberal centre would traditionally prefer an assimilationist or pluralist solution, and particularly the latter. Parekh, for example, condemns assimilationist policies as easily leading to the forcible indoctrination of the minority to be assimilated and as being, anyway, normally counter-productive.[22] He also condemns full-blooded pluralism, which refrains from criticizing and attempting to reform those minority practices that run directly counter to the shared values of the wider society. He refers to Muslim marriage customs (including summary divorce) and the Hindu practice of preventing teenage girls from attending school. What is needed, according to him, is a form of modified pluralism that accepts the right to be different and redefines Englishness to accommodate those differences but at the same time does not tolerate divergence from certain basic values.

The solution espoused by the left grows directly out of the way in which the "problem" is conceptualized – that is, as a threat posed to working-class solidarity by ethnic division. Such division is in part attributable to the racist attitudes of the white native working class, which are based on a misunderstanding of the role of immigrant labour in advanced capitalist societies. The native working class has to be made to realize that immigrant workers are not brought in as replacements so much as to do the jobs that native labour refuses to do, and that their economic contribution as producers of value, taxpayers, and consumers of goods and services is greater than their cost to the system. From the more traditional left perspective, racism has its roots in the perception of immigrant labour by the native working class as a threat to their existing levels and conditions of employment. The solution is to correct such misunderstandings and to emphasize the underlying class solidarity that needs to exist between native and immigrant labour.[23]

For the independent black movement the traditional conceptualization of the problem on the left is inadequate. Racism has much deeper roots in Britain's colonial past, and the only possibility of changing the situation is for the white left and the white working class to come to an understanding of the racist oppression to which they have been parties, at the same time as the black working class comes to a fuller understanding of its class position.[24] Amos et al. condemn traditional white sociology for seeking the cause of the black "problem" within the black community. The principal problem for blacks is white racism, and it is white racism that should be the focus of white sociology.[25]

The left thus seeks to expose the superficial character of ethnic barriers and prejudices and penetrate to the class structure that underlies and is concealed by them. On the other hand, the right seeks to impose its interpretation of the situation as an irreconcilable confrontation between two opposed and unequal ethnicities. On this latter interpretation, everything is reduced to ethnicity, and any class solidarity or opposition is ignored. The independent black movement seeks to demonstrate that the black working class is oppressed both on grounds of class and of race, and that racial or ethnic oppression is not just the empty mask that conceals class oppression but has its own reality. At the same time the liberal centre offers a number of watered-down class- and ethnicity-based explanations, and produces various socially cosmetic solutions. Alongside all these charges and counter-charges across class and ethnic boundaries is the heavy-handed response of the repressive apparatus of the state, which has little concern for the niceties of ethnicity and class but knows how to strike hard when the occasion requires.

I have earlier considered the way in which capitalist relations of production can bring about the possibility of full class formation on the part of direct producers who have been parcelled up in isolated rural communities – hence Lenin's optimism that the new working class thus created could eventually bring about the collapse and replacement of the system. The "problem" of ethnic minorities in advanced capitalist societies demonstrates how ethnicity as a dividing factor can intrude on and help to prevent the development of such class solidarity. Long-established working classes in such societies have two kinds of appeal made to them: from the left, in the name of a class solidarity that should override ethnic boundaries; and from the right, in the name of an ethnic solidarity that should override class boundaries, or at least those class boundaries that exist between different segments of the ethnic group so defined. The latter discourse can appeal to certain elements in the native working class where the ethnic barriers that the right seeks to maintain coincide with dividing lines within the working class itself, between, for example, native workers in the primary and immigrant workers in the secondary labour-market sectors.

To approach the "problem" of the ethnic minority purely in terms of white attitudes, however, can lead to the denial of the subjective choices and preferences of the immigrant worker, who tends to be considered "acted upon" rather than acting in his or her own right. This is Dahya's point in relation to Pakistani immigrants and housing.[26] They are not simply forced to live in the areas they do but choose to do so in the light of their preferences as well as the constraints operating on them in the form of hostility from the wider society. This provides a counterweight to such arguments as Piore's, in which labour migration is considered to be instigated by capital and the labour migrant is given no weight as an independent reflecting subject.[27] No one, presumably, would deny the element of careful calculation and premeditation that accompanies European middle-class migration to North America, but it is symptomatic of most studies of working-class migrants that they are presented rather as subject to the will of capital than as exercising their own.

The subtle difference between these two approaches emerges in the different treatments of the confrontation in Britain between young blacks and the state. The normal interpretation on the left is that young unemployed blacks are the victims of a system that has rejected them and that the system needs to be changed to accommodate them. The independent black movement, however, as represented by Darcus Howe and *Race Today*, maintains that it is the young blacks who have rejected the system rather than the other way round, particularly by refusing to do the jobs that their parents were forced into on arrival in Britain, and that it is the black section of the working class that is leading the fight against capital.[28]

The attitude in the liberal centre and on the left that suggests that the black section of the working class is the passive victim of white working-class racism or, alternatively, the grateful beneficiary of white middle-class reformism is presumably as much a relic of colonialism as racism itself, and indeed as much a form of racism as the more manifest variety. Underlying it is a colonial past in which the colonized was involuntarily subjected to the will of the colonizer, which subjection was then taken to suggest both the innate superiority of the colonizer and the lack of will of the colonized, whence the oppressive paternalism that characterized the British Empire and its agents and that managed to coexist with ruthless economic exploitation.

The question remains whether racism is really the monopoly of the white lower-middle and working classes, as upper-middle-class researchers, activists, and politicians are fond of suggesting.[29] If racism is understood as being based in part on delusions of superiority arising out of the colonial experience, it is worth considering which classes in British society had a direct hand in that experience, and not so much as foot-soldiers but rather as administrators, profiteers, and agents of cultural change. The answer might suggest that the ruling class is not only locked up in the keep of British ethnicity while the middle and working classes man the outworks, but that the beast of racism has its quarters in that same keep and is only occasionally let out to rampage around the outer walls.

CHAPTER TWELVE

From a Train Window: Ethnicity and the Landscape of Class in Britain

Labour migration, whether within states or between them, creates two simultaneous possibilities: the possibility that the mass of direct producers will be brought together so as to be able to associate politically and thereby stand some chance of gaining political and social control over the process of production, and yet the possibility for division within that same working class, based on differential role and reward allocation between and within sectors and on the congruence between those divisions and the ethnic markers that are themselves the result of labour migration. Such divisions are underscored by the monopolistic closure exercised by different sectors of the native middle and working classes, which seek to prevent the access of immigrants to their respective niches in the labour market; they are underscored as well, in the form of racism, by the attempt on the part of white society as a whole to retain its privileges by containing the black working and middle classes behind rigidly defined ethnic barriers.

I now turn to a different aspect of contemporary class societies, in order to get closer to the reality of class as experienced within those societies. To define class strictly on the grounds of relations of production, such that any individual is assignable to a given class, only allows us to construct in skeletal form the class relationships of a given society. If structurally determined class position is determinant of the different kinds of alignments and associations into which people enter and therefore of their identity as participants in those associations (following Marx), it is none the less clear that there can arise a sense of collective identity or brotherhood (following Weber) that does not use class itself as a marker – since class has no such visibility – but selects one or other of a set of "ethnic" labels.

At a theoretical level it is perhaps possible to stop at that explanation of secondary ethnic marking. It is impossible, however, to draw the line between the ethnic labels that classes or other associations use to demarcate themselves and the constitution of their identities as groups, and, ultimately, of the identities of the members within those groups. The problem is to sort out the relationship between class and ethnicity in a society where "class identity" and "class solidarity," which many participants in that society take to be the reality of class, is constructed around symbols and rituals and normative behaviour patterns that seem to have more to do with ethnicity than with class. How are we to understand class as it surfaces in such a society, and to what extent can it be said that ethnicity is determinant of action apart from class?

British society is divisible into classes both in the strict sense of relations of production but also in the looser descriptive sense (and one that comes closer to non-Marxist theory) of class endogamy, class dialect, class housing, class culture, class education, and, most strikingly, class patterns of consumption. In other words, the relatively straightforward distinctions in Marxian and Marxist theory among bourgeoisie, petty bourgeoisie, and working class – which may or may not include contradictory class locations in between – give rise to the most exotic and complex tangle of distinctions and identities at the level of social life. This may be particularly true of Britain, where capitalist relations of production have long been in a position of dominance and where the privileged classes to which those relations give rise have therefore long had the chance to indulge in the transmission of privilege to their offspring (transgenerational monopolistic closure in Weberian terms) that is so characteristic of established class societies. But the question arises of what these exotic growths are in terms of class and ethnicity, growths whose infinite subtleties are perhaps difficult to understand – let alone appreciate – for the non-initiated.

Cohen has isolated one small part of that tangle – the London financial elite – as constituting an ethnic group, and in so doing would seem to undermine the notion of a broader English ethnicity built up on several hundred years of colonial self-delusion, of which that particular group's identity would form a part.[1] But he also isolates one fraction of the dominant class as a self-contained ethnic unit, whereas there is little to separate top civil servants, decaying landed gentry, old-school Oxbridge academics, Church of England bishops, and Old Etonians generally, on the grounds of commensality and class endogamy, from their *confrères* in the City. Miliband would be closer to the truth than Cohen. The ruling class does not permit monopolistic closure within its ranks.

In discussing the altercation between Miliband and Poulantzas, I suggested that Miliband could be considered – from a Weberian point of view – to have discovered what amounts to a status group occupying the highest levels within the English bourgeoisie.[2] It is interesting to consider how far that Weberian notion can account for the experience of class in the form of the exotic outgrowths mentioned above. Weber maintains a rigid distinction between class and status group according to his own definition of the two terms, and that distinction is hard to maintain when one encounters the reality of class society. Whereas class for him is a question of the differential ability to control goods and services on the market (based ultimately on the possession of property or of marketable skills), status groups are a question of shared life-style based on empirical training or rational education, connubium, commensality, monopolistic patterns of consumption, and various status conventions.[3] Above all, status groups are conscious of themselves as groups and succeed in exacting from the wider society the recognition of their existence as a group. Such groups can arise out of a shared class situation, but they can also arise – as they have done in the past – for any number of reasons and can as well straddle class boundaries as be contained within them. The status group, for Weber, might therefore correspond to something of the monopolistic, mainly endogamous, class-based associations into which the upper levels of British class society can be broken down, but it can also refer to a variety of other kinds of grouping that are not class-based. This sets up the notion of the status group as a concept distinct from class, even if the reality to which it refers can on occasion overlap with it.

Closer to what I am suggesting to be the reality of class is E.P. Thompson's understanding, where class is "defined by men as they live their own history," with all the theoretical problems that that poses.[4] But if one is to talk of class in the full Marxian sense, and even in the full Weberian sense (that is, where negatively privileged classes come to be aware of their own class position, if only temporarily), one has to take into account the experience of class in consciousness. Class consciousness is above all the consciousness of the existence of a class or classes to which one does not belong, and in this it is close to ethnic consciousness. If, for Marx, classes presume the existence of one another, class consciousness also necessarily presumes that existence. One can therefore ask oneself about the form that one's consciousness of not belonging to other classes takes, or the grounds for believing oneself to be excluded from them. Optimistic abstractionists (optimistic in the sense that they believe that one day the world will come to accept their abstractions for the reality) might think that the consciousness of class is based on the realization of the objective relation of different groups in society to the process of production. The die-hard empiricist, by contrast, in defining class as lived experience, will necessarily look to that lived experience for the source of class consciousness.

I suggested above that where capitalist relations of production have long been established, the various class growths to which they give rise have had the time to produce a luxuriant and exotic tangle of foliage in the form of class-based dialects, customs, and so on. It would seem to be an elementary conclusion in relation to old established class societies that the consciousness of class and the consciousness of not belonging to other classes is constructed first around the appearances of class as experienced, in all the various forms of talking, thinking, behaving, eating, working, and housing in which class clothes itself. The consciousness of class can thus exist apart from any deeper understanding of the structures that lie behind the symbols and practices. But if this is the case, the relationship between class and ethnicity becomes that much more problematic, since the very labels and symbols that come to identify different classes in the experience, and therefore the consciousness, of class, can also be taken to be constitutive of ethnic differentiation. In a sense class could be said to become ethnicity, or class structure could be seen as taking the form of ethnic differentiation in those societies where capitalist relations of production have been long enough in existence for some degree of class endogamy and transgenerational monopolistic closure to have been established. This suggests that it would be mistaken to see class and ethnicity as mutually exclusive ways in which agents in society can conceive of themselves. However, before committing myself further to the notion that class becomes ethnicity, I shall look closer at the reality of British class society. In the following description I take into consideration three main aspects of class: coming to a consciousness of class (or growing up in a class society); class encounters between class-conscious agents; and class and social inequality.

In both Marxian and Marxist theory there is a fundamental distinction between the presence of class at the structural level and the coming into existence of fully self-conscious and politically organized classes under capitalism. Weber also makes the distinction between class as a way of classifying people according to their situation and class struggle arising out of the consciousness that such similarly situated people may come to have at particular periods where the reality of social structure becomes more visible.[5] In the experience of individuals coming to an understanding of the society in which they grow up, there is something of the same duality. Such children cannot help but be conscious of the differences between classes that are omnipresent in social life. That is not the same, however, as a consciousness of class (in the full Marxian sense). But inasmuch as those differences are the expression of class "relationships" (Marx) or "situations" (Weber), such a superficial class consciousness also contains at least the seeds of a deeper structural understanding of class. The second kind of class consciousness, therefore, would be one where that deeper structural understanding replaces the superficial grasp of class differences as the way in which those differences are explained.

Coming to a consciousness of class in a class society is, therefore, first coming to an awareness of the evident differences between classes without necessarily understanding why those differences exist. In contemporary British society every aspect of a child's experience comes to be constitutive of such differentiation. Every town, for example, reproduces on a larger scale the differences that already exist at the village level between the big house standing in parkland outside the village, the substantial houses of the local rector, doctor, and other notables, the respectable private housing of the teacher, shopkeeper, garage-owner, and perhaps electrician, plumber, and other providers of skilled services, and the newer local-authority housing on the edge of the village, which is invariably built at low cost and to standard design, quickly shows its age, and is rented to the locally based, mainly agricultural working class unable to compete on the market for the older housing in the village.

It has to be said, however, that such villlages are no longer typical of the English countryside. Any village within easy commuting distance of a town is liable to have been largely bought up by the various teachers, doctors, lawyers, representatives of upper and middle management, company owners, and indeed anyone who possesses a car, has sufficient capital or credit to compete on the village housing market, and wants to escape from the town. In addition, any village situated in attractive surroundings and whose houses are of some antiquity and architectural interest, however remote it might be from the nearest town, and particularly in the south of England, is liable to have a large stock of the pensioned-off relics of the genteel upper middle class, keeping bees, voting Conservative, wearing tweed, and living in the thatched, slated, or stone-roofed cottages that once housed the rural working class.

But even that does not suffice to characterize the English, Welsh, or Scottish village. Wherever those villages are not only beautiful but situated in mountainous, coastal, or other dramatically different areas (different, that is, from suburbia or the leafier parts of the inner urban landscape), they will have been largely bought up for holiday homes. There is thus the spectre of the Welsh mountain village, where one-third of the housing stands empty for forty-eight weeks of the year with darkened windows and smokeless chimneys and where the local teacher has to live in a caravan for lack of available housing. And then there are the endless villages within eighty to one hundred miles from London that contain the weekend cottages of better-off Londoners as well as the homes of long-distance daily commuters, retired colonels, bee-keeping widows, and professionals and managers from the local towns. To grow up in an English village is thus to find oneself in the midst (or more normally on the edge, if one belongs to a working-class family) of a strange amalgam of the imperial past and the entrepreneurial and professional present. To grow up in a Welsh village, by contrast, can be to grow up as a Welsh-speaker in poor-quality local-authority housing while a good proportion of the older slate-roofed and stone-walled houses in the village are silent and empty except during the English school holidays.

Growing up in a British town is perhaps less confusing for the increasingly class-conscious (in the primary sense) child. At the same time the differences may be less immediately striking than in the dormitory, holiday, or retirement villages, where the Industrial Revolution took off the working population to the towns and simultaneously provided a replacement population of emigrant petty and other bourgeois anxious to leave the new urban working class to its own devices. Any British town consists first of a working-class district, largely made up of early to mid-twentieth-century red-brick terraced housing interspaced between, and always downwind of, decaying factories, and criss-crossed by railway embankments, disused canals, and raised motorways. Here and there the terraces have been demolished and transformed into high-rise housing through the grandiose urban-planning mistakes of the 1960s, or displaced altogether to the outskirts of the town, where the fields of low-cost local-authority housing rise and fall with the contours of the landscape, occasionally giving way to a ring road, or the windowless regional-distribution centre of some multinational washing-machine company taking advantage of tax concessions and development grants on an otherwise unoccupied industrial estate.

Far to the southwest of this conglomeration of manufacturing industry on the decline in the face of foreign competition and the distribution centres of that foreign competition itself are the middle- and upper-middle-class preserves, in which the individual units become leafier and larger the further one moves out towards the golf-courses and annexed villages, which eventually give way to the retired bee-keepers and hunting farmers of the countryside. Where working-class housing stands eye to eye – and, in the old days at least, back to back – with one living-room window looking directly into another and with the view from the railway line being a monotonous succession of bottles of washing-up liquid in kitchen windows, the large, rambling houses of the upper middle class are concealed behind crumbling red-brick walls and privet hedges. Both of these features are reproduced on a newer, smaller scale on suburban middle-class housing estates, but with that inevitable hallmark of the aspiring middle class, an obsession with neatness and weedlessness.

Between these three urban enclaves, the public world of the working class, the more private domains of middle management, young professionals, and the occasional more highly paid worker, and the wooded seclusion of the upper middle classes, is the centre of the town. The centre is characterized by its faceless uniform department stores, recently cleaned nineteenth century municipal buildings, and two or three churches whose original congregations have moved away or stopped attending but whose windows have been repaired by Pentecostalists. Behind these various fronts of commerce and municipal pride is to be found the one-time housing of the old urban middle class, now given over to basement travel agents and multi-occupation on the part of those members of the native or immigrant working class who are unable or unwilling to obtain local-authority housing.

To grow up in a British town is to grow up in an already rigidly divided class landscape and one in which contemporary class divisions have slowly evolved out of the class divisions of the past. One's consciousness of those divisions is first an environmental one, in which a street, park, or railway shunting-yard constitutes the dividing line between "our" neighbourhood and "theirs," with perhaps large detached housing and quiet avenues on the one side and smaller semi-detached houses on the other. Beyond these immediate neighbourhood boundaries are the remoter areas of town, dense panoramas of municipal waterworks and working-class streets, glimpsed from a car or a train window. One's first consciousness of the existence of other classes and of one's own class (in the primary descriptive sense) is thus a vague awareness of other environments that are not like one's own. And since one rarely has cause to do any more than pass through those "other" environments, or skirt round them, that awareness can easily remain a state of comfortable or resentful vagueness, a realisation that such areas exist but no knowledge of what it might mean to live surrounded by three-quarters of an acre of lawns and flower beds on the one hand or by neighbours' washing lines on the other.

The various residential class domains already constitute closed realms of experience: closed from the inside, with those who belong only vaguely aware of other domains elsewhere, and closed from the outside to those belonging to other domains. To cross over the boundary from one class to another is not just to change territory but to find oneself in an unfamiliar and hostile environment. In a working-class street, doors open and close, faces disappear behind curtains, cars are dismantled and reassembled. In an upper-middle-class neighbourhood, by contrast, nothing moves apart from the occasional mid-afternoon pedestrian.

For the developing class consciousness of the child the various realms are not only separated from each other in space and on a scale of awareness running from familiarity and closeness to vagueness and distance, but remain separated over time. Working-class children go to overcrowded, neighbourhood, state-owned schools. Middle-class parents usually contrive to get their children into the more respectable state schools in middle-class catchment areas, when they are unable to purchase a third-rate upper-middle-class education in the less expensive private schools. And upper-middle-class parents buy their way out of the state system altogether by sending their children to the expensive local primary and regional preparatory schools, before despatching them to be trained as leaders of men in the private sector.

The social environment in which children are brought up in Britain thus precludes anything other than marginalized contact between classes. Children learn, play, and are generally socialized within – and in order to fit into – their own class environments. They learn to speak with particular class dialects, behave in accordance with class norms, and expect to find employment in the same class niches and live in the same class circumstances to which they have become accustomed, except where the possibility of upward social mobility allows them to aspire to cross over class boundaries. And no sooner have they crossed over as adults but they attempt to resocialize themselves into the ways of the new environment, with as little success in the case of ex-middle-class newcomers to the upper middle class as in that of conscience-stricken upper-middle-class intellectuals moving into what they fondly imagine to be working-class areas and life-styles. Class in Britain is therefore reduceable (at this primary level) to closed universes of action and meaning, whose closedness is in no way threatened by the upwardly and downwardly mobile. Indeed, mobility can reinforce closedness, inasmuch as new arrivals can be the most enthusiastic supporters of monopolistic closure against anyone inclined to follow in their footsteps.

The social and educational system in Britain produces a range of class products so as to guarantee the reproduction of existing social relationships against the background of the maintenance of a particular dominant mode of production. Because of the closedness of the different class domains, however, and particularly those of the upper and upper middle classes, which are not only socially barricaded behind the credentials of ancestry but physically barricaded behind high fences and thick hedges, the knowledge of what it means to belong to any other class, and more particularly to work in the niches reserved to those who belong to any given class, is necessarily limited. To emerge from childhood and adolescence is to be thoroughly familiar with one's own class domain and to be aware of where the boundaries lie between that domain and those above and below it, but to have little knowledge of what lies beyond those boundaries, unless one's mother was in service when she was young and can give an all-too-intimate account of bourgeois or petty bourgeois domestic bliss.

At the same time classes cannot live in isolation from each other, and indeed both exist and identify themselves in relation to each other. Living in a class society, therefore, involves "class encounters." By a class encounter I mean a more or less ritualized event where the members of different classes encounter each other. Given that they share neither the same class dialect nor the same class norms, the encounter comes to be a delicate compromise in which conversation is restricted to the banal and the essential and any reciprocal obligations do not go beyond those implied by the encounter itself. A whole range of service contacts are necessarily class encounters, where those receiving the service and those providing it belong to different classes, as in the case of homehelps, cooks, cleaners, hospital orderlies, shop assistants, drivers, porters, mechanics, secretaries, policemen, and anyone who is brought into contact with upper-middle and upper-class patrons.

The basic normative framework for such interactions is deference on the part of the servant, who is frequently required to be in uniform to symbolize the fact that (s)he "belongs" to the institutional or private employer, and condescension on the part of the patron. Generally the broader the social distance, the more polite the interchange, with the greatest hostility between, for example, supervisors and production-line workers in factories. Wholly informal encounters can only take place between class equals, where communication is instantly and easily possible on the basis of shared expectations, shared life-styles, and some equivalence in material circumstances. Any class encounter, by contrast, is necessarily formal. Domestic helps in upper-middle-class houses might be addressed by their first names but would rarely reciprocate; would normally be excluded from eating at the family table; and would probably never expect to be visited by their employers in their own homes other than for charitable or paternalistic purposes. Sometimes, exchanges within class encounters can be fairly free and unrestrained, but they are never permitted to go beyond the boundaries established by convention.

The underlying rationale behind the maintenance of such rigid spatial and social boundaries in a class society is to make social inequality possible. In a society where one-half the population has lower life expectancy, lower income, less job satisfaction, lower-quality education, worse housing, and longer working hours than the other half, and for no reason other than having been born in the wrong half, it is important that the awareness of those differences be kept vague and that interclass contact should be reduced to a minimum. Hence, the greater the privilege, the more private the setting in which those privileges are enjoyed. That state of affairs prevents the negatively privileged (in Weberian terms) from fully grasping the extent of the privileges from which they are excluded but also, since high walls are as difficult to look over from one side as they are from the other, prevents the privileged from coming too uncomfortably close to the reality of negative privilege. On these terms, a class society can only survive in so far as people do not know what it means to be a member of a more or less privileged class, since they are debarred from having experience of any class other than their own.

There are thus two areas of class consciousness that tend to be less accessible than the omnipresent but superficial awareness of class differences. The first would be a genuine consciousness of what it means to be brought up in and belong to another class, a level of consciousness that presumably can only exist – to a limited extent – for the socially mobile, and whose general absence makes possible the maintenance of social inequality. The second would be the understanding of the reality of class at the deeper structural level, an understanding that leads to seeing classes at the level of appearances as the more or less camouflaged outcrops of underlying class formations and relations of production. This latter understanding is full class consciousness in the Marxian sense. Closed class domains and ritualized class encounters are the surface features that either allow us to see or prevent us from seeing underlying social structure, depending on how we look at them.

The question arises of how these broad class domains and opposed identities should be conceptualized. Poulantzas, for example, makes the distinction between the structural determination of class on the one hand and class position on the other.[6] The former is one's objective class situation according to relations of production, and the latter the subjective class position that one chooses to adopt. An example of the latter would be the tendency of the skilled and better-paid fraction of the working class to adopt petty bourgeois or even bourgeois class positions in order to differentiate itself from other semi- and non-skilled categories of workers. As the material conditions of that skilled fraction of the working class improve, so it moves into increasingly non-traditional working-class residential areas, and particularly suburban developments aimed at young petty bourgeois or established skilled working-class would-be home-buyers. The difference between subjective class position and objective class situation can be seen where members of a skilled working class live in an area that corresponds to their subjective class identity, but work in a working-class environment.

This is not perhaps the way in which Poulantzas would develop his own argument, but it can show up one kind of relation between class domains (as I have been referring to them) and other aspects of class structure: one can work in one class domain and yet increasingly come to identify with another. The transition between domains, however, whether on a daily basis or in a once-and-for-all move, is not an easy one. The different domains are accompanied by complex cultural baggage, which children come to acquire and which serves for the construction of their identity. That identity will necessarily carry over into the new class domain and will tend to label the new arrivals as class migrants until such time as they blend into the new cultural environment. Such a cultural time-lag is most evident in the case of decayed gentry or the downwardly mobile of upper-middle-class origin. In both these cases they can still succeed in playing at the ritualized class encounters appropriate to their having been social-ized into a particular class domain. Impoverished aristocrats can rely on being able to elicit a deferential response even if their diminished material circumstances have long since prevented them from living in the style to which they once were accustomed. Sufficient of the class trappings remain for them to benefit from the deference normally accorded to those trappings.

There are two kinds of cultural time-lag. In the first case, upwardly mobile class migrants are identifiable and ridiculed by their being unable to get rid of the stigmatized cultural baggage that they bring with them. Such baggage can include car stickers, dropped "haitches," carefully fastened terylene net curtains, and a general confusion of the public and private domains, with hair-curlers being worn outside when they should be worn inside – if at all – and domestic quarrelling in the front garden when it should be restricted to the car. The second kind of cultural time-lag concerns the maintenance of socially valued cultural habits long after the individual has fallen from grace, examples of which would be the Old Etonian tramp or the countless elderly couples living in impoverished gentility in seaside towns. In certain cases the ability to maintain the appropriate style of life can be waived altogether as a criterion for remaining within the boundary of a class domain, but only where some other criterion explains and justifies that disability. The classic case is the upper- or upper-middle-class Church of England vicar, who is more often than not obliged to lead something of a threadbare existence but is none the less attributed the status honour due to his class origins.

There is a further element in the intricacy of the relationship between the different aspects of class, which is that of the criteria adopted for class determination. Poulantzas distinguishes between the working class and the petty bourgeoisie on, among other grounds, the intellectual division of labour.[7] He means that the intellectual content in the production process (that is, the planning that precedes and the overall control that accompanies production) has been separated from the mechanics of that process and been appropriated by technicians, managers, supervisors, and office staff. The production worker is left as an agent in a de-intellectualized production process. That criterion for what Poulantzas describes as structural class differentiation or determination is equally relevant, however, to class domains. The *secret du savoir* in the sense not only of the planning and organization of production but in the broader realms of history, philosophy, literature, and in the arts and pure sciences in general is carefully monopolized and jealously guarded as a class privilege. It comes to be a further way of differentiating among individuals socialized into different domains, in so far as private intensive education can succeed in inculcating something of the appearance of knowing and being "cultured" into even the most unpromising material.

There is thus a constant interplay between the different aspects of class. Class cannot be limited to one of its aspects, be it relations of production or patterns of consumption. The relationship between classes is a global, all-encompassing relationship that covers all phases of social life and not only that in which wealth is created and redistributed. Every element in that relationship is a constituent element. Prejudice and identity, class cultures, mechanisms of exclusion, coercive force, are all part of what class means and are all essential to the continuity of class. Class domains as perceived by actors in British society are thus not distinct from other aspects of class, including class as a relation of production. Relations of production can, however, subtly change while class identities – as closed universes of action and meaning – lag behind or move ahead or go in unpredictable directions. But all aspects of class remain co-determinant of all possible outcomes.

In the light of this global understanding of class I suggest that industrial capitalist society is no exception to the rule that can be seen to apply in other forms of society in which collectivities necessarily identify themselves in relation to each other in order to interact as collectivities. If we understand ethnicity as being the concept that most closely corresponds to such opposed collective identities, then the class domains or the closed universes of action and meaning that I have presented in this chapter are best understood not just as an aspect of class but as the necessary ethnicity of class.

PART THREE

Frameworks of Meaning: The Politics of Ethnicity

CHAPTER THIRTEEN

A Sense of Belonging:
Capitalism and the
"Nation-State"

We have, on one axis, been moving from the past to the present, and on another from the periphery to the centre, and these movements through time and space have been accompanied by the intertwining of class and ethnicity. I now turn to the role of the state in capitalist society in relation to class and ethnicity, and begin by looking at some aspects of the Marxian and Weberian notions of the state.

Marx was primarily concerned with the developed capitalist mode of production and with the way in which that mode of production developed from earlier systems. The central feature in his work is the relationship between the different classes that that mode of production brought into being, and particularly the class of those who managed to acquire ownership, through various political and economic means, of the material bases of production itself – land, raw materials, equipment – and those who were gradually excluded or separated from such ownership. The focus of *Capital* is what takes place behind the factory gates in the process of production. Lying behind and surrounding that process is the state itself, which might still be in the control of the old landed aristocracy (in early nineteenth-century England), or, in a case where the bourgeoisie actually won control of the state from the landed interest, passes out of the immediate control of that bourgeoisie, who find the process of running it a burdensome distraction from the more important business of making money (in Louis Napoléon's France as described in the *Eighteenth Brumaire*).[1] Both for Marx and for the Parisian bourgeoisie the important concern is the accumulation of capital, and the state is only of interest in so far as it bears on that process of accumulation. Marx produces an exhaustive description of the capitalist process of production, in which class and state are omnipresent both in and around that process, but neither the characteristics of class nor the role of the state are as closely scrutinized as is production itself.

Weber looks more closely at class and the state. Of the two, class remains in a secondary, classificatory role, except when the negatively privileged classes erupt on to the stage of history as the result of having suddenly become aware of the fact of negative privilege. The state, however, occupies a central position in *Economy and Society*, inasmuch as Weber is preoccupied with the development of institutions rather than production relations, and particularly with such issues as legitimate authority and economic and administrative rationality.

Weber distinguishes between charismatic, rule-based, and patrimonial authority.[2] Charismatic authority can come into play at times of warfare or crisis when authority comes to be vested in a leader who is held to be capable of confronting that crisis. It is also characteristic of religious movements, where the charisma of the founder can be institutionalized and handed on via a hierarchy or priesthood. Patrimonial authority, by contrast, is not so much based on the qualities of leadership or charismatic religious inspiration but on tradition, the tradition, for example, of the senior kinsman having absolute authority over a more or less extended kin-group. It is from this latter patriarchal origin that Weber traces the development of the patrimonial state, in which the ruler enjoys authority by virtue of tradition, according to which, among other things, succession to the kingship might be vested in a particular royal lineage.

The patrimonial state is thus the primitive household, or self-supporting budgetary unit under patriarchal control, in developed form, in which the ruler still wields personal authority, the officers of the state are bound to him personally and owe their positions to him, and under which merchant capital can flourish but only at the king's pleasure.[3] This form of the state was characteristic of the European Middle Ages. It was, however, unsuited to the burgeoning needs of capital, which required a more solid basis for accounting than the whim of royalty. It also tended to oppose the king to the development of alternative centres of power among the discontented nobility.

Even with the early development of the patrimonial state, however, there was already an alternative form of administration to that of the personal delegation of power to corruptible and untrustworthy notables. New Kingdom Egypt, for example, was not only an immense patriarchally dominated household but was also based on complex bureaucratic arrangements needed to control the waters of the Nile.[4] It is in the development of such bureaucracy that the future of the state lies. Authority within a bureaucracy is based neither on charisma nor on blind tradition but on rules. Weber considers the developed bureaucratic hierarchy to be the most efficient decision-making machine that has ever been devised, one that is almost impossible to uproot and that can defeat any less well-organized administrative structure. Since it is based on rules, fixed salaries, and promotion (ideally) through merit and experience, it is the direct opposite of administration via notables, who administer according to their own and the king's will, have no fixed salaries and therefore tend to use the office to their own benefit, and are appointed and occasionally decapitated through the king's personal decree. Central to the power of the bureaucracy is the bureaucratic "secret" (just as the commercial secret is the key to the success of the capitalist enterprise), which consists of the collection, processing, and storage of useful information, which can then provide the basis for bureaucratic decision-making. In contemporary complex societies, state bureaucracies can both control large populations and keep the elected representatives of the people suitably ill informed.

Alongside this ability to control and misinform, the development of bureaucracy also fits in to Weber's general portrayal of humanity as progressing from irrationality to rationality.[5] Bureaucracy is a highly rational form of administration and can be opposed to the various charismatic and patrimonial systems of the past. It keeps pace with developing rationality in law, religion, the economy, and warfare to provide the social structure in which rational capitalistic accounting can flourish. The bureaucratic state is thus the ideal, predictable, rule-based, and efficient administrative structure to accompany the development of full industrial capitalism from the early nineteenth century onwards. It represents a solid counterweight to the individualism, competitiveness, and necessary risk-taking of the capitalist enterprise. The bureaucratic state for Weber develops independently of but alongside capitalism and is part of the same drive towards rationality in administration and production. There is thus a close link between the two. Indeed, the developed state bureaucracy can come to depend on capitalism to provide the fiscal basis for its own existence at the same time as capitalism depends on state bureaucracy for the maintenance of social stability and social control in the broadest sense.[6]

This understanding of the role of state bureaucracy has echoes in various Marxist approaches to the state. The principal problem for Marxism is the existence and maintenance of capitalist relations of production – hence the classic Marxist approach to ethnicity, which is concerned with the functional role of ethnicity in the maintenance of a divided working class and the consequent inability of that class to organize itself politically and threaten the dominance of capital. The same is largely true of the state. Given that the capitalist mode of production is dominant in contemporary complex industrial societies, the state necessarily functions to maintain that dominance. The role of the state under capitalism, or of the capitalist state, is therefore to ensure the continuity of the system in which capitalism can flourish.

This is Lenin's point of view, who considered the democratic state, with its periodic elections giving the impression of popular control, to be the ideal shell for capitalism.[7] For Lenin, however, the state does not simply function to maintain the conditions in which the capitalist mode of production can be sustained but is an instrument of domination in the hands of the ruling class. He points out that the state did not exist in gentile or lineage-based societies but only comes into existence along with class struggle.[8] It is preceded by and develops out of the groups of armed retainers that all rulers and dominant classes in societies based on class struggle have been obliged to maintain. Over time it comes to have some independence as a structure from the dominant class, but it none the less remains an instrument in their hands. Lenin considers that the working class has to seize the state and turn it into its own instrument, although since there is not to be class struggle in socialist society, it will eventually and necessarily disappear. He is opposed to the view of the social democrats that the state can serve as a force for class reconciliation, or as a mediator between classes. It is an instrument of domination that itself has to be seized.

This sets something of the tune for the habitual Marxist or Leninist approach to the state; the question is invariably posed of how, if, and when it will eventually disappear. However, there are different shades of opinion concerning its relative autonomy or otherwise. For the empiricist brand of Marxism, as represented by Miliband, the capitalist state is in practice run by the ruling class, and therefore it makes no sense to conceive of it as separate from that class.[9] Miliband's approach suggests that the state is wholly under ruling-class control (at least in his British example), with that same class also controlling industry and banking.

Westergaard and Resler, working to some extent in the same tradition, or at least on the same side of the empiricist-abstractionist divide, also draw attention to the close links among the top personnel in state, financial, and industrial hierarchies.[10] This approach to the state is also functionalist rather than instrumentalist. In the three-cornered management of the economy, the state continually reinforces the privileged position of capital against the repeated attempts by organized labour to change the status quo. It also ensures the operation and continuity of the system by providing health care, transportation networks, electricity supply, housing, and, of course, social control. At the same time it steps in to nationalize vital but loss-making sectors of industry (coal-mining and steel, for example) and thus further helps to concentrate capital in the hands of the few, the former owners of those industries receiving generous compensation.

Some of the changes introduced by the state have been beneficial to society as a whole – as in the case of the British National Health Service – and there is no unitary group of capitalists in whose interests the state necessarily operates. On the contrary, different capitalists tend to play off the state against one another, competing for government contracts, developing area grants, employment subsidies, and tax concessions. For Westergaard and Resler, inequality in Britain is based on the extraction and maximization of surplus value by capital, and the role of the state is essentially to provide the framework in which that extraction and maximization can take place. This fits into a more general understanding in contemporary Marxism, which relates to the necessary tendency of profit levels to fall under capitalism, given the nature of capitalist competition as described by Marx. The role of the state is not therefore just to maintain the framework in which the extraction of surplus value can take place but to protect profit levels against their inherent tendency to fall.

The more abstractionist or theoretically oriented school of Marxism adopts a similar position but concentrates on the role of the state at the level of class and mode of production in theory rather than in practice. For Althusser, for example, what is crucial for the maintenance of the capitalist mode of production is the reproduction of the means, forces, and relations of production.[11] The reproduction of the means of production themselves (raw materials and machinery) takes place within the capitalist enterprise, or at least under the responsibility of the capitalist, but the reproduction of the forces of production – notably, the labour force – takes place outside the enterprise and not under capital's direct control. To a large extent the reproduction of labour-power – health, education, housing – is the responsibility of the state.

What particularly interests Althusser, however, are the relations of production themselves and their reproduction, that reproduction being as essential to the maintenance of capitalist relations of production as is the reproduction of means and forces. The reproduction of capitalist relations of production, or the relationship between a class of capitalists and a class of workers in which the former appropriates the surplus value produced by the latter, is guaranteed by the repressive and ideological apparatuses of the state: police, courts, and prisons on the one hand and the family, schools, churches, and the media on the other. On the whole, Althusser's understanding of the state is Leninist, in that he sees it as a tool in the hands of the dominant class, but his particular interest is with the role of the ideological apparatuses.

As a final example of contemporary Marxist approaches to the state I turn to Poulantzas. Poulantzas considers the state to be relatively autonomous from the opposed classes in struggle.[12] For him it guarantees the stability and cohesion of the system, and therefore cannot be under the direct control of any one class. However, where the system subject to the cohesive and stabilizing tendencies of the state happens to be capitalist, the various categories of person to be found in the higher ranks of the state bureaucracy have to be ascribed to the bourgeoisie since they fulfil one aspect of the role of capital, just as upper management does in industry. In Poulantzas' terms, they direct the different branches of the state's activities in the *service* of capital.[13]

Marxist approaches to the state relate generally to its function in the maintenance of a given mode of production and, more especially, the capitalist mode of production. It is curious that in some ways the classic non- and even pre-Marxist doctrine of the laisser-faire state echoes many of these views. Throughout the nineteenth century, direct involvement of the state in production was frowned upon, but the state was none the less required to provide the security in which industrial capitalism could take root, and above all the security of property. In cases of famine, however, or more than normally widespread destitution, the state had to step in to provide relief works. Essentially the doctrine was – and still is – that the state had to provide the structure within which private enterprise could flourish, while remaining uninvolved in any area where private capital could be profitably employed.[14] There are light-years between such views and Marxist approaches to the state, but the two sides none the less agree on the necessity of the state apparatus for the continued functioning of the capitalist system.

Central to all these approaches is the functionality of the state in the maintenance of a given system of production, with Weber going behind that functionality to the bureaucratic state as to some extent an autonomous administrative machine with its own history and increasingly concerned with its own interests and security. From a Marxist perspective such an approach would be written off for treating the state as an institution or set of institutions, without going beyond that purely descriptive concern.[15] Aside from function and description, there is the more interesting question of how the state manages to act as a stabilizer or socially cohesive force, given that that is its principal role. It is in this last case that one goes beyond institutional description and functionalist explanation to a deeper level of understanding, and it is in this case that the roles of class and ethnicity respectively come to be of critical significance. If we adopt the working hypothesis that the principal function of the state in capitalist society is to provide stability and social cohesion, we have then to ask how class and ethnicity fit into that function.

Class, by definition, is threatening to the state since it can cut up the social formation that the state is trying to maintain as a coherent unit into horizontally defined and politically opposed strata (given full Marxian or Weberian class consciousness). To fulfil its function the state is thus required to inhibit the development of class consciousness among the mass of the population. That preoccupation is identical with the principal concern of capitalists, who equally, as a self-conscious and politically aware privileged class, have to prevent the negatively privileged or exploited mass of the working class from coming to a consciousness of its class position. The immediate goals of both capital and the state, therefore, coincide, which is hardly surprising since we have assumed that the function of the state is to guarantee the continuing dominance of the capitalist mode of production.

Ethnicity can represent a different kind of threat to the state. In this case, different ethnic groups can introduce the danger of vertical fissuring of the social structure where those groups are represented at different social levels. Religious, linguistic, regional, or other differences can have a powerful impact in identifying, reinforcing, and even sustaining vertical divisions that can arise for a variety of different reasons. The state also has to be able to cope with such vertical divisions if it is to prevent itself from falling apart at the vertical as opposed to the horizontal seams. The key to the resolution of the problem for the state lies in the nature of ethnicity. In the case of ethnic-minority formation in industrial societies, ethnicity, along with occupational divisions within the working class, can effectively inhibit the development of a unified class consciousness (and therefore the threat of political action) within that class. Ethnicity can thus be functional for the state and for capital as long as the vertical fissuring does not cross class boundaries. Should it do so, there is an increased risk for the state that the ethnic segment so defined will split off from the pyramid. If the different class elements within that segment can be vertically integrated on the basis of shared ethnicity, however, the question arises why the state should not elaborate a similar set of labels that could weld together the social formation as a whole in an ethnic-based opposition to other social formations, thereby overriding dangerous internal ethnic and class divisions. The answer is, of course, that that is exactly what the state does and what states have always done, in the form of the "nation"-state.

The concept "nation-state" manages to merge the bureaucratic administrative structure of the state with the territorially, linguistically, or otherwise definable "nation" such that the nation becomes the state and the state becomes the nation, and one ends up using the word "state" both for bureaucratic administrative hierarchies and sovereign territorially bounded units. The idea of the nation comes to be as crucial in the consolidation of the established capitalist state as it is in resistance to colonialism. Hence what Lenin and others mean when they refer to the ideal character of the nation-state for capitalism. Its administrative efficiency guarantees the functioning of the capitalist system, and its ideological significance guarantees the mystification of that system.

Nairn explains the development of Third World nationalism in its more pronounced forms as the only way in which the dominant classes of those social formations can hold them together and override the various regional and ethnic subdivisions, particularly where it becomes clear that the formation in question is to remain excluded from the circle of wealthy industrialized nations.[16] Nationalism is thus a binding force but also a reaction to threat, a way of holding together a society that is in danger of falling apart at the seams, given the non-realization of shared economic goals. One has, therefore, to make a distinction between the normal, operational nationalism that is necessary for the functioning of the nation-state and the more pronounced forms of nationalism as a reaction to crisis. Northern Ireland is one area with a complex interplay between class, ethnicity, and state that can help to clarify some of these issues.

From 1921 to 1972 there existed in Northern Ireland what the republican left describes as the "Orange" state.[17] This regional form of government, which came into existence within the framework of the United Kingdom and following the partition of Ireland, was in a sense the consecration of the dominant position held by the Protestants in Ulster since the plantation of the seventeenth century. For the first time the Ulster Protestants constituted the dominant majority within their own regional state. The solidarity within the Northern Protestant community that provided the foundation for the Northern Ireland state arose largely as a reaction to republican nationalism.

Gibbon describes the way in which the localized sectarianism of the mid-nineteenth century suddenly gave way in the 1880s and 1890s to a new kind of politicized Protestant ethnicity.[18] Gladstone had, in 1886, the support of Parnell in Parliament, and as the price for that support introduced a Home Rule (for Ireland) Bill that was, however, shelved by the Conservatives when they returned to power. But it was sufficient to galvanize the Northern Protestants into a defensive reaction. Belfast in the nineteenth century was the only heavily industrialized part of Ireland and was an integral part of an industrial area that included Glasgow, Liverpool, and Manchester. It was also dependent on retaining access to imperial markets and building the ships that both serviced those markets and brought back raw materials. It was thus dependent on remaining part of the United Kingdom in order to maintain existing levels of production and capital accumulation. The prospect of a Dublin-dominated Irish republic in which Protestants would be outvoted by a Catholic majority and that would give access to no markets whatsoever (and hardly even a home market, since Britain had largely succeeded in preventing such a market from developing) represented a major threat to Northern capital. It also represented a threat to the Ulster Protestant labour aristocracy, the shipyard workers, who were equally dependent on the imperial connection.

In 1892 a convention was held in Northern Ireland as a direct result of the threat of Irish home rule, which not only saw the birth of Ulster Unionism but also the consecration of the "Protestant Ulsterman." In a process Gibbon describes as "ethnogenesis,"[19] the Ulster Convention glorified the sterling qualities of loyalty to his own kind and to the Crown, of steadfastness, of dependability, and of courage that were held to characterize the Ulsterman, in contradistinction, of course, to the not so sterling qualities of the Catholic Irish. There was thus created a political movement in which all the different classes of Protestant were brought together in a defensive reaction to the threat of a United Ireland and under the sign of Protestant Ulster ethnicity.

The creation of the Northern Ireland state in 1921 consecrated the movement of resistance that had begun with the Ulster Convention in 1892 by establishing an administrative structure that was to remain permanently and solidly under Protestant control until it was dissolved by the British government in 1972. It does not constitute an example of an ideology binding together an entire sovereign nation-state but rather one where a dominant class that happens to be Protestant allies itself on the basis of its Protestantism and common origin with the bulk of the middle and working classes and against those fractions of the working class and eventually of the middle class who happen to be Catholic, Irish in origin, and largely sympathetic to the goal of a united Ireland. Ethnic solidarity within the Protestant community serves as the guarantee of the ascendancy of Ulster capital over the Catholic and mainly working-class minority, and, equally importantly, as a bulwark against the development of any socialist or radical alternative among the Protestant working class.[20] On only one or two occasions has there been any sign of a working-class solidarity cutting across Catholic-Protestant divisions.[21]

The ideology of Protestant solidarity and the evocation of the heroic past and unlimited capabilities of the Protestant Ulsterman were not sufficient in themselves to bind together bourgeois, petty bourgeois, and working-class Protestants. From the inception of the state – granted that it remained under the aegis of Westminster – the Northern Ireland government was always at pains to act in such a way as to maintain its hold over popular Protestant opinion. At the same time it redrew electoral boundaries to reduce the level of Catholic representation at Stormont, although such Catholics as were elected generally refused to participate anyway.[22] Government strategy included a dominant strain of populism within the government, which consisted both in the cultivation of a certain accessibility on the part of the prime minister and in the introduction of a social-welfare program similar to that introduced in the rest of the United Kingdom after the Second World War.[23] It coincided with generally preferential treatment of Protestants, or, what amounts to the same thing, the non-preferential treatment of Catholics.

If populism and bias were the necessary adjuncts of an ideology of shared ethnicity to maintain Protestant working class-support, they equally had the effect of setting off permanent conflict within the ruling class itself, between populists and anti-populists. The latter saw populism, welfarism, and generally the cultivation of close links between capital and labour as too heavy a price to pay and too much of a threat to the maintenance of the dominance of capital. Bew et al., in their study of the Northern Ireland state, consider such divisions within the Protestant bloc to be as much a contributing factor to the collapse of the Northern Ireland government as the Protestant-Catholic division.[24]

The recent history of Northern Ireland constitutes an example of a particular kind of uneasy articulation of class, ethnicity, and state. The Protestant bourgeoisie unleashed ethnicity as the binding force of a multi-class Protestant political movement but then had to pay the price in the form of populism. Opposed to that Protestant ethnicity is an equally power-ful and deep-rooted Catholic Irish nationalism, which itself transcends class boundaries within Catholic Irish society, north and south. In another area of the world, class and ethnicity have an equally involved and intractable relationship with the state. In the nineteenth-century province of Lower Canada a Protestant English-speaking ascendancy was also confronted by a Catholic non-English speaking peasantry.

With the creation in 1867 of the Canadian Confederation, the imperial government intentionally introduced an element of structural instability.[25] Federal and provincial governments were balanced against each other, partly to prevent the emergence of a strong, unified Canadian state that might go the same way as the southern colonies, but also to prevent provin-cial governments from attempting to secede from the confederation. With reference to Quebec, Bourque and Legaré make the point that this had the effect of creating two kinds of state, neither of which was really capable of fulfilling the functions that capital required of it, given that the strong, centralized nation-state is the necessary prerequisite for the flourishing of capitalist relations of production. The federal government has never been able to impose successfully a form of pan-Canadian national identity, since most of the responsibility for the ideological apparatuses of the state was delegated to the provinces: "The separation of the branches of the state apparatus leading to the concentration of most of the ideological apparatuses at the provincial level ... makes it very difficult to affirm an ideology that might produce a historical 'memory' that would bring together the agents of the social formation and give to that formation the expected politico-ideological cohesion."[26]

Equally, the provincial government in Quebec finds itself in the posi-tion of being able to override internal class divisions by appealing to the profound cultural homogeneity and distinctiveness of the French-speaking population, but lacking the authority or the capacity to provide the struc-ture in which the nascent French-speaking regional bourgeoisie can properly establish its hegemony over the other classes. Canadian monopoly capital is thus frustrated by the non-national characteristics of the Canadian nation, while regional, non-monopoly capital in Quebec is frustrated by precisely the opposite: Quebec constitutes a nation without actually being a nation-state.

Dofny and Rioux adopt a different approach.[27] For them it is not the nation-state itself but rather the "total society" that is important, inas-much as social class can only be properly understood within the frame-work of that society. In Canada, however, what constitutes the total society depends on the perspective taken. Economically Dofny and Rioux consider that Quebec is part of a total society in which United States capital is dominant. Relations of production cannot be considered apart from that total society. Politically, however, Quebec remains part of the Canadian federation and therefore belongs to a different total society, while culturally it constitutes a total society in itself.

Dofny and Rioux see three possibilities for the future: either Quebec will be increasingly integrated politically and culturally into the United States, along with its already existing economic integration; or the Canadian state will assert itself over its provinces, and simultaneously the principal emergent class struggle will be that between the Canadian working class and Canadian monopoly capital; or the constituent classes in French Canada will unite as an "ethnic class" against English Canada and demand some form of sovereignty. It is notable that in all these three cases, the "problem" for capital, as defined by Bourque and Legaré, would be overcome, in that they all presume the resolution of the present instability by the consolidation of the nation-state at either the provincial or the federal level (within Canada) or the swallowing up of Quebec in the United States.

Quebec and Northern Ireland both represent the state in crisis, with on the one hand a Canadian federal administration anxious to increase its hold over the provincial government, and on the other a centralized British administration apparently keen to wash its hands of the Northern Ireland "problem" altogether, although perhaps not just yet. The role of class and ethnicity in the dismantling or construction of states through political action is critical in both these cases. But the same is true in a less pronounced way of any nation-state in less critical circumstances: the stability and cohesion of a social formation under capitalism is never guaranteed by the capitalist mode of production itself.

An overriding and all-important "national" identity, therefore, beside which class differences pale into insignificance, accompanies and mystifies class relationships within the framework of the capitalist state. It uses familiar signs and symbols and places them within a new realm of meaning such that the trivia of different hair-styles and eating habits come to be significant of deep national differences, and those who drive on the left are united against the barbarians who drive in the middle and occasionally on the right. This suggests, following Weber, that the state simply capitalizes on the universal tendency of human associations to accompany, justify, and protect that association by coming to believe in a form of brotherhood or fictional kinship that serves to bind the association together. From there it is a simple process to select the particular labels that can serve to identify members of the association and give them a sense of belonging.

If, however, ethnicity or nationalism can be used as a form of ideological cement to bind society together, we need to ask how states go about imposing such ideologies. In the following chapter I turn to multiculturalism in Canada as an example of a state's attempting to piece together an over-arching, ethnically based, "national" identity.

CHAPTER FOURTEEN

Keeping the Old World Going: Multiculturalism and the State in Canada

Multiculturalism as a way of understanding Canadian society emerged in the 1960s in the context of the Royal Commission on Bilingualism and Biculturalism. The report of the commission, published in 1970, does not, however, present Canada as primarily and essentially multicultural but rather as composed of two dominant cultures, those of the "anglophone and francophone societies."[1] Alongside those two dominant cultures and their associated languages are the variety of subordinate languages and cultures that the various immigrant groups have brought with them (native peoples being excluded from the mandate of the commission).

The commission considers the significance of these various culturally defined groups in two ways. First, "Canadian culture" has been the richer as a result of all the various cultural inputs.[2] According to the commissioners, that process of cultural enrichment should be safeguarded.[3] Second, they consider it to be of vital importance that individuals should not be cut off from their cultural and linguistic roots via assimilation to one or other of the dominant cultures. The objective should rather be that individuals integrate into either anglophone or francophone society without losing their own cultural identity.[4] Canadian society thus is portrayed in the commission's report as an uneasy compromise between biculturalism and multiculturalism. The domains of political institutions and economic life are primarily bilingual and bicultural, whence the necessity of integration on the part of newly arrived immigrants. But alongside those domains there are the parallel realms of the arts, religion, and family life, which can remain distinct cultural enclaves.

The contemporary (1969) White Paper on Canadian Indian policy is equally ambiguous. It maintains that the separateness of native peoples as a distinct category within Canadian society must come to an end. They must become an integral part of the great Canadian family and be entitled to the same rights and services as all other Canadians. At the same time, the family into which they are to be welcomed is a multicultural one, and native cultures and languages must be encouraged to develop.[5] The messages of these two documents are thus somewhat similar. There are the core Canadians, brought up in one or other of the two cultural and linguistic mainstreams, and then there are the various cultural minorities, who are supposed to be both integrated and different at the same time.

This picture began to clear in the early 1970s with the emergence of the federal government's multicultural policy. It has to be admitted that all was not peaceful at the time between the two Canadian "charter" groups, the English and the French. Perhaps for that reason, in Prime Minister Trudeau's 1971 statement in the House of Commons the image of a Canada composed of two dominant cultural and linguistic entities surrounded by a number of more or less marginal groups, which is essentially the position put forward in the royal commission's report, had come to be quite definitely an image of "multiculturalism within a bilingual framework."[6] In other words, the image of a Canada deeply divided between two dominant and parallel cultures (and therefore in some danger of falling apart along the lines of that division) was reworked into that of a Canada that was essentially *multi-* rather than *bi*cultural. The emphasis in the early seventies was on papering over the cracks rather than on drawing attention to them, as the following statement from *A National Understanding* serves to demonstrate: "Our two languages and our diversity of cultures in Canada are the expression of our spiritual values even as our vast country is the reflexion of our physical strength and variety ... Our linguistic duality and cultural diversity are both the condition and the safeguard of our continuing freedom and our unity as a country ... Let us not permit our country to be divided by what can so enrich us."[7] By 1973 Canada was well on the way to becoming officially multicultural with the setting up of the Canadian Consultative Council on Multiculturalism,[8] Trudeau having appointed a minister responsible for the implementation of the multiculturalism policy the previous year. The Multiculturalism Directorate had as one of its tasks "to increase awareness of the bilingual and multicultural nature of our country."[9]

Over the next five years the notion of Canada as essentially multicultural was to provide an underlying logic for the operation of a variety of government departments. External Affairs took care to present the image of a multicultural Canada abroad; the Canadian Radio-Television and Telecommunications Commission published a booklet on multicultural broadcasting,[10] and the National Museum of Man reoriented its activities to celebrate the newly discovered multicultural nature of Canadian society by, among other things, using "dolls, sculpture, cooking recipes, clothing, embroidery, archaeology, masks and music ... as themes to reflect the Canadian cultural mosaic."[11]

Two years after the election of the Parti Québécois in Quebec, therefore, the countervailing belief in the essentially multicultural nature of "Canada's great ethno-cultural family"[12] had become a recurring theme, a central organizing idea in the operations of federal government. Four years later, in 1982, the Parti Québécois government lost its referendum on sovereignty-association and refused to be a party to the passing of the new Canadian Constitution Act. Within the framework of that act it is affirmed that any interpretation of the Canadian Charter of Rights and Freedoms must be "consistent with the preservation and enhancement of the multicultural heritage of Canadians."[13] Hence came into existence a new kind of society to be set alongside the various other historically attested types ranging from the "primitive communist" to the "underdeveloped." From the mid-1980s onwards in Canada, any number of editorialists, politicians, bureaucrats, teachers, and other agents of persuasion writing on subjects as disparate as housing, eating, education, and immigration prefaced their remarks with a ritual genuflexion in the direction of the federal orthodoxy of multiculturalism. Biculturalism was dead; the bilingual framework was showing signs of disrepair; but multiculturalism had been elevated – by, for example, the Canadian Multiculturalism Act of 1988 – to the status of a "fundamental characteristic of the Canadian heritage and identity."[14]

At the heart of the idea of multiculturalism is the notion of unity in diversity. What is held to make Canada an entity distinct from other entities is its enormous physical extent and the diversity of cultural groups that are scattered across its surface. Distance and difference thus come to be – in the terms of Roland Barthes – the core symbols in a myth of unity and, as is appropriate in the context of myth, signify something that contradicts what would be normally associated with them.[15] A myth has meaning in two directions. It serves both to explain and either to justify or to undermine an existing reality. In the case of nineteenth-century Ireland, for example, the British justified their oppressive presence on the basis of the myth of the racial inferiority of the Irish. The Irish constructed a counter-myth on the basis of a distant heroic Irish past, a golden age that testified to those inherent qualities of the Irish people that had been temporarily suppressed by British brutality but would one day reassert themselves in an independent Ireland.[16]

Myth can thus be seen to grow out of a present reality, either reinforcing it or demolishing it. And in growing, it spreads its root system back into the past, which it reworks and reinterprets better to explain how the reality that it sees came into being, and on into the future in order to provide the basis for what it would like to see existing. Of the two great genres of myth – those that set out to demolish and recreate and those that set out to support and maintain – the myth of multiculturalism belongs to the second. For the moment we can suspend discussion of the future, but what of the Canadian multicultural past and present? The myth of the multicultural past begins, as do all myths, with a founding fact. That founding fact has to conform to the nature of the myth itself. Myths that set out to justify royal power and wealth begin inevitably with the divine origins of the dynasty in question. Multiculturalism does not, therefore, set out from the extermination of the Beothuk people or the conquest of New France as its founding facts since that would introduce elements at the very heart of the myth that would gnaw away at the central theme of harmony in diversity. The solution is simple. In looking back into the distant past of multiculturalism, what we find is none other than multiculturalism itself, well expressed in the Coolican report on the rights of native peoples, as the fundamental principle on which the Canadian Confederation was built.[17]

Logically this suggests that when the Beothuks were being massacred and other native peoples decimated and enclosed, when the Acadians were being expropriated and deported, and when the French were defeated at Quebec, the principle on the basis of which these various operations were carried out was that of multiculturalism. It suggests that the fur trade had as its central determining feature the will of the traders to coexist harmoniously alongside those who were different from them and in the celebration of that difference. That the Jesuits who set out to Christianize and civilize native peoples and to educate unco-operative native parents in the ways of European discipline did so in a spirit of respect for and tolerance of the *other*. That the railway companies and their corporate and political associates set out to develop a Canadian home-market in the face of British protectionism and American competition in order that the various immigrant groups and native peoples thus brought alongside each other could participate in a process of mutual cultural enrichment. That MacKenzie King's racially discriminatory immigration policy was designed to fit in with the multicultural nature of the Canadian state. That contemporary employers in the Canadian garment industry employ their multicultural female workforces in order to conform with the founding principle.

Different writers have at times sought to impose some kind of cultural causality on the historical movements of peoples that have always been a part of Canadian history. McCormack, for example, draws attention to the element of ethnic preference in the hiring of British workers in the period between 1900 and 1914, and to the way in which British immigrants attempted to maintain their ethnicity once in Canada.[18] But leaving aside the question of whether this is not rather evidence of monoculturalism than of multiculturalism, it is clear from Reynolds' detailed account of the British immigrant in Montreal[19] that employers always set out to satisfy their own needs in terms of expertise, as well we might expect them to do. In so far as that expertise was to be found among the British skilled working class, then the skilled workers in question were brought over in large numbers and came to staff the shipbuilding yards, steelworks, and railway-repair workshops in Montreal. Where unskilled labour was required, as in the case of canal and railway building, employers brought over the labour from whatever sources were available. Ethnicity only entered into the process in the form of ethnic prejudice or racism (given the availability of labour from a diversity of sources), according to which Chinese immigrants were penalized by having to pay a poll-tax and blacks were kept out altogether.[20]

Within Canada, apart from the unique success of French Canada in maintaining its language and identity, other non-anglophone, non-British groups have quietly gone the way of assimilation to the dominant Anglo-Canadian cultural group. Even the most culturally resilient of immigrant groups, the Ukrainians, has seen facility in the Ukrainian language decline from 92 per cent in 1921 to less than 50 per cent in 1971, with a much smaller percentage of the third generation now being able to speak the language.[21]

While multiculturalism sets out to reinterpret history, therefore, history makes a mockery of multiculturalism. There are different ways in which myth-makers can respond. If history cannot be brought into alignment with the way in which one wants to interpret the present and plan for the future, then it is better that it should be forgotten, as the Canadian prime minister suggested that it should be to the representatives of native peoples at the first constitutional conference in 1983. In addition, history can, if necessary, be reduced to the artefacts that different peoples produced: the musical instruments, sculptures, sleds, clothing, quill-stitchery, and so on, with never a word being breathed of the oppressive relationships between the peoples who were thus busily stitching and singing. This we might describe as the Museum of Man approach. Faced with the recalcitrance of history in allowing the relationships between peoples to be reinterpreted, the myth of multiculturalism has an answer: forget about them.

If multiculturalism rewrites history, it also rewrites the present. Or at least, it gives rise to a version of the present that is situated in a different realm of meaning from, for example, run-of-the-mill studies of social inequality, from whatever perspective they may be operating. The result is versions of the Canadian present in which some people see one thing and some another. Langlois, for instance, gives a descriptive account of the spatial distribution of different ethnic groups over time in the Montreal area. He explains the choice of Montreal for the study as follows: "We know the importance of the ethnic factor in the structuring of residential space in this town. Moreover it is this special characteristic of the socio-ecological structure of Montreal which differentiates it from the typical North American town where – as we know – residential space is differentiated above all according to socio-economic status."[22] In the case of the Italian community in Montreal, the fact that its spatial distribution has remained highly stable over time leads Langlois to conclude that this ethnic group has probably reached "in its spatial organization, a balancing point between its desire to affirm its identity and its desire to interact with other ethnic groups, notably the dominant ethnic groups."[23] This touches on an old debate over the relative importance of the will of a given ethnic group to inhabit a certain area and the will of surrounding ethnic groups to contain them within that area.[24] But beyond that debate, Langlois's description of Montreal is thoroughly multiculturalist, as opposed to other descriptions that might be occupational, meritocratic, or class-based (in the Marxian sense of the word).

It is notable, for example, that in Reynolds' study of British immigrants in Montreal, the spatial distribution of those immigrants and of their descendants is related to occupation and income. The skilled workers brought over at the turn of the century settled close to the shipbuilding yards and steel works in Hochelaga. Subsequently, as their material conditions improved, they moved eastwards to Maisonneuve and northwards to the cleaner air and more salubrious living conditions of Rosemont. As the skilled workers of British origin were gradually displaced by French Canadians, the second generation moved upwards into white-collar jobs and westward into the more solidly middle-class areas of the city, west of the Mont Royal.[25] Rather than seeing it as distinctive, Reynolds interprets the history of the residential distribution of ethnic groups in Montreal as following the traditional pattern well known from other areas of high immigration, the British immigrant gradually moving outward through a series of concentric circles and the most recent immigrants occupying the innermost circle. He also sees the process as being like a residential ladder, with one's social and economic status measurable by where one is living.[26] Langlois and Reynolds thus provide us with two versions of Montreal, two cities: the one multicultural and the other multi-occupational or multi-class; the one based on ethnic and cultural preferences, the other based on socio-economic differences that may coincide with ethnic differences.[27]

These two approaches represent two distinct frameworks within which contemporary realities can be interpreted. If one adopts the multicultural framework, one is led to ask certain kinds of questions rather than others. For example, in her study of a francophone community in northern New Brunswick, Nanciellen Davis takes as her problem the survival of ethnicity against a background of socio-economic conditions,[28] whereas the alternative approach might take as its problem the survival of socio-economic inequalities against a background of ethnic difference. If one sets out from the premise that Canada is by its very nature multicultural, the decline or survival of a particular minority language group can come to be of greater importance than the maintenance of high levels of unemployment.

What interests Davis is the question of contact between ethnic groups and the playing up of one factor or another in the articulation of difference between groups. She considers the key difference between francophone Acadians and the surrounding English-speaking population in the nineteenth century to have been religion, but with the relative decline in the importance of religion it has now come to be language.[29] Language, therefore, has come to be the key factor contributing to the survival of French Canadian ethnicity in the area, particularly given the relative isolation of the different language groups, with bilingual brokers maintaining the contacts between francophone fishermen and the Anglo-Canadian and American-owned processing companies.[30] Davis's analysis does not deny socio-economic differences, but ethnic survival rather than social inequality is the focus of interest.

In two parallel cases researchers have started from the same assumptions as Davis and Langlois but have, in the course of the research, altered the framework of the analysis as a result of the reality encountered. Stymeist, in his study of a town in Northern Ontario, expected to encounter the Canadian mosaic in miniature as predicted by multiculturalism.[31] The problem is that the "English" (of English, Irish, and Scottish origin), "Ukrainians" (Poles, Russians, and Ukrainians), "Finnlanders" (Norwegians, Swedes, and Finns), and "French" into which the town is supposedly divided hardly differentiate among themselves anymore. They live in the same areas, intermarry freely, and only maintain the vestiges of ethnic difference in the context of ethnic jokes.[32]

Confronted by the overwhelming cultural homogeneity of the non-native town-dwellers, Stymeist had to revise his approach. The one area in which major cultural and ethnic difference was evident and admitted was between the local population of European origin and surrounding native peoples. Native peoples are marginal to the town; few work in it, but most come in every now and again to attend hospital, shop, or go to the pub. They frequently get beaten up, are dealt with harshly by the courts, excluded from the informal job network, and have difficulty getting lodgings. They have what Stymeist describes as a clear class position in relation to everyone else in the town, and the fact that they occupy that position is more often than not "explained" by the non-native population in racist terms. *Ethnics and Indians* thus calls into question the multicultural ideal as a way of characterizing a fairly typical mid-Canadian railway town that has, ironically enough, been largely reoriented towards the dispensing of services to the surrounding native population. In cultural terms one would have to describe it as bi- rather than multicultural, but the cultural division in question so transparently follows the lines of social inequality that it would seem more reasonable to characterize the town on the basis of that inequality.

A second study that ends up calling into question the multicultural model has been done by Marguerite Cassin in Vancouver.[33] She gives the following account of her research:

When I began interviewing "East Indian" families I encountered a serious difficulty: I couldn't find ethnicity. I "saw" this first when I reviewed my field notes from an interview with a family where both the man and woman worked in the economy; she was a garment worker and he worked in a saw mill. In the notes I had taken I couldn't find anything that would distinguish them from other Canadian families in the same economic circumstances. It was with an increasing sense of horror that I found that the same thing was true of my notes from a very long interview with a couple who were both professionals. Assuming that I had just done "bad" interviews I determinedly set out to rectify this situation. The problem I encountered was that I had to make certain particulars about the home, life style, activities, food, clothing, etc. relevant in order to "see" these people as different from my own friends and acquaintances who were "non-ethnic", but in corresponding economic situations.[34]

Cassin concludes that ethnicity is a framework placed upon the evidence by the various agents of the state and private enterprise, into which people are made to fit. The health problems of overworked immigrant mothers can thus be seen as problems of cultural adaptation (in terms of the framework) rather than as deriving from the double day's work or working conditions themselves.[35]

Peter Li makes a similar point with reference to the Chinese Canadian family.[36] In the context of multiculturalism and immigration, much is made of the survival of the extended patriarchal Chinese family in Canada. According to Li, not only is the Chinese Canadian family similar to all Canadian families (4.63 persons per Chinese Canadian census family in 1971 as against 4.50 for all Canadians),[37] but the extended patriarchal family never really existed in China either, where average household size varied from 5.96 in AD 755 to 5.33 in 1812.[38] In the latter case, the existence of the extended family was more a question of ideology than of empirical reality. In Canada, Li concludes, belief in its existence flows in part from a "misconception of immigrant societies as mere extensions of old world cultures."[39] Here, of course, there is a double misconception, inasmuch as the extended family did not really exist in the old world either. The point is, however, that we are looking not really at a "misconception" at all but rather, as Li points out in relation to China, evidence of the continuing predominance of ideological over empirical versions of reality.

There are thus those who set out to look for ethnicity or multicultural-ism and fail to find it, and those who take the multicultural framework for granted. In all these studies one of the central problems remains the relationship between social inequality and ethnicity. If in Davis's case ethnicity displaces social inequality as the focus of interest, while for Cassin and Stymeist the contrary is true, in Porter's classic study of social inequality and ethnicity in Canada, *The Vertical Mosaic*, neither one is displaced by the other.[40] Porter adopts an "elitist" approach to the prob-lem of social causality, according to which social connections, inter-marriage, shared cultures, class solidarity (in non-Marxian terms – that is, in terms of similar socio-economic and occupational standing), shared religious belief, and all the other various ways in which human groups bond together and protect their own interests play in and out of each other in the maintenance of a socially inegalitarian society. At one level occupa-tional elitism leads to the over-representation of lawyers in Parliament;[41] at another ethnic elitism leads to the over-representation of the Protestant bourgeoisie of British origin in the boardrooms of Canadian corpora-tions;[42] and at a third Catholicism keeps French Canadians at a low socio-economic level in Porter's Weberian explanation of the relative social inequality of French and English Canadians: "It follows ... from Weber's thesis that the Catholic milieu is less favorable for the creation of those values – the acquisition of skills, orientation towards profit-making and personal accountability – which prepare a labour force for industrializa-tion. 'Other worldly' orientation, in education, for example, leaves less time for 'this worldly' knowledge. Consequently Catholics lose out on the general upward social mobility that comes from the increasing skills in the industrial labour force, and as a result they become over-represented in the lower unskilled occupations."[43]

Porter's account of the "vertical mosaic" thus draws on a mixture of culturalism, elitism, and collective self-interest as different kinds of causal factors that maintain a set of parallel, hierarchical elite structures. The account is, for that reason, out of joint with multiculturalism, which spe-cifically sets out to present Canadian society as one based on principles of mutual rather than self-enrichment, even if the enrichment in question is cultural rather than material. But at the same time, in the context of French Canada, Porter reinforces the idea that culture has been a deter-minant factor in relation to French Canadian poverty and that in part, therefore, socio-economic realities flow from cultural characteristics. This culturalist strand in Porter's argument serves to requalify Canadian society as being, at least in some respects, primarily "multicultural."

The problem with multiculturalism is not so much at the level of ideas, since what it expresses follows closely the lines of a certain humanism and sense of justice that can also be found in the Canadian Charter of Rights and Freedoms and that are generally held to be in accord with core

Canadian values. The problem occurs rather where the idea of multiculturalism touches down in the reality of contemporary Canadian society, whether that be in the context of social research or the Canadian census. While frustrated researchers try to make their data correspond to what they are supposed to look like according to the preconceptions of governmental and other agencies, those responsible for the census make endless attempts to ask sensible questions in order that the essentially "multicultural" nature of the society might be borne out by regularly gathered statistics.

In the 1981 census the "ethnic" question related to "sense of belonging" as against "geographical provenance" or "maternal language," the questions that had taken turns in previous censuses.[44] There has always been a certain amount of confusion over what was really being asked. In 1955 Ryder pointed out that "55% of the children, other than French, born in Canada in 1951, had origins different from those of their mothers."[45] This strange statement means that ethnic belongingness at the time related rather to the ethnic origin of the father than to that of the mother. This artificial way of classifying the children evidently had little to do with any "real" mixed ethnic identity they might have had, and curiously goes against the very notion of the "mother" tongue that, Ryder suggests at another point in the article, should be made the basis of the ethnic question. However, according to Ryder, individuals should not be asked about the mother tongue of their mother but rather about their father's mother tongue (sic).[46] Similar critiques are made by Anderson et al., who refer to the Canadian census prior to 1981 as counting in "its ethnic origin category only those who claim the ethnic origin of the original male immigrant or predecessor to Canada."[47] Thus, traditionally, census data both distort the evidence of ethnic origin by systematically ignoring female ancestors and also overestimate the homogeneity of existing ethnic groups, given intermarriage.

These various critiques suggest that the Canadian census has created the impression of continuing multiple ethnic distinctiveness in non-francophone Canada when, in reality, the mosaic has long been subject to a process of melting down. Ryder, in the mid-1950s, had already pointed out the endless confusion between the relative significance of language and birthplace and mothers and fathers, and also drew attention to the absurdity of attempting to make any sense out of the various confusions among English, Irish, and Scottish ethnic belongingness. To do so is to "accomplish little more than the satisfaction of idle curiosity."[48]

The search for ethnicity in the context of multiculturalism is reminiscent of Leach's "butterfly-collectors."[49] But it is butterfly-collecting in the pre-Darwinian sense of trying to find, observe, and protect as many varieties as possible without proceeding to an explanation of why and how those varieties came to exist and why they remain in existence. One approach that has more of an explanatory than a descriptive character is that which starts out from a preoccupation with social inequality and seeks to situate ethnicity with respect to that inequality. Porter was evidently on something of a similar road, although his study none the less remains more descriptive than explanatory and, when it does seek to explain, as often as not leads us back into culture as the determinant factor. Two contemporary accounts that tie ethnicity more closely into the process by which social inequalities are generated and maintained are those of Micheline Labelle et al. in *Histoire d'immigrées*[50] and François Moreau in *Le Capital financier québécois*.[51]

Labelle et al. explain the utility of immigrant female workers to the Montreal garment industry on the following lines:

The employer is keen on hiring such labour because of its acquired skills (in sewing, among other things), which he doesn't have to pay for since they were acquired in a different society with a different system of work. In addition, those particular qualities associated with female labour in less-developed countries or parts of the world are of interest to him: physical endurance stemming from manual work experience, dexterity, docility, non-absenteeism, availability for overtime work or work that prohibits normal social life (for example, night work in the cleaning industry) – in other words, a malleable labour force, subordinated to the imperatives of production, and which both desires and is obliged to work under any conditions, given that it is an emigrant labour force.[52]

Such an account differs from official multiculturalism in taking as the central determining factor of the presence of such women in the first place the need of certain categories of employer for a certain kind of work-force, just as Reynolds explains the bringing over of British workers in the early years of the century on similar grounds. Cultural attributes such as learned skills, dexterity, and docility are not secondary to that process but are a part of it. They may be considered to constitute cultural heritages that should be maintained for purposes of mutual "enrichment," in accordance with the official creed of multiculturalism, but that enrichment means minimum wages for the women and the maintenance of profit levels for the employer.

For François Moreau, in another context, cultural factors can be equally central to "enrichment." In the late 1970s there was a close interlocking between the Quebec state and francophone capital that led to the emergence and consolidation of a francophone bourgeoisie in finance, retail, and manufacturing, an emergence that took place at the expense of hitherto dominant anglophone interests.[53] This is an example of the juxtaposition of ethnically distinct bourgeoisies that Rousseau has illustrated in the case of Tanzania.[54] If we are to characterize central Canadian history over the last ten years in cultural terms, and in the light of Moreau's analysis, it would seem more appropriate to do so in terms of a struggle between francophone and anglophone capital than in those of a decline in Ukrainian folk-dancing.

The question remains of the overall significance of "multiculturalism" in the Canadian context and, pre-eminently, in relation to the central theme of this book, what it means to describe a socially inegalitarian society as being by nature "multicultural." Multiculturalism in Canada cannot be understood apart from questions of power and politics. Within the terms of the ideology itself, as expressed by the various agencies of federal government, the question of power is, of course, ignored. The emphasis is on "mutual enrichment," "maintaining cultural heritages," "unity in diversity." But the ideology itself was constructed and diffused by the government in power and in the context of heated political debate over the future of Canada.

The multiculturalism and bilingualism policy was born at a time of political crisis and for eminently political purposes. The policy has always been linked to the desirability of national unity and has had the effect both of heading off Quebec grievances via bilingualism and of buying the support of "other" non-charter ethnic groups via multiculturalism, as Peter, among others, has pointed out.[55] Moodley makes a similar point, but also draws attention to the way in which the policy has neutralized the special claims of native Canadians,[56] a process that we have already seen underway in the White Paper of 1969. Multiculturalism was thus from the outset a politically charged vision of Canadian society. That researchers subsequently set out to use it as a model for understanding social relationships on the ground in a northern Ontario town or in Vancouver, with the consequences referred to earlier in this chapter, was to mistake politically motivated vision for grounded social analysis. Both politicians and social scientists operate in the light of visions of how things should be, and both categories have to be careful when it comes to imposing those visions on to things as they are.

Wardhaugh makes a similar point in *Language and Nationhood* when he is careful to differentiate between government policy and the reality of Canadian society.[57] Whether or not it is desirable that Canada should be multicultural, he reminds us, in essence it isn't. Multiculturalism disguises the fact that Canada is divided into two distinct linguistic and cultural zones, the anglophone and the francophone, each of which is separated from the other by a bilingual buffer zone, which, to the west of Quebec, runs down the Outaouais valley, and to the east cuts across northern New Brunswick.[58] Apart from those zones, Canada is divided into two solidly monolingual areas, with a few marginal exceptions here and there.[59]

In a sense Wardhaugh's "real" Canada is the most cogent single refutation of the multicultural model on its own terms, with a variety of other attempts to grasp the multicultural nettle becoming entangled in a web of regionalisms, interest groups, ethnic stereotyping, and other factors.[60] Various other non-Marxist analyses go beyond Wardhaugh in linking the central dichotomy in Canada to the question of Quebec nationhood and traditional social inequalities between anglophone and francophone Canadians. The question of Quebec's being a nation-state within an ill-defined federation, for example, which is central to much French Canadian writing on the subject of Quebec,[61] is also to be found in Anderson et al. among other explanations.[62] And in the work of Van den Berghe, whom we have already considered in the context of non-Marxist approaches to ethnicity, the real impetus in Quebec nationalism is not, surprisingly enough, considered to be primordial ethnic sentiment but rather "class conflict in linguistic disguise."[63]

Approaches to Canadian multiculturalism thus range from the Museum of Man vision of Canada as a collection of cultural vestiges, via the overriding bicultural confrontation between English and French Canada, to social inequality as the impetus within that principal cultural confrontation. Van den Berghe, however, sees class (in its non-Marxian sense) as only a transient form of sociality that temporarily displaces ethnicity (understood in genetic terms) as the basis for social action.[64] As we move towards the left, class-based social inequality comes to be seen more clearly as the key to the unravelling of multiculturalism, with ethnicity a framework within which social controllers, whether in private enterprise or state bureaucracies, "constitute" the different segments of the population that they have to control.[65]

In chapter 18 I turn to the ultimate conundrum of who is really constituting what, or, alternatively, what is really constituting whom. In the present context, however, it is worth alluding to Jabukowicz's article on multiculturalism and neo-conservatism in Australia.[66] From the late 1970s onwards the two have been as close companions in Australia as they have been in Canada. According to Jabukowicz, the official ideology of multiculturalism has been particularly useful for neo-conservatives inasmuch as it has helped to forge links between them and ethnic-minority employers. As it happens, those employers have a significance that goes beyond their mere ethnicity, in that they are the neo-conservative small-capitalist folk-heroes who have been the pioneers in forcing down wages and rolling back union representation. In the Australian context multiculturalism has also been useful because it is easily tied into Social Darwinist notions of innate ethnic superiority. The key signifiers of the neo-conservative perspective on multiculturalism are the consistent assertion and reassertion of the cohesion model of society; the systematic denial of any material tensions or contradictions in contemporary Australian capitalism; and the legitimation of ethnic communal organizations as the "voice" of the ethnic communities.[67] All of this tends to suggest that the ideology of multiculturalism, whether in Canada or elsewhere, is not so much the incubator of a new world as one of the artificial lungs that keeps the old world going.

CHAPTER FIFTEEN

Collective Containment: Ethnicity and the Colonial Frontier

The confrontation between an exploding, urbanized, industrial civiliza-tion, constantly in need of raw materials and expanding markets in which to sell those raw materials transformed into finished products, and the more localized, repetitive, and traditional societies that preceded and surround it is, first, a material one. It begins with the exchange of material goods in the form of a long-distance trade in exotica, bringing, for example, spices, silks, and cloisonné-ware to late medieval Europe. It continues with the extraction of raw materials for transformation by industrial societies, as well as the more organized production of those same exotica for consump-tion, in the form of tea, sugar, and coffee plantations. And it culminates with the gradual displacement of the process of transformation to areas outside the old industrial heartlands.

In Marxian terms we could say that we are moving towards, or have already arrived at, global relations of production, in which the class differ-ences that exist within the old established industrial societies pale into insig-nificance beside those that now exist between producer and consumer states. As with all attempts, however, to reduce the complexity of social organi-zation to a set of clear-cut oppositions – whether between ethnic groups or between classes or among whatever constructions one chooses to place on that complexity – the rapidly changing system of production and consumption that one attempts to encapsulate within those constructions or oppositions continually manages to elude, deny, or refute them.

Alongside that material confrontation is a confrontation between peoples, in which differences in material standard of living and the ability to dominate and control by force of arms are taken by the dominant to be significant of inherent differences in capability among the peoples so brought into confrontation. It can be said that no people has been so duped by that confrontation as the British, who happened, by historical accident, to have ridden the crest of the first tidal wave of industrialization that swept across Europe and produced secondary shock waves in the non-European world. In terms of the Protestant creed, which succeeded in remodelling the Christian conscience in line with capitalist practice, the very success of imperial expansion was taken to be an indication of the possession of God's grace and the mission of the British to civilize, convert, and generally anglicize the unenlightened.

The material confrontation thus coincided with an ideological one, which served both to justify and mystify the first. Nor was that grand ideological scheme necessarily destroyed with the end of empire. The protected peoples who were finally "granted" independence in the post–Second World War world were considered to have "grown out" of their previous barbarism under British tutelage and to be ready to fulfil their adult role as independent nation-states. The divine mission accorded to the British in the nineteenth century was considered to have been successfully carried out, and the nuclear family of the Empire gradually evolved into the extended family of the Commonwealth, except for those few ungrateful individuals who cut their links with the family altogether. This was the ideological explanation of empire that grew up alongside it, accompanied its downfall, and survives in the British consciousness as the memory of Empire.

It would, however, be unfair to say that that view of non-British subject peoples was shared in any uniform way across British society. It contributed to the ethnically constituted, overarching "British" identity that served as the ideological cement of British class society, but the ruling class and its ideological lieutenants among the intellectual petty bourgeoisie were equally duped by the appearances of their own class-divided society. The nineteenth-century eugenics movement, for example, under the leadership of Francis Galton, expressed the belief that the working classes were genetically inferior to the upper classes and that society was for that reason marked by evident social and material inequality.[1] Social inequality flowed from biological superiority and inferiority. Hierarchical class society was the social expression of natural differences. Relations of material and political inequality were thus as mystified by the dominant classes within Britain on "natural" grounds as they were within the framework of empire.

The ideological confrontation between the colonizer and the colonized, or between the imperial power and those who were subject to that power is not, therefore, essentially one between two "peoples," although in certain circumstances it can come to take that form. It is rather the continuation at the colonial or imperial level of the ideological justification of social inequality within the metropolitan society. The crises of identity experienced by colonized peoples and referred to by Sivanandan or Fanon are matched by the crisis of identity experienced within English class society by the emigrant who leaves the working-class domain and is catapulted by selective education into the state bureaucracy, the professional petty bourgeoisie, or the upper middle class.[2] Similarly, the voyage to the end of the world by Lévi-Strauss in order to discover society in its Rousseauesque primitive state is paralleled by the voyages of Old Etonians such as Orwell into the depths of English working-class life.[3] In the case of both Lévi-Strauss and Orwell, members of a dominant class set out in search of the "other" who is necessary for the establishing of their own class identity. In this chapter I look particularly at the colonial encounter, but without forgetting the ethnic aspects of the class encounter within the industrial homeland.

In every empire from the Roman onwards, and presumably before, empire-builders have encountered two categories of peoples: those who live on the edge or beyond the bounds of the territory to be subjugated, and those who live within those bounds. Marginal peoples had to be prevented from erupting across the frontier into the subjugated zone and robbing that zone of precisely those riches that the imperial power had reserved to itself. In Roman Britain, for example, the productive cornlands of the southeast and the riches of the new urban civilization in the lowland areas were constantly under threat from the non-subjugated peoples living beyond the bounds of the settled zone.[4] The boundary between subjugated and non-subjugated territory tended to lie along the edge of the highland areas, which made penetration and subjugation difficult, and there was often no economic incentive to subjugate those areas, unless it was to exploit the tin mines of the Cornish peninsula or the silver and lead mines of Wales, except in so far as they threatened the economic life and security of the lowlands. Altogether the highland zones represented a difficult and expensive problem and one that was never resolved by the imperial administration. Roman armies were constantly tied down in expeditions that were successful only as long as they lasted (rather like contemporary police anti-street-crime operations in London). Supply lines were difficult to maintain, ambushes difficult to avoid, and the set-piece battles in which individualistic Celtic heroics inevitably came to grief against Roman discipline and superior military technology were difficult to engineer. The Romans were reduced to punitive expeditions across the lines of forts and occasionally walls that separated them from the hill peoples, and in the case of the Scottish Highlands, the "problem" was only finally resolved by the wholesale clearances of the early nineteenth century.

The British in India were confronted by a similar problem on the North-West Frontier, which equally was never resolved. Endless British expeditions set out from the plains of the Punjab to punish the Pathans for the murders of British officials and harassment of the trade routes into Afghanistan.[5] None of these expeditions succeeded in doing anything more than suffering heavier losses than anywhere else on the imperial frontiers and spurring on the hill tribes to more violent acts of revenge and resistance. According to Elliott's pro-imperial account of the North-West Frontier campaigns, the Pathans never understood that the British were not interested in subjugating the hill peoples but just in punishing them and preventing them from disturbing the Pax Britannica that applied to the east. They were thus incapable of understanding that the aerial bombing campaigns of the 1930s were ultimately for their own good and that the endless attempts to annihilate their fighting capacity were not intended to threaten their political freedom.

The other face of the coin for the British was that the frontier provided a never-ending challenge for military ingenuity and foolhardy courage (as Northern Ireland still does), and operational disasters only served to whet the appetite of the soldiery to try again. At the same time, defeat at the hands of the Pathans gave rise to an admiration for those same Pathans, and thus a deep ambiguity in the attitude of the would-be dominant power. The pro-imperial accounts, of course, fail to appreciate the moral imperatives operating in Pathan society, in which any military encroachment is an offence against honour and any casualties inflicted require revenge.[6] The British version of the North-West Frontier campaign, therefore, constitutes another example of the situation in which a dominant power mystifies itself about its own motives, while those subjected to that attempted domination are in no position to so mystify themselves.

Both the Roman and the British Indian examples relate to established, geographically fixed frontiers, which coincide with an ideological account of nations undergoing civilization for their own good on one side and thoughtless barbarians unhelpfully (but at the same time courageously) trying to disrupt that process from the other. The frontier is not, however, always so fixed. The process of colonial juxtaposition leading to articulation and eventual domination begins with the frontier surrounding the trading post, continues with the colonizer establishing his presence elsewhere in the territory from within the security of a mobile armed force, and ultimately can lead to the ending of resistance throughout the area by the establishment of an overall paramilitary presence. This is the process described in Jeffries' pro-imperial account of the colonial police,[7] which concerns the way in which the frontier dividing controlled from uncontrolled territory is gradually pushed back to more natural geopolitical boundaries. This again is accompanied by the ideological distinction between the "tame" and the "wild", with the remnants of the untamed natives being gradually harassed, pushed back, and encircled, and if possible brought within the fold of civilization or, in the case of the "wild" Irish, executed, deported, or otherwise disposed of. On the one side of the fixed or movable frontier, therefore, we find the wild and the untamed, and on the other the recently tamed, the latter being subjected to the self-mystified reforming zeal of colonial administrators.

British administrators were generally concerned to anglicize, Christianize, and generally "civilize" their colonial subjects out of their barbaric non-European habits, but they were careful to maintain rigid social barriers between themselves and those same subjects. This echoes Norwegian-Lapp relations as described by Eidheim, where Lapps are encouraged to Norwegianize themselves but are not accepted as Norwegians.[8] Thus the British expatriate community in India deplored the non-Englishness of their subjects from within the confines of their compound while at the same time maintaining the strictest possible controls over entry into the European club, which remained an island of exaggerated English ethnicity. As Gorer points out, however, the "natives" were frequently only a backdrop to the really important oppositions that were established within the community itself between the representatives of the different British classes.[9] The engineers, technical staff, and lower-grade functionaries would always be held at the greatest possible social distance by the higher-grade civil servants of altogether different social origins. The threat was not so much that of being overwhelmed and slaughtered by the surrounding population, which was something that had on occasion to be stoically accepted, but rather of being confronted by fellow British colonials of lower social rank who took advantage of the enforced intimacy of colonial life to get ideas above their station. However, if one's first loyalty was to one's class, one's second was still to one's fellow Britons, and the colonized population beyond the compound remained an object of suspicion, contempt, and paternalistic affection.

The most that could be hoped for from the colonized was that they should produce a pale copy of British discipline and virtue. As is stated in a pro-imperial history of British India (published in 1921), the great triumph of the British in India was to have "westernized" Indians, even if the process had not gone the lengths of producing a "class of 'Indians in blood and colour but English in taste, in opinions, in morals and in intellect.'"[10] That latter passage, as quoted, had been written in the previous century but none the less serves to illustrate the guiding principle of colonial administration. The problem for the administrator was twofold. First, the native had fundamental defects of character. He was lazy, fickle, untrust-worthy, cunning, elaborately deceitful, and yet honest to the point of simplicity, recklessly brave, cowardly, emotional, hot-headed, irrational, inexplicably attached to wasteful traditions and rituals, ungrateful, and unpredictable. In Darling's study of the Punjab, the native "problem" is summed up by such defects.[11] The administrator's second problem, however, was the tendency of the sterling British character, which had been reared in the invigorating atmosphere of the English Home Counties and was possessed of all the Protestant virtues, to be corrupted by the Indian climate. One had, therefore, to instil those virtues by example before they had had time to go to seed.

So the Indians were everything that the British were not, although to be fair, Darling does distinguish among different peoples. Conditions in any area are dictated by ecology and by character. By constructing irrigation canals in the Punjab, the British administration congratulated itself on having resolved the first of these two problems, and then set out to find the native character that was best suited to cultivate the land made available. The Rajput and the Mea are rejected as being innately lazy – because they prefer aristocratic warfare and live near Delhi – but the Jat are tall, hard-working, and strong, and the Ahirs are equally hard-working after many generations of struggle in the hostile environment of the sands.[12] The best of native character, however, having been brought into the best of environments, inevitably succumbs to the wiles of the money-lender, given the childlike attitudes of the peasant in questions of finance.[13]

The process of taming, domesticating, and anglicizing the "natives" within the imperial frontiers, and above all the encouragement of settled farming, the rationalization of holdings, and the attempt to put an end to the enactment of superstitious rites when the British veterinary surgeon should have been called for, all run headlong into the problem of native character. The distant Victorian father-figure, meting out punishment and doses of affection by turns, is thus more than matched by the paternalistic colonial administrator, punishing the impudence of the tribesmen beyond the frontiers and putting up in an affectionate, long-suffering way with the foibles and recalcitrance of his settled subjects. Such pro-imperial accounts of the British experience in India tend to restrict themselves to the political and the ideological, the particular domains of the administrator and the natural subject for recollection and contemplation in retirement. The material or economic rationale behind the imperial presence can be seen to be of little significance beside the battles and campaigns waged by the agents of the East India Company and the gradual extension of their control over ever-larger areas of India, or beside the perennial struggle of the administrator with the "defects" of native character.

The determinant role of the material encounter is equally submerged in relation to nineteenth-century Ireland, where the lack of security of tenure and lack of compensation for improvement combined to provide little motivation for the peasantry to improve their holdings. Indeed, to improve one's holding normally meant that one would be removed from it so that it could be let at a higher rent by the landlord (frequently resident in England).[14] The nature of tenure thus led to the demoralization and hopelessness of the Irish peasantry, which was itself interpreted in dominant English opinion to mean that the Irish peasant was inherently lazy, careless, and uninterested in improvement.[15] The Irish "problem" was seen to be one of Irish character rather than one determined by colonial policy. This was also true of attitudes towards Ireland as a whole, where the lack of industrial development and agricultural improvement was generally interpreted as a result of the defects of Irish character rather than of the inhibiting of Irish manufacturing industry by the dumping of British goods on the Irish market.

The history of empire and of colonialism from the pro-imperial viewpoint illustrates the Weberian thesis that the privileged will go to any lengths to legitimize and justify their privileges.[16] Officially one can say that the British considered themselves to have been divinely selected to remodel character along the lines of northern Protestant virtue and to confer the benefits of English political institutions on backward and disorganized peoples. That there was some profit to be made in this process was just a happy coincidence and, of course, a sign of divine approval for the whole scheme. There were certain cases, however, where the gap between civilization and barbarism was so wide as to make the possibility of Europeanization, and preferably anglicization (since non-English Europeans are themselves not untainted by barbarism), seem doomed from the outset. This was particularly so in the case of the American Indians. Colonists in South America tended to resolve the problem by eliminating the indigenous peoples altogether, whether by hunting them down or simply by introducing diseases against which they had no resistance. These methods were also usefully employed in North America, but administrators and missionaries were increasingly preoccupied with the necessity of Christianizing and Europeanizing the natives who survived.

In Canada colonial administrators were brought up against the problem of properly controlling and administering seasonally nomadic peoples who had no knowledge of their language and no understanding of their institutions. As long as Europeans and native peoples had only trading contact, which was mutually beneficial inasmuch as European guns and ammunition made hunting easier, there was little direct interference. But as the colonization developed, conflict over land and resource use developed alongside it and brought the colonial administration to restrict and delimit areas reserved to Indian use.[17] Again, alongside the restriction of native access to resources, there grew up an elaborate ideological structure that explained, justified, and mystified that restriction. According to the ideology, the natives had to be "civilized," and their salvation ensured. It was thus necessary to bring them within fixed bounds where they could be encouraged to settle down, cultivate the land, be converted, taught French or English, and generally be prepared for integration into the wider European society.[18] The ostensible reason for the system of reserves, therefore, was not economic or even political – although in terms of economics and politics there were certain convenient by-products – but to ensure the reform of native character such that the natives so reformed could disappear into the dominant Euro-Canadian population. In European ideology the purpose of this process was to introduce the Indians to the benefits of civilization, but at the same time it necessarily involved the eradication of Indian languages and customs, since, as Canadian federal legislators stated in 1891, as long as they spoke their own language, they constituted a separate people.[19]

The logic behind the ideology is similar to that found throughout pro-imperial and pro-colonial historiography. The difference between colonizers and colonized was not simply one between backward and advanced, or non-civilized and civilized, but between immaturity and maturity. As in Darling's account of the Punjab, the colonized peoples of North America were held to be in a state of chronic immaturity. The role assumed by the colonial administration was one of protective paternalism, since without such protection, it was maintained that incoming Europeans would ride roughshod over those whom the lieutenant governor of Upper Canada referred to circa 1836 as "red children."[20] The federal government thus took the Indians into wardship, with the idea that only when individuals could be considered to have reached a state of maturity – that is, to have lost their own language and culture – could they be let loose into the wider society. This rule referred principally to male "status" Indians. From 1869 until the mid-1980s Indian women who married whites were automatically barred from band membership, it being evidently presumed that the children of a white male would be *ipso facto* non-Indian, although here a political-economic counter-explanation tended to disguise that racist and sexist belief.[21] The explanation was that white males had to be prevented from taking up residence within reserves since they would tend to dominate and exploit the Indians.

The Indian peoples of Canada remain in the 1980s under the guardianship of the federal government, in accordance with nineteenth-century paternalistic ideology. The number of Indians who chose to be enfranchised and become part of the great adult Canadian family had dwindled to 1 in 1974–75, although in the same year 590 women were forcibly ejected from band membership by marrying whites.[22] The setting up of reserves thus failed to bring about the disappearance of Indian people as had been hoped, and the federal government has been obliged to seek other means to bring about the same end of disappearance through assimilation, as expressed in the 1969 White Paper, which was subsequently shelved but not forgotten in government circles.[23]

At the beginning of this chapter I made a distinction between the untamed peoples beyond the imperial frontiers and those who find themselves within those frontiers and who are subject to being tamed, anglicized, civilized, and generally rendered innocuous. The North American Indians both found themselves within the imperial frontiers and yet proved to be untamable. Hence the erecting of an internal frontier in the form of the reserve boundary, within which the wild and the unassimilable could be contained. The confrontation between marginalized indigenous peoples in Canada and the federal and provincial governments acting on behalf of major public and private corporations has long since come to a head with the development of mining, hydroelectric and forestry projects, and natural gas and oil prospection and extraction in the Canadian north. Native peoples who were forgotten and ignored as long as federal and provincial governments had no economic interest in the north have now become a central concern of those same governments. This was one of the factors that underlay the federal government's 1969 White Paper. The position put forward was that the protected status of Indians should be brought to an end, that reserve lands should be turned into disposable private property, and that Indians should become full, tax-paying Canadian citizens like everyone else and subject to provincial jurisdiction.[24] Ideologically, that process of assimilation was to put an end to second-class citizenship (and third-class citizenship in the case of Indian women), but underlying the ideology of equality is the more material and political question of Indian land-claims.

The federal government refused to recognize Indian claims to large areas of the north that are known to be rich in natural resources. The underlying intention of the White Paper is to resolve the Indian "problem" so as to make native peoples indistinguishable from the rest of the population and therefore in no position to press embarrassing land-claims on the basis of their existence as distinct peoples. In the event, the White Paper had the opposite effect as far as native peoples were concerned, making them even more sensitive to federal government attempts to nullify their campaign for the recognition of land rights and self-determination. This process of having to eliminate the threat posed by indigenous peoples who stand in the way of economic development can be seen in the case of the James Bay hydroelectric project in Quebec.

What is now northern Quebec officially became part of Quebec in 1912, but the Quebec government expressed no interest in or concern for the area until 1960, incidentally having failed to come to the aid of the Inuit during the famine of the 1930s.[25] The situation then changed, as the Quebec government came to recognize the north's immense economic potential, and the province began to duplicate the educational and social services already offered by the federal government. In 1971 the vast James Bay hydroelectric project was begun without any prior consultation with the Indian communities whose lands were to be flooded. In November 1983 the Cree succeeded in getting an injunction to have work on the project stopped, a decision by Judge Malouf that created something of a panic among the American and European financial backers, the provincial government, and the state corporations responsible for the development. In fairly indecent haste the judgment was reversed by a superior court, and the Quebec government decided to go for direct negotiation with the Indians and the Inuit rather than rely on the unpredictability of legal procedures. The Quebec Indian Association, however, insisted on negotiating within the framework of its overall land-claims, which called into question Quebec's sovereignty. This was unacceptable to the provincial government, which chose rather to negotiate directly with the native people most immediately concerned by the project, the Cree, as well as the Inuit to the north who were liable to be affected by later projects.[26]

The negotiating bodies of both these groups, the Grand Council of the Crees and the Northern Quebec Inuit Association, the latter of which appears to have been created in the Department of Indian Affairs in Ottawa in order to provide somebody with whom Quebec and Ottawa could negotiate,[27] both accepted the principle of Quebec sovereignty and also Quebec's rights to all subsoil resources. This involved the reciprocal recognition by both federal and provincial governments of the traditional rights of the native peoples to the land, but that recognition was only conceded by those governments in so far as the native peoples concerned were prepared to renounce those rights within the framework of the same agreement. By signing the James Bay and Northern Quebec Agreement, therefore, the Cree and Inuit negotiators won recognition of and simultaneously signed away the traditional rights of their peoples to the land, while the two governments both conceded those rights and had them extinguished.[28]

The simultaneous recognition and extinction of native rights is foreshadowed in the conclusion of the Quebec Dorion Commission's report in 1971:

An Indian title has existed. Its real nature is difficult to determine, but it seems to be usufructuary in character and above all related to traditional hunting and fishing rights linked to subsistence needs ... Whatever may have been the case ... it is necessary to find some way of replacing the "Indian title" in those areas of Québec which may be affected by it ... as a precursor to such replacement, it is obviously necessary to recognize the territorial rights linked to Indian title, with the intention of extinguishing them ... those rights, having disappeared, must then be replaced by such rights – individual or collective depending on the choice of the Amerindian people – as may include the right to hunt and fish for their own subsistence needs and those of their family, land grants, ... the enjoyment of all the monetary and other benefits that are available to citizens generally, in addition to a special development fund.[29]

The James Bay and Northern Quebec Agreement thus reflects the position of the Dorion Commission. It attempts to resolve the hitherto intractable problem of native title to land – in the case of those areas of northern

Quebec that are subject to the agreement – a problem that had threatened not only resource extraction but also federal and provincial sovereignty. In return for conceding that title, the Cree and Inuit obtained compensation, the spending of which was to be administered jointly by the recipients and the two governments, as well as exclusive rights to certain areas for hunting, trapping, and gathering, and semi-exclusive rights to other areas. In addition, all the communities were to be brought more closely into line with the south in terms of education, social welfare, communications, and justice.[30]

The James Bay Agreement was constructed on the basis of a particularly fragile premise, that it is possible to extinguish native rights. With the recognition of native rights in the Canadian Constitution Act of 1982, the federal government instituted a process of consultation with native peoples and provincial governments in order to clarify the nature and extent of those rights within the constitution. By the end of the five-year period allowed, the constitutional talks reached a stalemate. In a document published by the federal government in 1986, Murray Coolican concludes that all treaties arrived at with native peoples since Confederation and founded on the principle of the global extinction of rights accompanied by the granting of limited new rights are essentially indefensible.[31] The James Bay Agreement, as a recent example of that principle, thus stands condemned. The relationship between the various non-native governments involved and native peoples remains fundamentally one between colonizers and colonized. A majority of non-native provincial governments refuse to recognize native title to land and native rights to self-government, while the native peoples refuse to make any concessions. Following the failure of the constitutional talks, native groups suggest that they will proceed to exercise their rights to self-government whether or not they are recognized.

The case of native peoples in Canada represents the continuity of an old colonial frontier and the continuity in attitudes across that frontier: incomprehension, paternalism, and impatience, bonded together in a form of diffuse racism, towards a people who refuse to be tamed and assimilated. Every now and again the frustration of native communities emerges in the unilateral exercise of traditional rights, which is then peremptorily curtailed by police or game wardens, as in the case of the confrontation between the Micmacs and the Quebec police over salmon fishing at Restigouche in 1981 and between the Mohawks and federal police over the sale of cigarettes at Kahnawake in 1988. Native peoples continue to be seen as a dangerous, unpredictable element on the edge of mainstream Canadian society, just as the impoverished Irish peasantry remained equally dangerously and unpredictably on the edge of nineteenth-century British industrial society.

As the colonial encounter was continuing in the form of the violent confrontation at Restigouche, the British police was enacting its own version of the encounter in London, Manchester, and Liverpool. Lord Scarman's report on that encounter presents a curiously one-sided picture of the series of clashes between young unemployed blacks (for the most part) and the police in Brixton.[32] He describes the events from behind the police lines and through the testimony of the police officers, such that the "rioters" themselves constitute an undifferentiated and uncontrollable mass somewhere behind the burning police vans. Every now and again an unidentifiable individual emerges from the mass to hurl a projectile or petrol bomb at the police and then disappear. In the final encounter, the police charge down the street and the mob melts away into the darkness down side-streets and alleys. Throughout the account we are made familiar with the feelings and injuries of individual, named policemen, while their adversaries remain unnamed and unknowable. On the one hand the report emphasizes the calm courage of individual police officers, and on the other the blind, animal-like fury of the mob.

Scarman's account of the English riots recalls accounts of other confrontations across the colonial frontier: on the one side of that frontier, the coolness and discipline of the Irish Peace Preservation Force, the European club members in Orwell's *Burmese Days*, or the relics of the British forces retreating from Kabul; and on the other, the secret societies of *banditti* who, in pro-imperial accounts, are held to have terrorized the Irish countryside (although we might ask who was really terrorizing whom),[33] the rioting Burmese, and the merciless Afghan tribesmen from whom only one man escaped alive into India.[34] In all these cases the opponent is unidentifiable, incomprehensible, barbaric, vengeful, and violent, in fact the counterpart beyond the frontier of the indolent, deceitful, and childlike peoples within it. In the experience of empire the military wrestles with the one and the long-suffering administrator with the other, but all such peoples prove useful in showing up the inestimably superior qualities of the British character that they so thoughtlessly refuse to imitate.

There is, therefore, a general similarity between the attitudes of the North American colonial governments, the imperial administrators in India, the under-secretary for Ireland and his entourage at Dublin Castle in the early nineteenth century, and the impartial investigator into street disturbances in English inner cities in 1981, whether towards the different indigenous peoples under their control or, in 1981, the children of labour migrants subject to official scrutiny. In each case the economic or material logic for the existence of that subordination, which in Britain led to an outburst of frustration on the part of the young black British working class, is subverted in the ideology of colonialism into the confrontation between a superior British ethnicity and a de-individualized irascible mob.

CHAPTER SIXTEEN

The Dark Rose:
Ethnicity, Resistance, and
the Idea of Nationhood

According to the nineteenth-century ideology of Social Darwinism, the evolutionary pinnacle on the top of which the members of the English ruling class found themselves rose in inverse proportion to the chasms in which they discovered the various peoples subject to their oppression.[1] Things did not, however, look the same from the other side. If Social Darwinism was the necessary ideological framework in terms of which the colonizer could get on with the business of repatriating primary resources and extending territorial boundaries with a clear conscience, on the other side, and in the charged atmosphere of political and economic subordination, there emerged other frameworks of meaning.

For such frameworks, the past is no longer the set of low points on the human trajectory from which the present started out (as it was for Social Darwinism), nor is the history of cultural and social change considered in the same light as it was by the founding fathers of cultural and social anthropology, as one of "steady progression from a lower to a higher condition"[2] or the "general improvement of mankind by higher organisation of the individual and of society."[3] The past is rather the golden age of independence and achievement that was destroyed by conquest. Alien domination has prevented the potential of the people that was evident in its heroic past from coming to maturity and fullness in the context of a united, independent Ireland or a separate Quebec. In the form of nationalism, such frameworks of meaning can be married to evolutionism, but it is an evolutionism that emphasizes the barriers that have prevented "racial excellence" from manifesting itself rather than the process by which that excellence triumphed.

Within the framework of meaning constructed by a dominant power, the present demonstrates its superiority, the future is more or less irrelevant, and the past is manipulated to show how its natural superiority asserted itself in history. For nationalism, by contrast, the present is the denial of the natural superiority of the dominated people, the past is the proof of that superiority, and the future will provide the opportunity for that superiority to reassert itself. For the dominant, present political and economic subordination is the proof of natural superiority. This was clearly the case with respect to the nineteenth-century Irish tenantry. English superiority flowed as a necessary corollary from the fact of Irish poverty.[4] It was not open to Irish nationalists to make the same kind of deduction but in the reverse direction, and hence the belief in Irish superiority had to be substantiated from other sources.

Thus it is that the focus for nationalism tends to be the past, while the focus for belief systems justifying present domination is the present. The goal of nationalism as an ideology is to summon the individual in the name of a belief system that rejects the ideology of natural inferiority imposed by a dominant and identifiably alien people and replaces it with one that creates a framework for redressive political action.[5] It has, therefore, to frame itself in such a way that redressive action might flow from it. That framework is normally established through the notion of "destiny" – and it is interesting that in another context destiny is at the heart of the Marxian understanding of history. Thus two factors need to be clearly established: the existence of a heroic past that can serve as a model for political and, if necessary, violent action in the present, and the idea that such political action will necessarily lead to nationhood.

Both of these factors are present in the development of Irish nationalism as described by Lyons, or perhaps one should say the maintenance through time of an ideology of Irish resistance and its re-emergence in the second half of the nineteenth century.[6] Following the defeat of the United Irishmen in the late eighteenth century and the Act of Union in 1800, Ireland was flooded with English manufactured goods and subject to widespread cultural anglicization: use of the Irish language went into rapid decline; place-names and family names were changed into forms that attempted to conceal their Irishness, and locally produced clothing was spurned in favour of English mass-produced fashions.[7] Continuing economic subordination thus accompanied the political subordination of the Act of Union, and both gave rise to cultural provincialism. Douglas Hyde, in his essay on "The Necessity for De-Anglicising Ireland," quotes de Jubainville on Gaul and applies it to Ireland: "England 'has definitely conquered us, she has even imposed upon us her language, that is to say, the form of our thoughts during every instant of our existence.' "[8]

The second half of the nineteenth century saw the articulation of a new Irish identity, which was partly an awakening to the Irish side of their Anglo-Irishness on the part of some members of the Protestant ascendancy and partly the ideological accompaniment to the increasingly significant political movement for home rule. One aspect of that reaction to British dominance was the rediscovery of an Irish heroic age that could serve as the refutation of the dominant British myth concerning the natural inferiority of the Irish "race" and as the blueprint of the new Ireland that was to rise from the ashes of provincialism. The characteristics of that heroic age were contained in the ancient Irish epics and sagas and dated from a period when Ireland was divided into a number of warring kingdoms ruled by native Irish aristocracies. But even when written down, the tales were merely semi-mythical recreations of an even older heroic past and were designed to entertain, spur on, and terrify as well as to glorify the semi-legendary heroes of the peoples to whom they were addressed. The ancient Irish tales are a curious mixture of myth and history, but more than one contemporary authority has considered them to offer a unique (if highly embellished) description of life in an Iron Age society.[9]

For Irish or Celtic revivalism in the nineteenth century, however, the interest of the tales lay not so much in their historical veracity or otherwise but in the image that they presented of a heroic, warlike, aristocratic, and wholly Irish society prior to foreign intervention. They could thus be held to represent the first stirrings of a people whose progression to mature nationhood had been cut off by alien domination. But more than that, the extravagant heroics of the sagas, in which the main protagonist vowed to lead a short and valiant life in the defence of his people rather than a long and nondescript one (when given the choice), came to serve as the model for militant nationalism, and a model that was explicitly present in the minds of the 1916 rebels when they undertook their suicidal action against the British.[10] The nineteenth-century writer who best captured and transmitted the atmosphere of the early Irish epics and thereby served (in Duffy's terms) to "warm the souls of men with the divine flame of patriotism"[11] was Standish O'Grady.

O'Grady had been through the nursery of the Protestant ascendancy (Trinity College Dublin) without realizing that Ireland had a history. It was only when he found himself shut in in the library of a country house in the west of Ireland on a wet day that he alighted on an account of Ireland's heroic past.[12] He was subsequently to publish works on early Irish society and history in which legend and fact are as openly mixed as in the sagas themselves and in a style that is quite as vivid and evocative as that of the originals. Thus the infant Ulster hero Cuchulainn proves too strong for all the weapons except those of the king of the Ulstermen, Conchobar, and on his first day under arms rides beyond the southern boundaries of Ulster, returning with the severed heads of three of Ulster's most feared enemies attached to his chariot.[13] O'Grady weaves into his account of ancient Ireland the exploits of Cuchulainn as told in the *Táin Bó Cualnge*, his slaughtering of innumerable Munster heroes at the ford in defence of his people, his wooing of Emer, and his tying himself up to a standing stone when finally overwhelmed by his enemies so as to instil fear into them even when dead. Cuchulainn is the type of the national hero spending his life terrifying and decimating the enemies of Ulster, but the stories of Cuchulainn are not simply tales of mindless, unremitted bloodletting. One of the heroes he is forced to fight and kill at the ford is his own foster brother Fer Díad, and after long days of fighting, when Fer Díad is finally despatched, no one is more grief-stricken than Cuchulainn himself.

O'Grady uses the stories to demonstrate the courage and dignity of the Irish before they were subjugated by the foreigner and explicitly to provide an alternative account of Irishness that could be opposed to English attempts to pass off the Irish as racially inferior. His work constitutes an attempt to reappropriate the definition of Irishness in the cause of nationalism. The Irish of the heroic age are described by O'Grady as possessing "warlike prowess, physical beauty, generosity, hospitality, love of family and nation."[14] English racism is turned against itself in a discourse in which it is Irish rather than English racial superiority that is asserted and ancient heroism rather than present domination that comes to be the means of establishing that superiority. According to O'Grady, the best work of the ancient Irish bards is "probably hidden in the blood and brains of the race to this day. Those antique singing men, with their imagined gods and superhuman heroes, breathed into the land and the people the gallantry and the chivalrousness, the prevailing identity, the love of action and freedom, the audacity and elevation of thought, which underneath all rudeness and grotesquerie, characterises the remants of their imaginings, and which we would believe no intervening centuries have been powerful enough wholly to annul."[15] Irish racial excellence has thus been suppressed, cut off in its early life, eternally prevented by alien domination from asserting itself.

Alongside the notion of the "blood and brain of the race" is that of the nation and of the destiny of nations to come to full independent nationhood as inevitably as a child becomes an adult. Most national historians have the task of watching the first rays of dawn gradually break into day as the nation comes of age,

but for the historian of Ireland no such delightful task is reserved; not for him to trace the track of the many springs and rivulets, to mark how they converge, and, uniting, form the strong undivided current of the history of a nation moving forward between its firm shores, freighted with the destiny of a single people accompanying its fate; not for him the slow glorious growth of a nation among the nations of the earth. Beginnings, ever beginnings; noble actions without end, that shine and vanish, characters as great as any, but resultless, movements full of hope but leading no whither, flashing glories ever dimmed and blasted, travail and labour unceasing, expectation and labour ever baffled; through all the centuries, Ireland, as in birth pangs with many cries, labouring to bring forth the Irish nation, and that nation still unborn.[16]

O'Grady was probably one of the most influential of the rediscoverers of the Irish past through the very vividness of his vision of that past and of the character and potential of the Irish nation. The discourse that he puts together is one of pure resistance, countering the notion of the preordained destiny of the English to rule and to civilize with that of the equally preordained destiny of the Irish to come to nationhood and, by implication, to throw off the English yoke. Along with others, he provided the ideological framework for the nationalist movement as it ebbed and flowed between political and military tactics from the rise and fall of Parnell and the Irish party in the British Parliament to the 1916 rising and beyond.[17]

The ideology of nationalism, however, was not built up merely on the recollection of a heroic past and a belief in the destiny of Ireland. It was also built up on the encouragement of all things Irish: speaking Irish, reading Irish books, wearing home-produced Irish cloth, ridding Irish place- and family names of their anglicized trappings, playing Irish games, and glorifying rather than ridiculing traditional Irish rural life. "In a word," according to Douglas Hyde, "we must strive to cultivate everything that is most racial, most smacking of the soil, most Gaelic, most Irish, because in spite of the little admixture of Saxon blood in the north east corner, this island *is* and will *ever* remain Celtic at the core, and far more Celtic than most people imagine."[18]

The nationalist movement reached a point of crisis during the First World War. Ireland was increasingly prosperous following the outbreak of war, and popular support for nationalism was under threat. The leading actors in the events of 1916 hoped to be the spark that would reignite nationalist sentiment, even in the knowledge that their own action was doomed to failure in military terms.[19] It is an irony of sorts that it was not so much their own action that had the desired result but the punishment meted out by the British government afterwards, in the form of executions, which effectively generated a wave of public sympathy for the nationalist cause.[20] Those involved in the rising had different reasons for so doing, but all were more or less fired by a belief in the destiny of Ireland to achieve independence and nationhood. Among the most celebrated was Patrick Pearse, who explicitly set the action that he took within the framework of meaning that had been constructed by O'Grady and by those other "wild writers" (in A.E. Russell's terms) "that had been let out by O'Grady from the neglected *dun* of Gaelic tradition."[21] Pearse's was a mystical nationalism that found its well-springs in the heroic past and in the destiny of Ireland that was to be "more glorious than that of Rome."[22] That destiny had to be made possible by the sacrifice of blood, and in the occupation of the General Post Office at Easter 1916 there is more than a hint of Cuchulainn giving his life in the defence of Ulster. "Bloodshed," Pearse wrote, "is a cleansing and sanctifying thing, and the nation which regards it as the final horror has lost its manhood. There are many things more horrible than bloodshed; and slavery is one of them."[23]

The shedding of blood in 1916 was thus the partial reddening into bloom of the dark rose that had come to be the traditional image of a subjugated Ireland.[24] That year was the highpoint in the cultivation of the particular kind of politicized Irish ethnicity that had come into existence in the context of resistance to English domination. It was an ethnicity that had been cultivated in its more purely aesthetic form by the Anglo-Irish school represented notably by Yeats and Lady Gregory[25] and had provided the ideological basis for the militant nationalism of the Irish Republican Brotherhood.[26] In the post-war years, and with the setting up of the Free State in 1921, the preservation of the Irish language and the cultivation of the Irish past came to be official government policy. To a large extent, however, the republic continued to be an English cultural province, as Corkery was to lament in 1931.[27] Economically it remained tied to the British market and, at least since the Second World War, has come increasingly under the sway of British capital.[28] The political tie had, however, been broken, and the urgency of having an ideological framework expressed through the medium of ethnicity as the basis for a national liberation movement was no longer present, except in the North of Ireland, where the political and economic subordination of the Catholic minority still go hand in hand.[29]

Nairn writes that nationalism, once unleashed, is impossible to control, much as Russell lamented that the wild writers of ancient Ireland could not be returned to their *dun*. The lesson of Irish nationalism, however, is that the system of meaning that nationalism brings into being only retains its power as long as the political and economic conditions that brought it into being remain in force. Nationalism in the south of Ireland reached its political dénouement in the 1920s and is only now kept alive as a flame of varying intensity by events in the North. Nationalism or separatism in Quebec, by contrast, has never known such a dénouement.

In the very decade when nationalism in the south of Ireland was going into government-sponsored decline – the 1920s – nationalist thought in Quebec was entering an active phase in the work of Lionel Groulx. It was a period during which Quebec was being rapidly swallowed up into the North American mass market, and the Catholic Church in particular was concerned at the emergence of an urbanized, secularized, industrial proletariat that was increasingly detaching itself from what were held to be the traditional values of Quebec rural society as it had evolved under the aegis of the Church.[30] There thus evolved what has been described as a "clerico-nationalist" ideology, which glorified the past and condemned the large industrial town as the "tombeau de la catholicité québécoise."[31]

Groulx's vision of the French Canadian "race" is articulated in terms of the two poles of nationalist thought, the heroic past and the destined future, in which present economic and political subordination will be eradicated.[32] The heroic period of colonization is established partly on the backs of the Iroquois, who are used to demonstrate both the bravery and the religious fervour of the colonizers. On the one hand, the small farms and stockaded settlements that were strung out along both banks of the St Lawrence River were constantly subject to Iroquois attacks, and therefore called for indefatigable courage among the colonizers; on the other, the early settlers were devoted to the task of converting those same Iroquois.[33] Hence the heroic age of the French colony, with its morally upright population (only one recorded illegitimate birth up to 1661, according to Groulx),[34] its courage, religious devotion, and commitment to clearing and cultivating the land. It was also a "racially" pure population (Groulx refuses to accept that there was a strong admixture of native blood in québécois veins) built on the strong peasant stock of western France, with certain elements of a more bourgeois and aristocratic origin.[35] The *habitant* was the ideal type of peasant virtue: "There was nothing in him of the half savage or half barbarian ... a hero, simple, ideal and courageous in make-up; a founder of a country and a race, a pioneer of civilization and faith with the dignity that goes with it. In the history of those early, heroic times, his bearing is rather like that which has been attributed to him in bronze. He needs to be visualized as having a demeanour characterized by faith and hard work, bare-headed under the broad expanse of sky, the bill-hook in one hand, and in the other, raising up the first sheaf of wheat to the Creator."[36]

The early colonists were devoted to the faith, to the land, to the family and to freedom.[37] Above all they were possessed of the French language, which – according to travellers from France – they spoke with an outstanding purity. Groulx asks whether the language is not their most priceless possession: "a wonderful cultural instrument, an element in their survival."[38] Behind that characterization of the heroic age is the idea that, with the colonization, a new race had come into being: "of all the events in human history, few are more precious in the eyes of God than the birth of races and peoples, vast spiritual organizations, so much a part of divine plans."[39]

Groulx's construction could hardly be closer to the portrayal of the Irish heroic past as the source from which the nation had sprung and whose potential would one day be realized through independence. In the Irish context the nation was also conceived of, in the spirit of the time, as a spiritual thing for which one could go to a martyr's death. Nationalism could thus be described as a "force" that might, in Corkery's words, flow from some historically datable event, or be something whose "origins will never be known, that we come upon ... as upon some natural thing – a torrent flowing headlong from the hidden recesses of crowded mountain ranges that never can be explored. Such a force therefore is not to be reckoned according to the extent of territory after which it is named; it is ... a quasi-spiritual essence."[40] In Ireland, too, language was considered to be the "soul of a nation," while the "three great forces of Irish national being" are held – by Corkery – to consist in the religious consciousness of the people, Irish nationalism, and the land.[41]

In both Ireland and Quebec the basic ingredients of nationalism as an overarching, ethnically constituted belief system constantly recur: the heroic past, religion, language, the destiny and purity of the "race," the land, and the family. There are also the personal qualities that are held up in defiance of the contempt of the politically dominant people: courage, virtue, pride, and loyalty. The central theme remains, however, the control of land. It is the vision of a united Ireland as a territorial unit that still underlies the hopes of Irish nationalism, and the fact of the Protestant presence in the North, the rock against which those hopes are continually dashed. Built into the idea of the land and the nation, according to Corkery, is the importance of locality: of Synge immersing himself in the Wicklow countryside or the Aran Islands and thereby breaking out of the framework of his Anglo-Irishness and becoming familiar with the "real" Ireland.[42] Allied to the question of locality is that of climate, with the French Canadian character – according to Groulx – being moulded by the harshness of the Canadian winter.[43]

There is thus something fundamentally irrational about nationalism, which is presumably what is meant by its being a "quasi-spiritual essence." At the same time, in its late nineteenth- and early twentieth-century form it is shot through with nostalgia for a pre-urban and less materialistic existence. It is in many ways close to nineteenth-century socialist utopianism, which equally rejects contemporary industrial, materialist society and casts that rejection in the form of a nostalgic evocation of a more rural past. There is in fact much common ground between, for example, William Morris's *News from Nowhere* and the mystical retelling of the legends of ancient and rural Ireland in Anglo-Irish literature. In both cases we detect a refusal to accept an existing social system, in the first on the grounds of class-based inequality and in the second on those of national oppression. Indeed, there are cases where class and nation weave in and out of each other in the rejection of the urban industrial present. When Synge returned to the Aran Islands after an absence of several years, he remarked: "As I sat down on my stool and lit my pipe with the corner of a sod, I could have cried out with the feeling of festivity that this return procured me."[44] For Corkery this is clear evidence that Synge was in close communication with the real Ireland, as are all his essays on the Aran Islands, whether it be a recollected voyage in heavy seas and in an open boat to Connemara, or the sight of a girl in a red Aran skirt sitting in a doorway. It was a similar closeness to the real Ireland that Corkery describes Synge as having felt on watching the men and women walking across the fields to mass on the Dingle peninsula within sight of the Atlantic and the Blasket Islands. Corkery refers to the "partly local and patriotic emotion that he felt among the people who were truly Irish."[45]

William Morris at a slightly earlier period felt the same immediacy and reality in the Oxfordshire countryside and, transporting that countryside into an idealized medieval future, made it the focal point of a voyage into an alternative society in which what is left of the towns has been invaded by the countryside, and the countryside itself is given over to festivals, harvest homes, and craft production.[46] The Romantics also felt it at an earlier period of industrialization, with Wordsworth's return to the Cumberland hills.[47] Groulx's clerical nationalism is equally a hymn to a rural golden age in which the rigours and high mortality of early colonial life are eclipsed by the virtue and heroism to which they gave rise. And it is no coincidence that his vision of that age was produced at a time of rapid industrialization and urbanization in Quebec, a process to which the Church was fundamentally opposed.

There is therefore a common theme running through the writings of William Morris, Lionel Groulx, and J.M. Synge that has nothing necessarily to do with nationalism, except in so far as the new urban industrial civilization is identifiable (as it was to a considerable extent in Ireland and Quebec) with an alien presence. That theme is expressed by Ruskin in *Unto This Last* and can be summed up as the rejection of the ugliness and brutality of industrial civilization combined with a nostalgia for rural life.[48] Thus, the festivity that Synge felt on lighting his pipe in the corner of an Aran cottage was not so much the joy of discovering the real Ireland but rather that of having escaped from a class-based urban society to find himself in the intimate, heated atmosphere of an Aran cottage. Here the past belonged to and was manipulated by the people themselves in the form of folksong and folktales, on an island where they wrung their livelihood from the arable patches of ground between the rocks and from the sea. It was the exact opposite of an alienated, urban middle-class existence with no direct contact with the past, no culturally creative practices in the present, and, perhaps more importantly, no direct involvement in the production of the necessities of life.

There are a number of different themes mixed together in the bits and pieces that go to make up nationalist thought on the one hand or a certain kind of socialist thought on the other. Nostalgia for the rural past and a passionate attachment to the rural present (normally accompanied by an unwillingness to give up the comforts of urban middle-class life for that same rural present) can have roots that have nothing necessarily to do with nationalism. In Quebec, for example, the rural past is still present in the ideology of nationalism, but it no longer plays the role that it played for Groulx. It is no longer the ideal alternative that haunts urban civilization but is rather the heroic beginning that preceded an industrial present that is equally heroic. In contemporary Quebec the promise of the past is in the process of being realized in a war of attrition against Canadian anglophone capital. The winning of the New York metro contract by Bombardier is as much grist for the mill of contemporary québécois nationalism as were the heroics of the early colonists. Nationalism is, however, an ideology of resistance, and the increasing self-confidence of francophone capital in the face of its competitors is presumably one of the reasons for the contemporary decline in evident nationalist sentiment, since its motive force in the recent past has come in large part from the ranks of a frustrated francophone bourgeoisie and petty bourgeoisie.

As in the case of all ethnically constituted belief systems, nationalism is linked to some form of political or economic condition, which in the case of nationalism means some form of external or internal threat or actual state of oppression. Ultimately it can only be understood in the context of the overall struggle to gain possession of the way in which society is explained, in order, in the case of nationalism, that the explanation advanced might have as its consequence the removal of the grounds for the explanation in the first place.

PART FOUR

Inequality and Pluralism: The Ethnicity of Class

CHAPTER SEVENTEEN

Structural Seclusion: Making Social Inequality Possible

In the various theoretical approaches to class and ethnicity, we can distinguish between class and ethnicity as analytical constructs that can help us to make sense of complex social structure, and class and ethnicity as ways in which participants in society consciously represent that society to themselves and act in accordance with that representation. This corresponds to the normal distinction between the analyst's construct and the cognitive perception of the actor, which Mitchell, for example, describes as being of "entirely different epistemological status."[1] In the case of Marxist approaches to class, however, the situation becomes complex. Here the distinction is not between analytical construction and cognitive perception, since it has been maintained from Marx onwards that class is neither the one nor the other. In other words, class is a reality in social structure and not just a construct placed on society by the analyst. By the same token it cannot be reduced to cognitive perception, inasmuch as the reality of class itself determines perception. From the Marxist point of view underlying both analysis and perception is the reality of class structure and class struggle. Alongside the more customary epistemological distinction is thus the Marxian one: class underlies social structure in pre-capitalist society and comes out into the open with capitalist relations of production. In the first case class would seem to be in the no-man's-land of being neither an analytical construct nor something that is perceived by agents in society, while in the second it passes into perception and comes to be – in E.P. Thompson's words – "present in the evidence."[2]

Whereas one might question the extent to which class is or is not an analytical construct for Marxists – and the wide range of theories of class within Marxism would suggest that it is not just the evident reality of class that surfaces within theory – there is also a problem with Mitchell's "entirely different epistemological status" of constructs and perceptions. In order to act consequentially, and perhaps even inconsequentially, in the world, we first need to have explained it, and any work of theory is simply that same explanation in a more controlled and rarified form, preceding or at least allowing for action. There is no place for a fundamental epistemological distinction between the explanation that the analyst pieces together as an acting analyst in the world and the explanations that the same analyst lives with as an acting non-analyst in the same world – that is, outside the laboratory or study. The form of the explanation might change, but the one is no less of an explanation than the other.

In approaching class in consciousness one needs, therefore, to make a threefold distinction between class in its standard sociological guise of analytical construct versus cognitive perception; in its Marxian form at the levels of structure and of consciousness; and in the more unitary context of explanation in general. The latter context also requires that one break down the distinction between actors and analysts. All actors analyse and all analysts act. In the case of class there is also the problem that on certain definitions of class (and notably the Marxian), one has to accept that class is itself determinant of the way one thinks about it. In setting out to understand class in consciousness one is, on those definitions, working within and from the perspective of an already existing consciousness that is itself determined by class. And this is apart from what is apparently the case in British class society, where class, on the terms presented above,[3] has its own ethnicity.

The role of the state in capitalist society is considered both from a pro- and an anti-capitalist standpoint to be to ensure the social stability and coherence that will allow capitalist enterprise to flourish.[4] Left to itself industrial capitalism has no such stability, nor can it ensure the security of property on which it depends and the reproduction of the forces and relations of production necessary for its survival. That is to say, it cannot fulfil those functions as capital, since stability, security, and the reproduction of forces and relations are not in themselves productive of surplus value but only help to establish the situation in which surplus value can be produced and appropriated. The state, therefore, as a fiscally based, non-capitalistic, bureaucratic, and coercive machine takes on those responsibilities. The principal enemy of the capitalist state as guarantor of the system is working-class and, to a lesser extent, petty bourgeois consciousness. Since the state has to maintain cohesion, it necessarily has to be preoccupied with the class divisions that threaten that cohesion.

Class divisions understood in a structural or analytical sense are not in themselves threatening to system-maintenance and are indeed essential to the system. They are only threatening in so far as they are accompanied by a consciousness of negative privilege (Weber) or of fundamental class opposition (Marx) that can give rise to political action. The focus of interest for both maintainers and defenders of the status quo is thus not so much class itself as the consciousness of class. To a certain extent, whether classes exist at all and what form they may take is not as important as what the mass of the people believe to be the case and the action they are likely to take in consequence of that belief. The aim, therefore, is not simply to produce the explanation of society that most closely approximates what is observed but to produce one that can serve as the vehicle for die-hard conservatism or radical opposition, as the case may be.

One of the central preoccupations of Marxist and non-Marxist theory is thus the way in which a politically organized working class comes or might come into existence and the way in which it might come to the consciousness of itself as a class, that consciousness being the precursor of political organization and action. Within Marxism it is maintained that the establishment of capitalist relations of production created the possibility of full class consciousness, not only because it brought together direct producers into densely populated industrial conurbations and therefore into contact with each other, but also because class came to be the explicit organizing principle on which society was based. Whereas previously society had been organized on the basis of kinship, estates, or vertically integrated power blocs (as in Swat),[5] and the consciousness that participants would have of those societies would have been principally constructed around those evident alignments, under industrial capitalism class becomes the evident organizing principle. That at least is the reason and the justification for Marx's holding that industrial capitalism creates the possibility for full class consciousness. In attempting to understand where their allegiance lies in capitalist society, the working class, confronted by the reality of class opposition, will necessarily come to a consciousness of class, which then, on both Weberian and Marxist terms, is liable to lead to political action. We need, therefore, to consider both the transition to full class consciousness and the transition from consciousness to action.

There is a distinction to be made between the ordinary consciousness that workers or others have of their class position, which accompanies and grows out of their experience as workers, and the consciousness they would have were they aware of the totality of the system in which they exist as a class. According to Lukács, it is only in the latter case that they come to a full consciousness of class in the Marxian sense, and it is only the proletariat that can come to an awareness of that totality and therefore to full class consciousness.[6] For Lukács, as the crisis of capitalism advances, so the nature and unity of the capitalist system becomes clearer and more comprehensible to the working class. Thus the point of full, revolutionary class consciousness on the part of that class – and as a result of it, the historically necessary passing of the capitalist order – comes nearer to being attained.[7]

There is a distinction maintained here between a working-class consciousness that is incomplete and pre-revolutionary and one that grasps the totality of the system in which it exists and will necessarily lead to the overthrow of that system. This gradually emerging understanding can be set alongside Thompson's description of the English working class, where that class does not continually make and unmake itself but rather gradually emerges in all its fullness out of the crucible of early nineteenth-century industrialization.[8] Lukács's distinction can also be compared to "class domains" as I have defined them,[9] inasmuch as the ordinary consciousness of class that necessarily arises as the result of being brought up in a class-divided society and that is constructed around the existence of class domains is distinguishable from the consciousness of what underlies those class domains.

But can the second arise from the first, and how? Peter Gutkind, for example, distinguishes between standard sociological class consciousness (that is, an awareness of different life-styles, income groups, and so on) and proletarian class consciousness, with only the latter necessarily leading to political consciousness and action.[10] But what does proletarian consciousness consist of in its incipient state if it is not an awareness of proletarian conditions of existence, or the characteristics of the working-class domain – in other words, of all the trappings of housing, income, working hours, and life-style of which sociologists are normally so fond, coupled with an awareness that other groups in society are not subject to those same conditions? One has evidently to distinguish between the awareness of proletarian conditions of existence that is necessarily the result of being brought up a proletarian and the awareness of those conditions of existence as "proletarian" – that is, as characteristic across society of a particular class standing in a relationship to other classes. But the question arises of the extent to which that second awareness results from an intellectual effort to grasp the nature of deeper class structure on the one hand or from working-class experience and struggle on the other.

That this is a false distinction, in that it suggests that working-class experience and struggle is not itself necessarily accompanied by the intellectual effort of understanding the system in which that struggle takes place, is reinforced by Matza and Wellman's study of the "ordeal of consciousness."[11] For them, working-class consciousness is the product of working-class experience, in particular the experience of being subject to the necessity of working to survive, to being disciplined, and to the lack of freedom of expression. The boredom of life on the production line creates ample opportunity for workers to reflect on the nature of class exploitation and to come to a consciousness of that exploitation. It is not the worker who has difficulty understanding the nature of profit.

This suggests that there is no clear distinction between the two levels of working-class consciousness. In so far as one is directly involved in production as a producer, whether as a subsistence agriculturalist, a share-cropping tenant, or an assembly-line worker, there is no dislocation between one's productive role and the understanding that one might have of that role. If, on Marxian terms, class is taken to be a relation of production, the working class is immediately involved in and confronted by that relationship in the day-to-day necessity of having to sell its labour-power to capital. The working-class domain is built around the immediate experience of class, or rather class, at the level of social structure, surfaces in daily working-class experience. It is thus that working-class ethnicity cannot conceal its basis in relations of production either from itself or from others, more particularly since it is the expression of the confraternity – or consorority – of workers within the process of production and in the working-class residential community. If we follow Lukács, therefore, and say that the working class necessarily comes to be conscious of the oppression to which it is subject,[12] in the terms of the present argument that is equivalent to saying that its ethnicity is directly expressive of that oppression. In the case of the bourgeoisie, however, the situation is different. If working-class consciousness is to some extent given in working-class experience, bourgeois class experience tends to obstruct the development of a clear consciousness of class,[13] to the point where we might imagine that those who dispense mystification in the form of the "nation"-state or the national "family" are precisely those who have the tendency to believe in it.

One aspect of self-mystified bourgeois consciousness is considered by Lewontin et al.[14] In their analysis, the eighteenth-century ideology of equality was essential for the transition from a system where wealth was based on aristocratic privilege and status to one where all capitalists (at least) were equal. The ideology that accompanied the French Revolution was primarily anti-aristocratic and for social equality among the bourgeoisie. It led, however, to the awkward situation in which other categories in society made political demands in the name of that same equality. Lewontin et al. suggest that bourgeois ideology has thus been forced to move to a position of biological determinism. According to this ideology, the rigid hierarchical structure of pre-capitalist society prevented the natural differences between individuals from coming out into the open, since birth established status. Under capitalist society, however, free or nearly free social mobility allows individuals to find their own levels according to their natural abilities or capacities, this process being made possible by a selective educational system. Inasmuch, therefore, as capitalist society allows individuals to find their "natural" levels, such a society is "natural" in precisely the way that pre-capitalist society was not. And if "natural" in dominant ideology is the equivalent of "proper" and "right," capitalist society finds its self-justification.

This is one aspect of a bourgeois class consciousness that has direct links with a past where ruling dynasties elevated themselves to divine status backed up by an elaborate mythology.[15] Indeed, if an overarching, ethnically constituted belief system – as in the case of multiculturalism in Canada – is the ideological cement of the nation-state, one could equally refer to the constant hammering home of the supernatural abilities of the capitalist hero (from chamber of commerce awards much publicized in the local press to knighthoods for export achievement) as the ideological basis for hierarchy under capitalism.

Bourgeois self-mystification, however, is as much based on the experience of class as is the consciousness of the working class. If, in the nineteenth century, the capitalist mill-owner tended to be personally involved in the running of his mill, and was thereby brought into daily contact with his work-force as the purchaser and consumer of their labour-power, that is now true only of small and marginal capitalist enterprises. Whereas in the nineteenth century typical capitalist entrepreneurs had direct experience of relations of production and of their place in those relations, they have now largely given way to professional administrators. That does not mean that they have ceased to exist, just that they have withdrawn into the back-rooms of finance capital or have restricted themselves to control at a distance in the form of majority or minority shareholding. Capitalists have thus removed themselves from the scene of production, but even their agents, who might be assignable – on Poulantzas' terms – to the bourgeoisie on the basis of their function,[16] tend to operate as controllers and directors of the production process only from the remoteness of the company or group head office. In broad terms, therefore, and with the exception of the small-scale entrepreneur, the bourgeoisie no longer has direct experience of relations of production but only experience that is mediated via the reports of company accountants or upper management. It is precisely that disloca-tion from the process of production that makes bourgeois self-mystification possible, just as the impossibility of the working class's dislocating itself from that same process prevents them from enjoying any comparable degree of mystification.

Whereas the proletarian condition is to be separated from the means of production and only to have access to those means on capital's terms, the bourgeois condition is thus increasingly to be separated from the process of production itself – whence the fundamental dislocation between the idea that the class has of itself, built around its ethnicity, and the reality of the relations of production that underlie that ethnicity. In the case of the old, established British bourgeoisie, and of all those categories in British society that have either served the interests of the bourgeoisie by providing profes-sional services or who have ancestral links with, and derive inherited finan-cial benefit from, nineteenth-century accumulators of capital, the dislocation is not just from the process of production but is also realized in residential terms. All these categories can be grouped together loosely under the non-Marxist term "upper middle class." This is a significant classification for the cognitive perception that participants have of British society and therefore the way in which they act in that society, but it also has some relationship to range of income and the ability to maintain a certain material standard of life.

Residential dislocation applies first within the neighbourhood itself. Whether they live in an upper-middle-class neighbourhood or, as is frequently the case, in one of the more picturesque houses in an urban satellite village, members of the upper middle class (as defined both by themselves and by others) have few links with the immediate community. In the village context communal contacts are generally restricted to ritualized class encounters, whereas in the upper-middle-class urban neighbourhood one might have some conversational contact with the neighbours in time of war, but more often than not neighbourly communication is via solicitors' letters. The real upper-middle-class "community" is based rather on professional associations, select church membership, and old-school networks, only the second of which creates certain links within the immediate residential community, but links that are restricted to a ritualized weekly display of respectability, material well-being, and piety.

The normal pattern of socialization for the upper-middle-class child is to be uprooted from such an environment and to be schooled expensively in some remote converted country house into upper-middle-class culture and expectations. Such children are thus dislocated from an environment in which their family is already living in a state of dislocation, and subsequently find themselves in one in which there are no ties whatsoever to the surrounding community. It is in these two dislocated environments that upper-middle-class children come to a consciousness of class and develop a sense of solidarity with fellow class members. And the upper-middle-class culture itself into which such children are socialized is also thoroughly dislocated and dislocating, inasmuch as the literature, music, history, and art thought fit for study are normally pre-1900 and preferably pre-1800, since the nineteenth century tends to give rise to awkward questions.

There is no aspect of upper-middle-class life in Britain, and of bourgeois or professional petty bourgeois experience, that can help the offspring of the upper middle class to locate themselves in relation to production. This is particularly so because direct involvement in production is held to be inappropriate behaviour for full upper-middle-class membership. Wealth is not considered to be something that is created in production, but rather, in the form of inherited capital, is the reward conferred by providence on ancestral virtue, or alternatively, in the form of high salaries or profits, is the just return gratefully yielded up by society for valued services. Being brought up in such a series of dislocated environments and within the framework of borrowed and suitably remote literatures and art-forms – more often than not created to entertain a pre-capitalist European monarchy – it is not surprising that upper-middle-class adolescents, on emerging into adulthood, find themselves in a state of more or less complete mystification. They have a thorough grasp and competent mastery of all the trappings of their class domain, but that domain is constructed around the masks and stage-settings specially created for the playing out of bourgeois mythology. The bourgeois or professional petty bourgeois child is thus brought up in a setting that is entirely removed from the scene of production and from any community of direct producers. It is precisely that dislocation that permits bourgeois self-mystification in the form, for example, of a self-flattering meritocratic belief system, as a way of "explaining" and "justifying" social inequality.

The working-class child, by contrast, is brought up in immediate contact with the reality of production and of relations of production. Those relations surface in the working-class domain, even if the localized nature of working-class experience can inhibit the development of a more historically and comparatively based understanding of class at the level of the social formation. Such an understanding is further inhibited by the fact that – as Weber points out – the working class finds itself in daily confrontation not so much with its real opponents, the capitalists, but with their local representatives in the form of works managers and supervisors.[17] Bourgeois or petty bourgeois absence from the scene of production can thereby help to inhibit the development of an awareness on the part of the working class of the exact nature of the classes to which they are opposed.

Each of the two principal opposed classes under capitalism is thus characterized by a particular kind of limited class consciousness: the bourgeoisie is conscious of itself as a class and acts in its own class interests, but only within the framework of a self-flattering mythology that substitutes itself for the reality of production relations; the working class is too close to that reality either to flatter or to deceive itself about its own relationship to production. But alongside these various forms of mystified or restricted class consciousness is the ability or otherwise to translate that consciousness into political association and action, and it is in that context that the bourgeoisie and the working class find themselves on entirely different planes.

Hobsbawm points out that even informal organization and action on the part of those categories in society who already have positions of authority has an effect altogether out of proportion to the numbers involved. He refers to the "modern professional strata" who oppose themselves to the "location of an airport, the routing of a motorway, or some other piece of administrative steam-rollering."[18] Where such pressure groups do not themselves control the levers of power, they know somebody who does. The working class, however, cannot get anything done other than by organizing on a vast scale. Nor can it organize in an informal way, as can professional pressure groups and letter-writers to the *Times*, but has to set up a complex, formal political organization that can overcome the problems of mobilizing at the base when all the channels of communication, administration, and finance run vertically rather than horizontally.[19]

The existence or otherwise of working-class consciousness is thus not the main issue, since that, to a certain extent, necessarily exists inasmuch as a working class exists. What is important are rather the avenues that are open to the working class to translate that consciousness into organization and action. And it is at that level that the system intervenes to inhibit trade-union development or prohibit working-class political organization. If, however, following Hobsbawm, the key question comes down to the immense problems of translating working-class consciousness into working-class political organization, one is brought to the conclusion that political organization is as problematic for that class as it was for pre-capitalist peasantries, and to a large extent for the same reasons. If an oppressed peasantry has some consciousness of itself as an oppressed class but has no way of translating that consciousness into political organization, being in a number of ways localized and brutalized, then there would seem to be certain fundamental similarities between that peasantry and the working class under capitalism. There would thus be a continuity in the experience and consciousness of class oppression, and in the difficulty of political organization at the base, from pre-capitalist to capitalist society. The difference between the two would not be one of kind but rather of degree, in that the amount of surplus value produced by contemporary working classes exceeds by many times what was remotely possible under pre-capitalist modes of production.

Class domains have a formative influence on consciousness, and inasmuch as those domains are a part of what class is, class determines consciousness. We can say, therefore, that class determines consciousness without our necessarily being fully conscious of class. At the same time I hold that those domains are ethnically constituted, in the sense that the "upper-middle-class" domain in Britain is none other than "upper-middle-class" ethnicity. This brings us to the relationship between class and ethnicity in the context of consciousness and action.

Whether from the Marxian or the Weberian point of view, relations of production or negatively and positively privileged property classes exist outside of and only occasionally within consciousness. They exist outside in that such classes exist whether people are aware of them or not according to the respective theories. And they exist within consciousness at the point where classes come to be aware of themselves, whether as the result of the development of capitalist relations of production (Marx) or at a moment of social clarity (Weber) when negatively privileged classes come to see through the normal opacity of social structure to the existence of negative or positive privilege.[20] Ethnicity, however, only exists within consciousness. That Scythian women put butter and Greek women perfumed oil on their hair is at one level only an ethnic distinction, in so far as Scythians and Greeks are conscious of it as such. But we are at liberty to say that ancient Greek versus Scythian ethnicity is inclusive of everything that Greeks as against Scythians were, or vice versa, and that therefore whatever cultural or other distinctions we might come up with are part of that inclusive ethnicity. In the case of English class domains, for example, everything is significant of the ethnicity of class, or, put another way, there is no aspect of upper-middle-class life and experience that has no part in the constitution of that ethnicity.

The relationship between the inclusive ethnicity of the domain and the ethnic boundary marker is thus an arbitrary one, in that any aspect of that domain can have a similar symbolic function, depending on context. Even given an all-inclusive approach to ethnicity, however, such an ethnicity can only exist within consciousness, in that it refers to the way in which groups define and identify themselves in relation to other groups. Ethnicity has no existence apart from that process of definition and identification. On this understanding ethnicity would refer to that area of consciousness in which individuals identify themselves as belonging to a particular ethnically definable group as against another. The differences on which ethnicity are based are thus objective differences that exist outside consciousness, as in the case of class, but their being perceived as "ethnic" is itself a question of consciousness.

The ethnically constituted class domain, within which children are brought up in class society, is the foundation on which they construct their social identity. It is on the basis of that perceived or constructed identity that children, and eventually adults, act, and prior to and along with that action attempt to understand and explain society to themselves sufficiently to be able to act rationally and consequentially in it. On this understanding class informs identity, explanation, and action via an ethnicity that may itself serve to reveal class as a relation of production – as in the case of the working class – or conceal it – as in that of the bourgeoisie.

A key moment in the maintenance or the transformation of an existing social system remains that at which consciousness translates itself into action. The state, as system stabilizer and protector, is required to take a particular interest in the prevention of such action, and in its containment should it break out. It is a priority of the state to explain society so as to make potentially transformative action less likely, thereby avoiding the expensive and generally counter-productive brutality of repression. The real battleground in society, therefore, between defenders and assailants of the status quo, is at the level of explanation. Explanation precedes action, and violent protest on the streets, or the institutionalized violence of the state that can give rise to such protest, is only the logical result of a particular kind of explanatory process. It is in this context that class and ethnicity, as explanations, have such potential for encouraging or restraining group action. Both refer to groups that are definable in opposition to other groups. Class – in its Marxian definition – refers to categories in society whose interests are opposed, while ethnicity refers to groups that are identifiably and visibly differentiated. As long as these two factors can be kept apart, then the lack of visibility of class and the apparent dislocation of ethnicity from production relations prevent either of them from becoming ways in which opposed categories in society can both understand the material basis of that opposition and identify the groups so opposed at the level of appearances.

In any established class society, however, there is the inevitable Weberian tendency of classes to mark out the particular niches they occupy in ethnic terms, in which the sense of "brotherhood" that accompanies association within the class comes increasingly to constitute a class-based ethnicity, which is reinforced when subsequent generations are brought up within the semi-closed class environment.[21] A class-divided society thus inevitably gives rise to an ethnically divided society, inasmuch as class privileges have to be protected through monopolistic closure made possible by ethnic labelling. All the ethnic attributes of class follow from the existence of class: class dialects, residential practices, education, culture, and patterns of consumption. Hence class relations have the inevitable tendency to become visible, in that the material inequality that follows from such relations is by definition visible inequality, even if the relations themselves are not. Alongside the increasing contradiction between classes in relations of production, and between the state and its citizenry, there is therefore the increasingly visible contradiction of the material inequality of class.

The combination of class and ethnicity is thus present in such societies, with all the threat that that poses for the state. One factor that prevents that combination from becoming an explosive one is that the greater the degree of material inequality, the more it can come to be hidden from view in select neighbourhoods, clubs, expensive hotels, and private schools. This is one of the reasons why the necessary visibility of material inequality – and therefore class – is not translated into open class struggle. The very privacy that makes the existence of private property in the means of production possible is also backed up by limitations on what people can be conscious of. Our normal operational consciousness is built around familiar social and physical environments, and we learn, through socialization into those environments, of the kinds of statuses we will occupy and the various role-expectations that are associated with those statuses. We thus come to "take our place" in a ready-made social environment. But we live up to those expectations and occupy those statuses in a series of known physical environments. Our ordinary, operational consciousness is restricted to our residential and occupational class domains. What happens outside those domains or in other domains remains largely unknown to us. We can be "class conscious," inasmuch as our consciousness is determined by our class, and yet remain in a state of ignorance of what it might mean to belong – in Weberian terms – to a more negatively or positively privileged class. We seldom go into other class neighbourhoods, let alone houses, and only meet members of other classes in ritualized encounters. And even if we succeed in penetrating into such neighbourhoods, it is difficult to visualize the sort of life that is led in them other than by transposing the life that one is familiar with into that environment. Privileged minorities can thus be said to have class consciousness on their side, inasmuch as nobody can ever be really conscious of what it means to belong to another class.

All this reflects the Weberian notion of the opacity of social structure,[22] which is not so much a question of its complexity or of the difficulty of understanding how the different classes relate to production but simply of concealment and non-visibility. We cannot extend our consciousness to include all those areas with which we are unfamiliar. It also suggests that the celebrated "English" ethnicity, which consists in an almost paranoid defensiveness and unwillingness to open up oneself and one's private life to the threatening intimacy of friendship, is a key element of upper-middle-class ethnicity. It is the equivalent, at the level of behaviour, of the structural seclusion and privacy of the upper-middle-class domain. Members of the English upper middle class have simply too much to lose in terms of material and social privileges to be able to operate on anything other than the defensive, unless they are dealing with someone of similar class status. The more visible, therefore, class becomes, the more opaque social structure is required to be in order to prevent the coming into existence of a consciousness of what class means in terms of material and social inequality on the part of those who are debarred from the privileges arising out of the existence of class. Should that opacity be allowed to clear, then open class struggle (following Weber) can develop.

Where different classes live and work in different physical and social environments and where material and social inequality is largely concealed from view within those environments, the need to explain away the inequality is correspondingly reduced. In so far as there is some intrusion of one environment on another, however, privileged classes can always console themselves either by seeing their privileges as having been merited

– through biological determinism or simply successful performance according to dominant values – or by believing themselves to have been singled out by providence for special treatment. Negatively privileged classes, by contrast, tend to be reduced to believing in their own bad luck and to cherishing the hope that luck might turn in their favour with some help from the state lottery or the football pools, while generally encouraging themselves with the belief that present injustices will be righted with the transformation of the present system or, failing that, in the life to come. Material inequality translated on to the ideological plane, therefore, can come to be seen in terms of merit or luck, depending on which side one is looking from, but neither the one nor the other in themselves call the existence of that inequality into question.

Ethnically constituted class domains become increasingly complex the longer capitalist relations of production are maintained. They are not, however, just the by-product of those relations of production but represent the form that relations of production take outside the process of production. The relationship between class domains, however ritualized, formalized, and distorted, is still a relationship between classes. Those domains are the framework that makes the reproduction of existing relations of production possible, or, put another way, they guarantee that reproduction quite as much as does any ideological apparatus of the state. Ethnically constituted class domains mystify and conceal the very relations of production they stand for, as well as rendering material inequality largely invisible, where that invisibility is not already guaranteed at the level of normal operational inhibitions on consciousness. But they also guarantee the production of personnel who are already socialized into particular class environments and who emerge from that process of socialization ready to "take their place" in the various preordained positions that are ready for them. The work-force and the various agents and administrators of capital, as well as the apprentice capitalists themselves, already emerge on to the labour- or money-market "thinking" class and ready to take up their particular class positions. That process of preparation and socialization is largely attributable to the ethnic constitution of the class domain. Ethnically constituted class domains thus guarantee the supply of a work-force that is not only socialized to accept class relations of production as normal but already carries the class labels that enable the individuals concerned to be assigned to their place in production. The reproduction of those production relations is thus dependent on the ethnically constituted class domain as a primary ideological apparatus.

CHAPTER EIGHTEEN

The Tangled Foliage

In the pursuit of an adequate social explanation of the phenomena referred to in different theoretical contexts by the concepts of class and ethnicity, I start out from two basic principles: the specificity of concepts within theoretical systems, and the specificity of phenomena within social systems. According to the first principle, a given concept only means something in the context of the theoretical system wherein it was formulated. It is as impossible to produce hybrid concepts of different theoretical origins as it is to blend theoretical systems.

The importance of this principle is evident in relation to class. In each of the four principal theoretical systems that were considered in the opening chapters of this book, the Marxian, Weberian, Parsonian, and Dahrendorfian, class means something different. This necessarily places constraints on any discourse concerning society that uses the concept class. Within a given theoretical tradition, that of Marxism, for example, the problem is to some extent resolved, since class can come to be one of the central concepts within the tradition. In such a case there is the possibility of arguing about the same thing even if there may be considerable latitude for disagreement over what exactly the concept refers to in the world and whether it should be understood primarily in an empirical or an abstract frame of reference. Indeed, a theoretical tradition is in many ways nothing more than a continual and gradual redefinition of an agreed set of core concepts.

In non-Marxist theory, however, class is far from being a central concept. In two of the three representative theoretical systems that I have chosen, the Weberian and the Parsonian, it tends to have the status of an awkward irrelevance, hanging about on the edge of the analysis as a relatively inconvenient way of bundling similarly situated people into the same category. The really generative factors are elsewhere, in the domain of values, action, and rationality. Dahrendorf is as much opposed to the

Marxian concept of class as Weber and Parsons are – even if he pretends not to be so. Rather than marginalizing class as a useful concept, however, he converts it into the core concept in his theoretical system, but in a way that has little to do with the Marxian usage.

The debate over the relative significance of the concepts of class and ethnicity, therefore, starts out from bases that tend to lead to confusion rather than clarity. On the one side, in the Marxian tradition, class means one thing, and on the other, in the non-Marxist, it means a multitude of different things. Among those who dismiss class as of no great importance in the attempt to understand ethnicity – which is what most non-Marxist accounts do – it is by no means clear what is being dismissed. Where class does come to be central in such accounts, as in the case of Porter's *Vertical Mosaic*, the "Marxian" concept of class that is set up to be summarily dismissed bears little resemblance to what is normally understood by class within the Marxist tradition. Porter concludes the subsection on Marx with the statement: "In the nineteenth century it may have been the case that two groups classified by the criterion of owning or not owning property were sociological groups, but in the present day such classes are statistical categories and nothing more."[1] This is a clear example of the attempt to incorporate a concept into an alien theoretical system. Within the context of the Marxian theoretical system, class cannot be a statistical category since it is constructed around the idea of opposition and relationship. Classes for Marx do not exist in isolation from other classes but in relationship to them and in relation to the production process. Above all, in the Marxian system, class is a central, dynamic concept. It is held to stand for phenomena that exist at the very core of social processes and that are independent of the will of individuals, be they actors in those processes or academic observers of them, to decide whether they exist or not.

The same point could be made in reverse in the case of ethnicity. In dismissing ethnicity as the mask behind which relations of class-based exploitation conceal their real identity, Marxists ride roughshod over the various primordialists, boundary theorists, and idealists who have carefully made ethnicity into the pivot around which all social relationships revolve. There is really no way in which the argument can be joined as long as concepts are allowed to float around from one theoretical system to another. We need to construct coherent theoretical systems that stand in clearly defined relationships to existing theoretical systems and that can then be let loose as alternative ways in which social reality can be understood.

This can stand as the first principle: one cannot dismiss a concept without taking into consideration the theoretical system in which it has meaning and, if necessary, dismissing the system, or at least that part of it in which the concept is to be found. Equally, if one takes over a concept from an existing theoretical system, as Dahrendorf claims to do in the case of the Marxian concept of class, without bringing either the system or that part of the system that serves to define the concept with it, then one has not really taken over a concept at all. One has simply created a new concept in a new system and sent it out into the world under an old name. If we are to formulate a theory in which class in the Marxian sense and ethnicity are to be related to each other, we need to have a concept of ethnicity that fits into the Marxian theoretical system, or that version of it that we choose to adopt. We can thereby avoid the error that is frequently made in non-Marxist discussions of class, in which a parody of what one thinks is meant by class in the Marxian tradition is constructed in such a way that no sooner has it been stood up than it falls down as a result of lack of encompassing theoretical support.

If we need to respect the integrity of theoretical systems, we also need to respect the integrity of social systems. Two kinds of specificity need to be taken into account. First, the phenomena we are attempting to explain are specific to a given society and at one level can only be understood within the context of that society. Second, those phenomena are specific to a particular type of society, and at another level can only be understood in the context of that particular social type. This is a position that is common to both Marx and Weber. Weber draws attention to the need to develop ideal type concepts – such as feudalism – in order to situate a given society under study within the range of different types of society and to begin to get an understanding of its basic operating principles.[2] At the same time he emphasizes that a real, historical society can never be deduced from an ideal type. All societies are unique, and subsequent to seeing a society as belonging to a particular social type, we have to proceed to understand it in all its historical or, in Weberian terms, "cultural" uniqueness. The same point is made within the Marxist tradition. We have first to place a society within the range of different social types characterized by different modes of production and then to arrive at a precise understanding of the individual society at a particular historical moment.

We need, therefore, to devise a theoretical model that respects these two kinds of specificity. For example, we may be able to study a whole range of societies from a Marxist perspective and decide that in many if not most there are opposed categories of persons that we choose to describe as classes. At the same time, we discover that all observable or knowable societies can be grouped into distinct social types and that the various phenomena that are to be found in such societies – including class – have to be understood primarily with reference to the type of society in which they are to be found. But within a given type of society the actual forms that class takes at any given moment can vary according to historical circumstances, and it is only through the empirical study of individual societies within the context of the social type to which those societies belong that we can understand what class means in those societies.

This suggests two priorities if we are to understand and explain social phenomena. We have first to be clear about the different types of society. In other words, we have to have a theory of social types that can provide us with the framework in which we can set about understanding phenomena. A large part of sociological explanation is devoted to arguing what the range of social types really is. Depending on the tradition in which one is operating, a given society might be feudal, proto-feudal, post-capitalist, industrial, underdeveloped, plural, slave, primitive communist, hunter-gatherer, late capitalist, complex, compound, primitive, subsistence-oriented, transhumant pastoralist, urbanized, peasant, Third World, marginal, multicultural, or be described in a variety of other ways. What-ever way we choose to describe it obliges us to see it as belonging to a particular social type opposed to one or more other types within a given general theory of social types. And whichever general theory we choose to follow will oblige us to see the social phenomena we are looking at in certain specific ways.

In order to respect the specificity of phenomena to certain social types, we have therefore to have some idea what those social types are. But in order to understand phenomena within the context of a given society we also have to have a close empirical knowledge of the society in question, or at least that part of it that bears on the phenomena we are looking at. Here is the interface between general theory and empirical practice. In the context of the debate within Marxism over what class means, for example, it is clear that on the one hand there is the tendency to sacrifice close, empirical knowledge of individual societies for the sake of "improv-ing" the general theory (as in the case of Hindess and Hirst),[3] while on the other general theory is abandoned in the attempt to communicate what was going on at a given moment in the history of a particular society (Thompson).[4] In order to understand ethnicity and class, or any other phenomena, therefore, we need to respect these two specificities, the theoretical and the social. Ethnicity is a case in point. If ethnicity is generally definable as the way in which opposed groups either within societies or across societal boundaries identify themselves and each other, or alterna-tively as the sum total of the life-styles and cultural practices of the group, then it is clear that we can only hope to understand the nature of those ethnicities at a given social moment by looking at the type or types of society in question as well as the precise characteristics of the particular moment in time we are seeking to understand.

For example, traditional Scottish Highland ethnicity in the sense of a total identity can be broken down into the variety of social, productive, and cultural practices that distinguished Highlanders from those with whom they came into contact. Any given cultural phenomenon that is considered to have been a component part of that ethnicity can only be understood as part of the whole. Gaelic "waulking" songs, for instance, are the reflection of a society that produced its own material necessities of life and did so in a collective way. Even if the plots of land in post-Clearance Highland society – that is, in the marginalized and fragmented coastal and island communities left behind after the Clearances – were held by individual family units, much of the work was done collectively, whether working the cloth, lifting the peat, or clipping the sheep. The working song was thus frequently the expression of collective work-patterns in a subsistence-oriented community. But it was also the vehicle for handing on the traditional information necessary to do the work, or simply for handing on traditional stories or the recollection of critical moments in the life of the community (typically drownings, massacres, or emigration to Canada in the case of the Outer Hebrides). In all such songs there is a close relationship between the song and the work, both the rhythm and the length of the song being dictated by and dictating the rhythm and length of the work.[5] Highland working songs are thus "explicable" in the context of a subsistence-oriented society heavily dependent on collective work patterns for survival in a hostile environment. But they are also explicable in terms of the precise historical context that particular society had arrived at as a result of forced emigration, the decline in Gaelic speaking, and the falling away of the traditional clan solidarities.

There is thus a close and necessary link among social type, historical moment, and the nature of the phenomena that are to be observed. We might think that this goes without saying, but part of the confusion over the understanding of the significance of ethnicity in contemporary industrial societies results precisely from a failure to respect these specificities. The problem lies in the nature of ethnicity itself, since it draws on a variety of factors to signal difference, many of which may relate to cultural practices that pre-date the arrival of the group in the society in question. Ethnicity can easily be explained in the light of origins and of the survival of patterns of behaviour that had their *raison d'être* in different social systems. That Gaelic working songs may still be sung at Scottish evenings in London, Boston, or Toronto, or elsewhere is held to be a sign of remarkable cultural longevity and, at another level, of the richness of cultural and ethnic diversity that is to be found in contemporary industrial societies.

A Marxist theory of social types can provide a different bearing on the problem of ethnicity. According to Marxist theory, contemporary advanced capitalist societies are examples of a highly specific and historically localizable social type. We can only come to a satisfactory explanation of class and ethnicity as phenomena in such societies by setting them within the context of that social type and within that of the specific example of the type that we happen to be looking at. We could, of course, follow a different theoretical system, the Weberian or the Dahrendorfian, for example, and come up with an alternative account of ethnicity (in terms of the theory in question). It is a question of choice, depending on our interests in following one theoretical system rather than another.

Contemporary industrial capitalist societies are increasingly part of an integrated world economy in which peoples at different levels of consumption are characterized more by uniformity than by difference. Given a certain level of income, the car I drive, the work I do, the language I speak, the television programs I watch, the clothes I wear, the opinions I have, the holidays I go on, the food I eat all tend towards a uniformity imposed by the globalization of a particular kind of production and consumption controlled by a diminishing number of giant supernational corporations. If ethnicity is the expression of difference, then in the world context and at the same socio-economic level ethnic distinctions are becoming a thing of the past. What does it mean, therefore, to see ethnicity as an emergent phenomenon in Britain; as having unexpected powers of survival in the United States; as being a part – in the form of ethnic pluralism – of a supposedly distinctive Canadian identity? If we say that ethnicity is linked with difference, then how is it, in an increasingly uniform world, that ethnicity still seems to be important as a way in which collective identities are expressed?

If we start out from the link between ethnicity and difference, then the survival of ethnicity in contemporary industrial societies means the survival of difference within those societies. In spite, therefore, of the apparent uniformity of consumption patterns within such societies and across them, we are still in the presence of real social difference. Within the framework of Marxist theory there is only one area in which real social differences are not only being generated but intensified in such societies – the area of social inequality. It is self-evident – that is, within the context of the theory – that contemporary capitalist production starts out from the historical premise of inequality (and therefore of difference) in terms of the possession of property in the means of production, and serves to intensify that inequality via the unequal distribution of the wealth produced. Inequality of result can only be intensified in a system that accords a higher percentage of the wealth that is collectively created to one-quarter of the population than to the other three-quarters. We thus participate in a system that intensifies uniformity within similarly placed class brackets (again in terms of the theory) across a whole range of societies, and at the same time intensifies difference between different categories of the population who find themselves differently situated with respect to the production and the distribution of wealth and the necessities of life.

Ethnicity in established industrial capitalist societies is thus not so much the expression of primordial identities, regionalisms, linguistic differences, or differences in way of life (understood as the way in which different human groups maintain themselves in existence) but the expression of social inequality. In established capitalist societies, class relationships and the different patterns of consumption to which they give rise generate the collective awareness and articulation of difference that I have referred to in preceding chapters as the ethnicity of class. In North American society, where different waves of immigrants have found themselves contained within particular class brackets, the inequality and therefore the difference generated by the system and to which they are subject comes to be symbolized by the various visible, religious, linguistic, or cultural markers that they have brought with them.

In the light of this explanation, contemporary ethnic pluralism is none other than the pluralism of social inequality in the context of an inegalitarian system of wealth distribution. Long-term ethnic distinctiveness in such societies is thus the emergence of class inequality on to the stage where social collectivities identify themselves in relation to each other. Ethnicity as a system-specific phenomenon in contemporary advanced capitalist societies is not the expression of distinct cultural heritages nor of primordial ethnic identities but of the inequalities generated within those societies. In this theoretical formulation ethnicity is not the mask that conceals class, nor an alternative to class as the basic explanatory concept, but an integral part of class: the luxuriant, tangled foliage that both conceals and reveals, nourishes and is nourished by its roots, and is thus part and parcel of the plant.

Not only are contemporary capitalist societies of a highly specific type in the range of historically known social types, but the age-old phenomenon of ethnic identification and allegiance takes on a specific form in such societies. If one of the clearest examples of that phenomenon is to be found in British ethnically constituted class domains, given that Britain constitutes the longest-running example of industrial capitalism, it is clear that any emerging capitalist society conforms relatively quickly to the same pattern. In the case of industrial-capitalist societies characterized by high levels of immigration, such as Canada and the United States, and particularly where immigrant groups have been brought in to occupy particular class levels, this theoretical position would require us to see two phases: first, the phase in which the pre-existing ethnic identities of labour migrants are brought up against or coincide with the ethnically constituted class boundaries in the new society, and in which the old ethnic identities of the migrants can appear to predominate; and second, the phase in which the gradually evolving ethnicity of class within the new society imposes itself over such pre-existing ethnic identities in the second and third generations. If, as is frequently the case, the descendants of the original immigrants find themselves collectively contained over time within particular class brackets, then some of the old trappings of the distinctive ethnicity of the first generation can re-emerge in the foliage of a new ethnicity – in the form of language revivalism, for example. But the meaning of that new ethnicity is different from the old, and can only be grasped within the context of the specific social type within which it emerges. It is not so much a question of the richness of difference as of the pluralism of increasingly divergent standards of living.

Notes

1 Weber, "'Objectivity' in Social Science," 100.
2 Below, chap. 3.
3 See the discussion below, chap. 4.
4 Weber, "'Objectivity' in Social Science," 61.
5 Parsons, "A Revised Analytical Approach," 121. See also K. Davis and W.E. Moore, "Some Principles of Stratification," *American Sociological Review* 10 (1945): 247, for a clear statement from a functionalist, meritocratic point of view concerning the "problem" of inherited wealth.
6 Dahrendorf is at times more explicitly supportive of social inequality than at others (see Dahrendorf, *Life Chances*, passim).

1 Marx and Engels, *Die deutsche ideologie*, 18ff.
2 Marx, *Einleitung*, 631–9.
3 The following argument is based on Marx, *Das Kapital*, Band 1, chaps. 1–4.
4 Marx, *Einleitung*, 631–9.
5 Marx, *Das Kapital*, Band 1, chap. 5 and following chapters.
6 Ibid., 701 and 704, and Marx and Engels, *Manifest*, 472. In the brief unfinished section on social class in volume 3 of *Capital*, Marx refers to the three principal classes under then contemporary English capitalism as being composed of landowners, capitalists, and wage-workers respectively (*Grundeigentumer, Kapitalisten, Lohnarbeiter* 892). It is to be noted that in late nineteenth-century usage, "middle class" normally referred to the manufacturing class as opposed to the landowners on the one hand and the working class on the other (see Arnold, *Culture and Anarchy*, for the dis-

tinction between "upper," "middle," and "working" class). In any discussion of the use by Marx of the concept "class," one has to be wary of the pitfalls of translation. *Mittelstände*, for example, literally "middle-status groups," is at times translated "middle classes" (see Marx, *Capital*, vol. 1, 847n), while at ibid., 303, where the English translation refers to the alliances made by *workers* with other *classes in society* (my italics), the original refers to the alliances made by the *Arbeiterklasse* ("working class") with other *Gesellschaftschichten* ("social strata"; German version, 313). The translation thus succeeds in turning Marx's original sentence upside down!

7 Marx, *Das Kapital*, Band 1, 683.
8 Marx, *Capital*, vol. 1, 794ff.
9 Ibid., 319–20.
10 Ibid., 817.
11 Marx and Engels, *Manifest*.
12 Marx, *The Eighteenth Brumaire*.
13 "Die Mittelstände, der kleine Industrielle, der kleine Kaufmann, der Handwerker, der Bauer, sie alle bekämpfen die Bourgeoisie, um ihre Existenz als Mittelstände vor dem Untergang zu sichern" (Marx and Engels, *Manifest*, 472; my translation).
14 Marx, *The Eighteenth Brumaire*, 149.
15 "Insofern Millionen von Familien unter ökonomischen Existenzbedingungen leben, die ihre Lebensweise, ihre Interessen und ihre Bildung von den andern Klassen trennen und ihnen feindlich gegenüberstellen, bilden sie eine Klasse. Insofern ein nur lokaler Zusammenhang unter den Parzellenbauern besteht, die Dieselbigkeit ihrer Interessen keine Gemeinsamkeit, keine nationale Verbindung und keine politische Organisation unter ihnen erzeugt, bilden sie keine Klasse" (Marx, *Der achtzehnte Brumaire*, 198: my translation).
16 Marx, *Das Kapital*, Band 1, 723.
17 Marx, *Capital*, vol. 3, 814ff.
18 Cf. Marx and Engels, *Manifest*, passim.
19 Marx, *Der achtzehnte Brumaire*, 198.

CHAPTER THREE: CLASS IN WEBER

1 Weber, *Wirtschaft und Gesellschaft* (English translation: *Economy and Society*).
2 Weber, *Economy and Society*, 24.
3 Weber, *Economy and Society*, 8.
4 Weber, *Economy and Society*, 5–6.
5 "For the subjective interpretation of action in sociological work these collectivities must be treated as *solely* the resultants and modes of organization of the particular acts of individual persons" (ibid., 13–14).
6 Ibid., chap. 2, part 3.

7 Ibid., 63ff.
8 Weber, *Wirtschaft und Gesellschaft*, 78 (*Economy and Society*, 138).
9 Weber, *Economy and Society*, 882.
10 Ibid., 337.
11 Ibid., 224.
12 Ibid., 212ff.
13 Ibid., 224. For Weber's theory of bureaucracy, see further below, chap. 13.
14 Weber, *Economy and Society*, 611ff. and 1158ff.
15 Ibid., 481ff and 630.
16 Ibid., 486ff.
17 Ibid., 611ff, 506, 477–80.
18 Ibid., 302ff.
19 Ibid., 302ff.
20 Ibid., chap. 2, part 2.
21 Ibid., 302ff.
22 Ibid., 304–5.
23 "Die Gesamtheit derjenigen Klassenlagen ... zwischen denen ein Wechsel (a) persönlich, (b) in der Generationfolge, leicht möglich ist und typisch stattzufinden pflegt" (Weber, *Wirtschaft und Gesellschaft*, 179; my translation).
24 Weber, *Wirtschaft und Gesellschaft*, 179 (*Economy and Society*, 305). What is translated in the English version as the "working class as a whole" is, in the original, "die Arbeiterschaft als Ganzes," "the collectivity of workers as a whole".
25 Weber, *Economy and Society*, 927.
26 Ibid., 305ff.
27 Ibid., 929.
28 Ibid., 931ff.
29 Ibid., 929.
30 Ibid., 928.
31 Ibid., 635.
32 Cf. H.J.S. Maine, *Ancient Law* (1861; London: Murray 1924), 174.

CHAPTER FOUR: CLASS IN
NON-MARXIST SOCIAL SCIENCE

1 Parsons, *The Social System*, chap. 1.
2 Weber, *Economy and Society*, 24.
3 Parsons, *The Social System*, 24ff and 249ff.
4 On the "personality system," the "social system," and the "cultural system" see Parsons, *The Social System*, chap. 12.
5 Ibid., chap. 7 and 480ff.

6 Ibid., chap. 10.

7 Ibid., 68ff.

8 Ibid., chap. 5.

9 Parsons, "A Revised Analytical Approach," 124.

10 Ibid., 95.

11 Ibid., 109.

12 Ibid., 97.

13 Ibid., 98.

14 Ibid., 106.

15 "Its place [that of inherited wealth] in the upper reaches of the system, including what is ordinarily called the upper middle class is ... undoubtedly worthy of more careful study than it has yet received" (ibid., 121).

16 Ibid., 120.

17 Dahrendorf, "Homo sociologicus."

18 Dahrendorf, "On the Origin of Inequality," 151.

19 Ibid., 151.

20 Dahrendorf, *Class and Class Conflict*, 36.

21 Ibid., 42.

22 Ibid., 57.

23 Ibid., 217–28.

24 Parsons, "A Revised Analytical Approach," 123–4.

25 "All that we can infer from what patchy data we have is what anybody living in a modern society can observe for himself, in post-capitalist societies there is a great deal of movement, upwards and downwards as well as on one social level, between generations as well as within them, so that the individual who stays at his place of birth and in the occupation of his father throughout his life has become a rare exception" (Dahrendorf, *Class and Class Conflict*, 59).

26 Ibid., 205.

27 Weber, *Wirtschaft und Gesellschaft*, 171 (*Economy and Society*, 292).

28 Dahrendorf, *Class and Class Conflict*, 142–3 and 248ff.

29 Ibid., 149.

30 Although what is at stake in the conflict between "classes" – in Dahrendorf's terms – in a chess club is of an entirely different order from that in an industrial enterprise, he none the less places these two forms of association at either end of the same continuum of "class" conflict (ibid., 211–12).

31 Ibid., 201–2 and 213ff.

32 Ibid., 276.

33 See Max Gluckman, *Custom and Conflict in Africa*, (Oxford: Blackwell 1956), and Lewis Coser, *The Functions of Social Conflict*, (Glencoe: Free Press 1956).

34 Marx and Engels, *Manifest*, 459ff.

35 Dahrendorf, *Class and Class Conflict*, 124.
36 "In the present context, all structural changes will be understood as changes involving the personnel of positions of domination in imperatively coordinated associations" (ibid., 231).
37 Ibid., 220.
38 I use "Marxian" to refer to Marx's own theory of society and the concepts of which that theory is composed, while "Marxist" refers to that body of thought that explicitly or implicitly derives its principal inspiration from the work of Marx.

CHAPTER FIVE:
CLASS IN CONTEMPORARY MARXISM

1 Thompson, *The Making*, 9.
2 Ibid., 11. See Thompson, *The Poverty of Theory*, 238, where he defines class as a "self-defining historical formation, which men and women make out of their own experience of struggle."
3 Thompson, *The Poverty of Theory*, 196ff.
4 Thompson, *The Making*, chap. 10, part 2.
5 "What Miliband avoids is the necessary preliminary of a critique of the notion of élite in the light of the scientific concepts of Marxist theory. Had this critique been made, it would have been evident that the "concrete reality" concealed by the notion of "plural élites" – the ruling class, the fractions of this class, the hegemonic class, the governing class, the state apparatus – can only be grasped if the very notion of élite is rejected. For concepts and notions are never innocent, and by employing the notions of the adversary to reply to him, one legitimizes them and permits their persistence. Every notion or concept only has meaning within a whole theoretical problematic that founds it." (Poulantzas, "The Problem of the Capitalist State," 70).
6 The following account of Miliband's position is based on Miliband, *The State in Capitalist Society* and "Poulantzas and the Capitalist State."
7 Miliband, *The State*, chaps. 2 and 3.
8 Aron, "La Classe comme représentation."
9 Westergaard and Resler, *Class in a Capitalist Society*.
10 Ibid., 249.
11 Ibid., 58ff.
12 Ibid., 74.
13 Ibid., 116.
14 Ibid., 297ff.
15 Poulantzas, *Les Classes sociales*, 207ff.
16 Ibid., 11–12.
17 Ibid., 192, and "The Problem," passim.

18 Ibid., 35ff.
19 "Bourgeoisie intérieure" (ibid., 48ff).
20 Ibid., 207ff.
21 Ibid., 226, 231.
22 Ibid., 248, 257.
23 Weber, *Economy and Society*, 956ff.
24 Poulantzas, *Les Classes sociales*, 10.
25 Wright, "Class Boundaries," 10–11 and 24.
26 Poulantzas, *Les Classes sociales*, 207ff., 325ff.
27 Wright, "Class Boundaries," 24.
28 Ibid., 15, referring to Karl Marx, *Capital* (London: Penguin Books 1976), 644.
29 Wright, "Class Boundaries," 30.
30 Ibid., 28ff.
31 Ibid., 25ff.
32 "It matters a great deal for our understanding of class struggle and social change exactly how classes are conceptualized and which categories of social positions are placed in which classes. Above all, it matters for developing a viable socialist politics how narrow or broad the working class is seen to be and how its relationships to other classes is understood" (ibid., 3–4).
33 Rey, *Les Alliances de classes*, 171ff.

CHAPTER SIX: ETHNICITY IN
NON-MARXIST THEORY

1 Bell, "Ethnicity and Social Change," 156–7.
2 "Unter Bedingungen geringer Verbreitung rational versachtlichen Gesell-schaftshandelns attrahiert fast jede, auch eine rein rational geschaffene, Vergesellschaftung ein übergreifendes Gemeinschafts-bewußtsein in der Form einer persönlichen Verbrüderung auf der Basis 'ethnischen' Gemein-samkeitsglaubens" (Weber, *Wirtschaft und Gesellschaft*, 219; my translation).
3 Weber, *Economy and Society*, 390.
4 Ibid., 395.
5 Ibid., 388.
6 Ibid., 391.
7 Ibid., 390.
8 Ibid., 320.
9 Ibid., 395.
10 Parsons, "Some Theoretical Considerations," 53.
11 A comparable distinction is to be found in the study of language. Should we understand the individual phonemes as occupying a particular space in a range of sounds irrespective of the spaces occupied by other phonemes, or should we rather see them as only existing and being identifiable in

relation to each other? In the latter case, it is not so much the isolated units of sound that are significant but the features that differentiate them from or oppose them to each other. "Une *opposition phonologique* est une 'différence phonique susceptible de servir dans une langue donnée à la différentiation des significations intellectuelles'; chaque 'terme d'une opposition phonologique quelconque' est une *unité phonologique*; le phonème est 'une unité phonologique non susceptible d'être dissociée en unités phonologiques plus petites et plus simples' " (Troubetzkoy, "La Phonologie actuelle," 232, himself quoting from the *Travaux du Cercle linguistique de Prague*). "A *phonological opposition* is a 'difference of sound which may or may not be used in a given language for differentiating between different meanings determined by the intelligence'; each 'term in any phonological opposition' is a *phonological unity*; the phoneme is 'a phonological unity which cannot be broken up into smaller or simpler phonological unities' " (my translation). See also De Saussure, *Cours de linguistique générale*, 140ff., and Jakobson and Halle, "Phonology and Phonetics," 13ff.

12 Van den Berghe, *The Ethnic Phenomenon*, 35.

13 Ibid., 256.

14 "The model of individual, fitness-maximising choice is closely analagous, not to say homologous to that of classical micro-economics" (ibid., 255).

15 For Bentham's celebrated definition of utility see W. Stark, ed., *Jeremy Bentham's Economic Writings*, (London: George Allen and Unwin 1954), 439. Jevons placed the calculating individual of the Benthamite tradition at the heart of his new "science" of economics. See W.S. Jevons, *The Theory of Political Economy* (1871; London: Macmillan 1931), 10.

16 Van den Berghe, *The Ethnic Phenomenon*, 37.

17 Ibid., 20.

18 "Socialism has always foundered on the rock of individual selfishness. We are an organism biologically selected to maximize our individual inclusive fitness" (ibid., 242).

19 Ibid., 239.

20 "Ethnicity is an extension of kinship and ... the sentiments associated with it are of the same nature as those encountered between kin, albeit typically weaker and more diluted. I have gone one step further to link ethnicity with the sociobiology of kin selection" (ibid., 239).

21 See Wilson, *On Human Nature*, 20–1.

22 Van den Berghe, *The Ethnic Phenomenon*, 172.

23 Sahlins, *Culture and Practical Reason*, passim.

24 "Car il [l'homme] ne peut échapper à la nature qu'en se créant un autre monde d'où il la domine; ce monde, c'est la société"; "because Man cannot escape from nature other than by creating another world from which he dominates it: that [other] world is society" (Durkheim, *De la division du travail social*, 381; my translation).

25 Tylor, *Primitive Culture*, 8.

26 Ibid., 6.
27 Referred to in Dumont, "Caste," 28–9.
28 Barth, ed., *Ethnic Groups*, 11.
29 In Cohen, ed., *Urban Ethnicity*, 77–118.
30 Rex and Moore, *Race*, 19ff.
31 Dahya, "Pakistani ethnicity."
32 Cohen, ed., *Urban Ethnicity*, ix.
33 See above, chap. 5.
34 Therborn, *Science*, 219ff and 424.
35 Schneider, *American Kinship*.
36 Barth, ed., *Ethnic Groups*, 11ff.
37 Parsons, "Some Theoretical Considerations," 65ff.
38 Schneider's term, quoted by Parsons, ibid., 65.
39 Ibid., 82.
40 Ibid., 65.
41 See Wallman, "The Boundaries of 'Race,'" and Barth, ed., *Ethnic Groups*, 9ff.
42 Wallman, "The Boundaries of 'Race,'" 202.
43 Ibid., 209–10.
44 Hannerz, "Ethnicity and Opportunity."
45 Wallman, "The Boundaries of 'Race,'" 210ff.
46 Hannerz, "Ethnicity and Opportunity."
47 Wallman, "The Boundaries of 'Race,'" 212ff.
48 "The economic order in almost all advanced industrial societies has become increasingly subordinated to the political system" (Bell, "Ethnicity," 162).
49 "Ethnic groups, being both expressive and instrumental, become sources of political strength" (Bell, "Ethnicity," 171).

CHAPTER SEVEN: MARXIST
APPROACHES TO ETHNICITY

1 Above, chap. 5.
2 "Die theoretischen Sätze der Kommunisten beruhen keineswegs auf Ideen, auf Prinzipien, die von diesem oder jenem Weltverbesser erfunden oder entdeckt sind. Sie sind nur allgemeine Ausdrücke tatsächlicher Verhältnisse eines existierenden Klassenkampfes, einer unter unsern Augen vor sich gehenden geschichtlichen Bewegung" (Marx and Engels, *Manifest*, 475; my translation).
3 "Il serait tout à fait faux de concevoir les classes sociales comme un 'modèle,' en les concevant ainsi, on est précisément amené à accepter la possibilité d'existence, dans la réalité d'une formation sociale, de certains ensembles extérieurs aux classes, qui seraient l'effet d'une 'richesse' du

'réel concret' débordant son 'modèle abstrait.' Les classes sociales ne seraient ainsi qu'une schématisation du réel, son 'squelette' en quelque sorte, extrait du réel par une simple opération d'abstraction, les ensembles extérieurs aux classes étant précisément la richesse de détermination du concret échappant à sa grille d'intelligibilité. On sait qu'il s'agit là d'une vieille conception *nominaliste* des classes sociales, relevant finalement d'une conception empiriste de la connaissance et des rapports abstrait-concrets" (Poulantzas, *Les classes sociales*, 214). "It would be completely wrong to think of social classes as a 'model': in thinking of them in this way, one is led to accept the possibility that there exist, within the reality of a social formation, certain entities external to classes which would be the effect of the 'richness' of 'concrete reality' overflowing its 'abstract model.' Social classes would thus be just the outline plan of the real, its 'skeleton' so to speak, extracted from the real by means of a simple process of abstraction, the entities external to class being exactly the richness determining the concrete that eludes the framework for understanding. As we know, what that amounts to is an old *nominalist* conceptualization of social class, itself stemming from an empiricist conceptualization of knowledge and abstract-concrete relations" (my translation).

4 Marx and Engels, *The Manifesto*, 124,142.

5 Labelle, *Idéologie de couleur.*

6 Ibid., 180, 271.

7 Ibid., 171.

8 Above, chap. 6.

9 Tinker, *A New System of Slavery.*

10 Black, *Economic Thought*, 1–14. Ireland had been the victim of English mercantilist policy throughout the first part of the nineteenth century. For the dumping of goods on the Irish market and the destruction of nascent Irish manufacturing industry, see Lebow, *White Britain and Black Ireland*, Jackson, *The Irish in Britain*, and more especially Marx, *Capital*, vol. 1, 773–89.

11 From the mid-nineteenth century onwards there were periodic outbreaks of violence on the part of British workers faced with the hiring of Irish immigrants at lower wages (Jackson, *The Irish*, 77, 82, 116–7, O'Tuathaigh, "The Irish in Nineteenth Century Britain," Millward, "The Stockport Riots"). The situation was not helped by the fact that in mines, iron works and textile mills, Irish workers were regularly used by employers as strike-breakers (Jackson, *The Irish*, 87). The fears of British workers were aggravated by the introduction of steam packets on the Irish Sea from 1818 onwards, thus facilitating labour migration into Britain (Jackson, *The Irish*, 7).

12 Quoted in Jackson, *The Irish*, 116, from Marx's letter to S. Meyer and A. Vogt dated 9 April 1870 and included in *Marx-Engels in Britain*, (Moscow 1954), 506.

13 A Canadian federal law of 1952 states that preference in the selection of immigrants should be given to "whites if possible" (Labelle, Lemay et al., *Notes*, 22).

14 "L'ignorance de la langue renferme bien des immigrants dans des ghettos d'emplois, à l'intérieur d'entreprises dont les patrons sont de même origine ethnique ou dans des entreprises où on isole les travailleurs par groupes ethniques. Dans tous les cas, la forte concentration des travailleurs immigrés dans ces secteurs a une double fonction. D'abord maximiser ou empêcher la baisse du taux de profit chez les patrons. Ensuite diviser les travailleurs sur une base ethnique par la manipulation et les préjugés" (Labelle, Lemay et al., *Notes*, 40). "The fact of not knowing the language leads to many immigrants being contained within employment ghettos in companies where the employers are of the same ethnic origin or in companies where workers are isolated according to ethnic group. In all instances, the high concentration of immigrant workers in these sectors has a double function – first, to maximize or prevent a decline in profit levels for the employers; and secondly, to divide up workers on an ethnic basis by means of manipulation and prejudice" (my translation).

15 See Bernier, Elbaz et al., "Ethnicité."

16 See Labelle, Lemay et al., *Notes*.

17 Bonacich, "The Past, Present and Future."

18 Ibid., 38.

19 "The dynamic is a class dynamic. Race, sex and nationality become the symbolism in which the conflict is expressed, but are not in themselves its cause" (ibid., 35).

20 Saul, "The Dialectic"; Rey, *Les Alliances de classes*; Laclau, "Fascism"; Nairn, "The Modern Janus."

21 Mafeje, "The Ideology."

22 Rey, *Les Alliances de classes*, 74ff.

23 Saul, "The Dialectic."

24 Above, 49ff.

25 Nairn, "The Modern Janus." Zubaïda's critique of Nairn (Zubaïda, "Theories of Nationalism") slightly misses the point. Nairn's primary intention is not so much to produce a watertight conceptualization of nationalism as to force Marxists to face up to the reality of nationalism as a multifaceted and powerful force that frequently conflicts with and nullifies the possibility of class-consciousness and class-based solidarity. On the question of nationalism in the context of resistance to internal and external threat, see below, chaps. 13 and 16.

26 Laclau, "Fascism."

27 Saul, "The Dialectic'."

28 The strategic error of failing to take ethnic factors into account is equally evident in the case of the relationship between the Nicaraguan government

and the Miskito Indians. It was not until 1984 that the Sandinistas agreed to the Miskito demand for some degree of regional autonomy and adopted the policy of enhancing the culture and identity of the different ethnic groups in the Atlantic coast region (see Rooper and Smith, "From Nationalism to Autonomy").

29 Rousseau, "Classe et ethnicité."
30 Althusser, "Comment lire *Le Capital?*"
31 Sivanandan, "Alien gods."
32 Fanon, *Peau noire, masques blancs.*
33 Sivanandan, "Alien gods," 108-9.
34 Ibid., 106-7.

CHAPTER EIGHT: THE PROBLEM OF PRE-INDUSTRIAL SOCIETY

1 Sahlins, *Social Stratification*, 3.
2 By "egalitarian," Sahlins understands those societies where stratification is based solely on age, sex, or personal characteristics.
3 Firth, *We, the Tikopia*, 333ff.
4 Sahlins, *Social Stratification*, 2-3.
5 See above, chap. 2.
6 See Rousseau, "Kayan Stratification."
7 See Barth, *Political Leadership* and "Pathan Identity," and Asad, "Market Model."
8 As in the case of Pospisil's various studies of the Kapauka Papuans. Pospisil defines Kapauka Papuan society as "primitive capitalism combined with individualism" (Pospisil, *Kapauka Papuans*, 78).
9 Weber, *Economy and Society*, 231ff.
10 Ibid., 63ff.
11 On bureaucracy and the patrimonial state, see further below, chap. 13.
12 Barth, *Political Leadership*, 127ff.
13 Ibid., 1ff.
14 Asad, "Market Model."
15 Ibid., 92ff.
16 "In the case of economic contracts and house tenancy contracts, this argument [concerning the freedom of choice] may appear specious, since a person who has no land of his own is, in practice, forced to enter into a contract of some kind to obtain a house and make a living; but at all events he is free to take any kind of available contract he likes" (Barth, *Political Leadership*, 42-3).
17 See above, chap. 2.
18 Dahrendorf, *Class and Class Conflict*, 173ff.
19 Thompson, *The Making.*

20 Thompson, "Eighteenth Century English Society," 148. Hobsbawm makes a similar point in relation to "class consciousness" as such as a product of the Industrial Revolution (in Hobsbawm, "Class Consciousness," 7).

21 See especially Thompson, "Eighteenth Century English Society," 146ff.

22 "People find themselves in a society structured in determined ways ... they experience exploitation ... they identify points of antagonistic interest, they commence to struggle around these issues and in the process of struggling they discover themselves as classes, they come to know this discovery as class-consciousness" (ibid., 149).

23 Ibid., 151.

24 Alavi, "The Politics of Dependence."

CHAPTER NINE: ETHNICITY AND
SOCIAL ANTHROPOLOGY

1 Above, chap. 7.

2 Above, chap. 6.

3 See above, chap. 6, n. 11.

4 Lévi-Strauss, *Tristes tropiques*, 227ff.

5 Galaty, "Pollution."

6 Leach, *Political Systems*.

7 Ibid., chap. 1 and 279ff.

8 Ibid., 197ff and passim.

9 Drummond, "The Cultural Continuum."

10 Harris, *Prejudice and Tolerance*.

11 Ibid., 184–5.

12 Ibid., 194–5.

13 Ibid., 178–9.

14 Barth, ed., *Ethnic Groups*.

15 Blom, "Ethnic and Cultural Differentiation."

16 Above, chap. 8.

17 Haaland, "Economic determinants."

18 Eidheim, "When Ethnic Identity Is a Social Stigma."

19 Siverts, "Ethnic Stability."

20 In Barth, "Pathan Identity."

21 Knutsson, "Dichotomisation."

22 Goldmann, *La création culturelle*.

23 Harris, *Prejudice and Tolerance*, 189.

24 "J'étais allé jusqu'au bout du monde à la recherche de ce que Rousseau appelle 'les progrès presque insensibles des commencements.' Derrière le voile des lois trop savantes des Caduveo et des Bororo, j'avais poursuivi ma quête d'un état qui – dit encore Rousseau – 'n'existe plus, qui n'a peut-être point existé, qui probablement n'existera jamais et dont il est

pourtant nécessaire d'avoir des notions justes pour bien juger de notre état présent.' Plus heureux que lui, je croyais l'avoir découvert dans une société agonisante, mais dont il était inutile de me demander si elle représentait ou non un vestige. Traditionnelle or dégénérée, elle me mettait tout de même en présence d'une des formes d'organisation sociale et politique les plus pauvres qu'il soit possible de concevoir. Je n'avais pas besoin de m'adresser à l'histoire particulière qui l'avait maintenue dans cette condition élémentaire ou qui, plus vraisemblablement, l'y avait ramenée. Il suffisait de considérer l'expérience sociologique qui se déroulait sous mes yeux. Mais c'était elle qui se dérobait. J'avais cherché une société réduite à sa plus simple expression. Celle des Nambikwara l'était au point que j'y trouvai seulement des hommes" (Lévi-Strauss, *Tristes tropiques*, 339; my translation).

25 Ibid., chaps. 14–16.

CHAPTER TEN: CAPITALISM AND
THE EMERGENCE OF CLASS

1 Thompson, "Eighteenth Century English Society" and *The Making*, passim. See above, chap. 5.
2 Marx, *Der achtzehnte Brumaire*, 198. See above, chap. 2.
3 Above, chap. 3.
4 Weber, *Economy and Society*, 929, 953.
5 See discussion above, chap. 8.
6 Rudé, *The Crowd*, 19ff.
7 Barth, *Political Leadership*, 104ff.
8 Alavi, "The Politics of Dependence."
9 The following account is based largely on MacPherson, *A Reconstruction of the Human Geography of Some Parts of the Scottish Highlands*, and Hunter, *The Making of the Crofting Community*.
10 See above, chap. 8.
11 MacPherson, *A Reconstruction*, chap. 2.
12 Ibid., 138ff.
13 Ibid., 83.
14 See Hobsbawm, "Capitalisme et agriculture."
15 Smith, *An Inquiry*, 258ff.
16 See Hunter, *The Making*, chap. 1, and Cregeen, "The Changing Role."
17 See, among others, Hobsbawm, "Capitalisme et agriculture," and Cregeen, "The Changing Role." The underlying theme of "improvement" is central in Adam Smith's *An Inquiry*, and generally in early nineteenth-century political economy.
18 Hunter, *The Making*, 6–14.
19 Ibid., 15ff. Kelp was (and still is) used in the manufacture of soap, glass,

and other items. For the effect of the Napoleonic War on kelp supplies and prices, see Youngson, *After the Forty-Five*, 134ff.

20 Hunter, *The Making*, 146ff.

21 Ibid., chap. 6.

22 Rey, *Les Alliances de classes*.

23 See Hunter, *The Making*, 81, where the Canadian immigration authorities at Quebec are quoted as saying that the condition of the West Highland immigrants, notably in terms of health and clothing, was the worst that they had seen.

24 Marx, *Capital*, vol. 1, 794ff, and Marx, *Pre-capitalist Economic Formations*, passim.

25 Lenin, *The Development of Capitalism in Russia*.

26 Ibid., chap. 5.

27 Hunter, *The Making*, 107-8.

28 Rey, *Les Alliances de classes*, 215.

29 Darling, *The Punjab Peasant*, 164ff.

30 Ibid., 169.

31 "The necessity of seeking a foreign market ... demonstrates the progressive historical work of capitalism, which destroys the age-old isolation and seclusion of systems of economy (and, consequently, the narrowness of intellectual and political life), and which links all countries in the world into a single economic whole" (Lenin, *The Development*, 46). "Unless the population becomes mobile, it cannot develop, and it would be naïve to imagine that a village school can teach people what they can learn from an independent acquaintance with the different relations and orders of things in the South and the North, in agriculture and in industry, in the capital and in the backwoods" (ibid., 262).

CHAPTER ELEVEN: LABOUR
MIGRATION AND RACISM

1 See above, chap. 5.

2 In Lenin, *The Development of Capitalism in Russia*. See above, chap. 10.

3 See Myrdal, *An American Dilemma*, 1018ff.

4 Above, chap. 7.

5 Piore, *Birds of Passage*.

6 "Dual labour-market" theory, as exemplified by Piore, is easily confused with the "split labour-market" theory of Bonacich (see above, chap. 7). The principal differences are that split labour-market theory, albeit focusing on the same process of division and pay differentials within the working class, puts greater emphasis on the roles of both colonialism and organized labour in the creation and preservation of differentially paid work-forces, and exists as a theory principally to explain the phenomena of ethnicity and racism as based on such divisions, within the general frame-

work of a Marxist perspective. Dual labour-market theory, by contrast, was set up within the framework of non-Marxist economics. Apart from certain differences in nuance, however, split labour-market theory could be described as a marriage between the theory of the dual labour market and traditional Marxist approaches to ethnicity.

7 Foot, *Immigration and Race*, 119ff.

8 Ibid., 173ff.

9 Piore, *Birds of Passage*.

10 Lack of trade union support for black workers is a recurrent theme in the pages of *Race Today*. A particularly notable example was the strike at Imperial Typewriters (Leicester) in 1974, when striking Asian workers received no support from the Transport and General Workers' Union (*Race Today* 6, no.7 (1974): 201–5, and 6, no.9 (1974): 249–51).

11 Dahya, "Pakistani Ethnicity" (see above, chap. 6).

12 Rex and Moore, *Race*, chap. 1.

13 See Parekh, "Postscript," 220–1.

14 The ambiguous character of the relationship between the police and the National Front was never more in evidence than on the occasion of the National Front meeting in Southall in 1979. The police commissioner insisted that the meeting should go ahead at all costs in spite of the protests of the local Asian community. The resulting clash between 6,000 anti-racist demonstrators and 3,000 police led to the death of Blair Peach (*Race Today* 11, no.3 (1979): 52–4).

15 Rex and Moore, *Race*, 19ff.

16 See Myrdal's theory of the "vicious circle" in *An American Dilemma*, 75ff.

17 Lambert, *Crime, Police and Race Relations*.

18 Ibid., 26ff. Even so, there is evidence from other sources that the police give particular attention to the black community, an attention that distorts the statistics in their disfavour (Stevens and Willis, *Race, Crime and Arrests*).

19 "Nothing can justify, nothing can excuse, and no one can condone the appalling violence we have all seen on television" (Margaret Thatcher, quoted in *The Times*, 8 July 1981).

20 Scarman, *The Brixton Disorders*.

21 Quoted in *The Times*, 10 July 1981: 2.

22 Parekh, "Postscript," 220–1.

23 See above, chap. 7.

24 See Sivanandan, "Alien Gods," and above, chap. 7.

25 Amos, Gilroy, et al., "White sociology," 39ff.

26 See above, chap. 6.

27 See Piore, *Birds of Passage*, passim.

28 Howe, "From Bobby to Babylon."

29 See Henry in *The Dynamics of Racism in Toronto*, who concludes that racists tend to be of low social and economic status.

CHAPTER TWELVE: ETHNICITY AND
CLASS IN BRITAIN

1 In the introduction to Cohen, ed., *Urban Ethnicity.* See above, chap. 6.
2 Above, chap. 5.
3 Weber, *Economy and Society*, 302ff, 938, and *Wirtschaft und Gesellschaft*, 180.
4 Chap. 5.
5 Weber, *Economy and Society*, 929.
6 Above, chap. 5.
7 Poulantzas, *Les Classes sociales*, 257.

CHAPTER THIRTEEN: CAPITALISM
AND THE "NATION-STATE"

1 Marx, *Der achtzehnte Brumaire.*
2 Weber, *Economy and Society*, 954.
3 Ibid., 1006–7.
4 This, and the following points on bureaucracy, are from ibid., 956ff.
5 Above, chap. 3.
6 Weber, *Economy and Society*, 65 and 224.
7 Lenin, *State and Revolution.*
8 Ibid., chap. 1.
9 Miliband, *The State*, 46ff.
10 Westergaard and Resler, *Class in a Capitalist Society*, 252ff.
11 Althusser, "Idéologie," 67ff.
12 Poulantzas, *Les Classes sociales*, 89ff.
13 Ibid., 192.
14 As in the case of many of the leading ideas in mainstream nineteenth-century thought, the idea that the state should provide the security in which capitalism might flourish had already been well articulated by Adam Smith in the eighteenth century: "The increase of manufactures and agriculture [in Europe] ... has arisen ... from the fall of the feudal system, and from the establishment of a government which afforded to industry the only encouragement which it requires, some tolerable security that it shall enjoy the fruits of its own labour" (Smith, *An Inquiry*, 1: 400). In 1817, Ricardo attributes the "unimproved" state of Ireland in part to "bad government ... [and] the insecurity of property" (Ricardo, *On the Principles*, 99), while in 1861, John Stuart Mill describes one of the primary ends of government as "the security of person and property" (Mill, *Considerations*, 298). Black provides an illuminating example of the British government's limiting itself to certain areas of involvement in Ireland in the nineteenth century – setting up a police force and stabilizing the currency, for example – while at the same time it carefully avoided

making loans for the establishment of industries, in line with the doctrine of *laisser-faire* (Black, *Economic Thought*, 134ff).

15 Poulantzas, *Les Classes sociales*, 106.
16 Nairn, "The Modern Janus."
17 See Farrell, *Northern Ireland*.
18 Gibbon, *The Origins of Ulster Unionism*.
19 "An ethnic group is one recognising itself (and being popularly recognised) as sharing a common visible, or establishable, inherited trait – religion, race, language, etc. – marking them off from other groups. Ethnic collectivities arise through the process of 'ethnogenesis'; the process is socially determined, and collectivities arising through it can do so on the slenderest cultural affinities" (Gibbon, *The Origins*, 89).
20 "[Populism's] 'solution' to the danger of a united working class was to weld ever more tightly the links between the Protestant bourgeoisie and the Protestant masses, to the visible exclusion of the Catholic masses" (Bew, Gibbon, et al., *The State*, 89).
21 For example, on the occasion of the Outdoor relief riots of 1932, but the state was quick to reassert its hold over the Protestant community (Bew and Norton, "Class Struggle"). See Gibbon, *The Origins*, 145, where he states that it is not the absence of working-class unity that is problematic in Belfast but rather its presence in, for example, 1907, given the lack of integration between the two communities.
22 Farrell, *Northern Ireland*, chap. 5.
23 Bew, Gibbon, et al., *The State*, chaps. 3 and 4.
24 Ibid., 187ff.
25 Bourque and Legaré, *Le Québec*, 68ff.
26 "La séparation des branches de l'appareil d'Etat concentrant la plupart des appareils idéologiques au niveau provincial ... rend extrêmement difficile l'affirmation d'une idéologie apte à produire une mémoire 'historique' rassemblant les agents de la formation sociale et donnant à cette dernière la cohésion politico-idéologique attendue" (Bourque and Legaré, *Le Québec*, 94; my translation).
27 Dofny and Rioux, "Les Classes sociales."

CHAPTER FOURTEEN:
MULTICULTURALISM AND THE
STATE IN CANADA

1 Canada, *Report of the Royal Commission on Bilingualism and Biculturalism*, 4:11.
2 Ibid., 4:197.
3 Ibid., 4:3.
4 Ibid., 4:5.

5 Canada, *Statement of the Government of Canada on Indian Policy.*

6 Quoted in Canada, *Multiculturalism*, 46.

7 Quoted in Wardhaugh, *Language and Nationhood*, 3.

8 Canada, *Multiculturalism*, 15.

9 Ibid., 16.

10 Ibid., 21.

11 Ibid., 26.

12 Ibid., 26.

13 Canada, *Canadian Charter of Rights and Freedoms*, para. 27.

14 *An Act for the Preservation and Enhancement of Multiculturalism in Canada* (C-93) 1988, 3(1)(b).

15 "Le monde entre dans le langage comme un rapport dialectique d'activités, d'actes humains: il sort du mythe comme un tableau harmonieux d'essences. Une prestidigitation s'est opérée, qui a retourné le réel, l'a vidé d'histoire et l'a rempli de nature, qui a retiré aux choses leur sens humain de façon à leur faire signifier une insignifiance humaine" (Barthes, *Mythologies*, 230). "The world enters into language as a dialectical relation of activities, of human actions: it emerges from myth as a harmonious portrayal of essences. A sleight of hand has been enacted, which has turned reality around, emptied it of history and filled it with nature, which has taken away from things their human meaning in such a way as to make them signify a human insignificance" (my translation).

16 See Lebow, *White Britain*, passim, and below, chap. 16.

17 Canada, *Traités en vigueur*, 125.

18 McCormack, "Cloth Caps and Jobs."

19 Reynolds, *The British Immigrant.*

20 Basran, "Racial and Ethnic Policies."

21 Wardhaugh, *Language and Nationhood*, 185.

22 "On sait toute l'importance du facteur ethnique dans la structuration de l'espace résidentiel de cette ville. D'ailleurs, c'est cette particularité de la structure socio-écologique de Montréal qui la différencie de la ville nord-américaine type où, on le sait, c'est surtout par rapport au statut socio-économique que l'espace résidentiel se différencie" (Langlois, "Evolution," 50; my translation).

23 "Dans son organisation spatiale, un point d'équilibre entre son désir d'affirmer son identité et celui d'interagir avec d'autres ethnies, notamment les ethnies dominantes" (Langlois, "Evolution," 23; my translation).

24 See the Dahya/Rex debate, above, chap. 6.

25 Reynolds, *The British Immigrant*, 119ff.

26 Ibid., 154.

27 Interestingly enough, Reynolds does give some weight to ethnicity, but in a way that runs counter to the ideology of multiculturalism as expressed in the federal government's 1971 document, i.e., that immigrants should not

be cut off from their cultural roots. On the contrary, British immigrants had to adapt quickly to the different working, clothing and eating habits of what was essentially a North American working class. Within a period of years British workers underwent radical cultural change (ibid.).

28 Davis, *Ethnicity*.
29 Ibid., 174.
30 Ibid., 85.
31 Stymeist, *Ethnics and Indians*.
32 According to which, among other things, Ukrainians are not supposed to know what good sausages are.
33 Cassin and Griffith, "Class and Ethnicity."
34 Ibid., 116.
35 Ibid., 117.
36 Li, "The Chinese Canadian Family."
37 Ibid., 93.
38 Ibid., 88.
39 Ibid., 87.
40 Porter, *The Vertical Mosaic*.
41 Ibid., 388 and 391.
42 Ibid., 81.
43 Ibid., 99.
44 Langlois, in the article cited above, laments that he was not able to use the 1981 census data on ethnicity on account of the question asked (Langlois, "Evolution," 52).
45 Ryder, "The Interpretation," 476.
46 Ibid., 477.
47 Anderson and Frideres, *Ethnicity in Canada*, 46.
48 Ryder, "The Interpretation," 476.
49 Above, chap. 6, n 27.
50 Labelle, Turcotte, et al., *Histoires d'immigrées*.
51 Moreau, *Le Capital financier*.
52 "L'employeur convoîte cette main-d'oeuvre à cause de ses acquis (entre autres en couture), non-rémunérables parce que relevant d'un système de travail autre dans une société différente. De plus, ce qui l'intéresse, ce sont des qualités précises attachées à une main-d'oeuvre féminine de pays ou de régions moins développés, l'endurance physique liée à l'expérience de travail manuel, la dextérité, la docilité, le non-absentéisme, la disponibilité pour le travail supplémentaire ou contraire à toute vie sociale normale (par exemple le travail de nuit dans l'entretien ménager) – soit une force de travail malléable et soumise aux impératifs de la production, et qui, parce qu'émigrée, veut et doit travailler à n'importe quelle condition" (Labelle, Turcotte, et al., *Histoires d'immigrées*, 208; my translation).
53 Moreau, *Le Capital financier*, passim.

54 See above, chap. 5.
55 Peter, "The Myth," 64.
56 Moodley, "Canadian Ethnicity," 320.
57 See Wardhaugh, *Language and Nationhood*, 200.
58 Ibid., 65 and 71.
59 Montreal remains something of an exception to this spatial dividing up of Canada, with its anglophone (west) island surrounded by a francophone sea.
60 See, among others, Anderson and Frideres, *Ethnicity in Canada*, and Ley, "Pluralism."
61 See particularly the résumé of Bourque and Legaré's arguments in chap. 13, above.
62 Anderson and Frideres, *Ethnicity in Canada*, 327.
63 Van den Berghe, *The Ethnic Phenomenon*, 211. For a discussion of Van den Berghe's central thesis, see above, chap. 6.
64 Ibid., 244.
65 In Cassin and Griffith's terms (Cassin and Griffith, "Class and ethnicity").
66 Jakubowicz, "Ethnicity."
67 Ibid., 43.

CHAPTER FIFTEEN: ETHNICITY AND
THE COLONIAL FRONTIER

1 Galton, *Inquiries*, 201.
2 On Sivanandan and Fanon, see above, chap. 5.
3 On Lévi-Strauss's voyage to the end of the world, see above, chap. 9. For an Orwellian voyage into English working-class life, see, for example, Orwell's *The Road to Wigan Pier*.
4 Frere, *Britannia*.
5 See Elliott, *The Frontier*.
6 The moral imperatives operating within Pathan society are well brought out in Ahmed, *Pukhtun Economy*.
7 Jeffries, *The Colonial Police*, 32-3.
8 Eidheim, "When Ethnic Identity Is a Social Stigma," and see above, chap. 9.
9 Gorer, "English identity." The classic accounts are, of course, to be found in Orwell's *Burmese Days* and Forster's *A Passage to India*.
10 Roberts, *History of British India*, 649.
11 Darling, *The Punjab Peasant*.
12 Ibid., 90-1.
13 "The Indian peasant (and sometimes too, his more educated brother in the town) is a child at finance and has all the timid child's disposition to meet discovery with deception" (ibid., 235).

14 See Lebow, *White Britain*, 35ff.

15 "Is it not ... a bitter satire on the mode in which opinions are formed on the most important problems of human nature and life, to find public instructors of the greatest pretension, imputing the backwardness of Irish industry, and the want of energy of the Irish people in improving their condition, to a peculiar indolence and recklessness in the Celtic race? Of all vulgar modes of escaping from the consideration of the effect of social and moral influences on the human mind, the most vulgar is that of attributing the diversities of conduct and character to inherent natural differences. What race would not be indolent and insouciant when things are so arranged, that they derive no advantage from forethought or exertion?" (Mill, *Principles*, 1:311).

16 Weber, *Economy and Society*, 490ff.

17 Thus the Micmac people of the Gaspé peninsula ended up on a small area of land surrounding the church at Restigouche (Lee, "La Gaspésie"). The creation of Indian reserves – officially to encourage assimilation to European life-styles and Christianization – had already begun in the seventeenth century. It was consolidated in a series of acts of Parliament from the mid-nineteenth century onwards (Jamieson, *Indian Women*, 16 and 25–38).

18 Ibid., 16–20 and 21ff.

19 St-Jean and Lemay, *Les Nations autochtones*, 71.

20 Jamieson, *Indian Women*, 21.

21 Ibid., 30.

22 Ibid., 64.

23 Weaver, *Making Canadian Indian Policy*, 190ff.

24 Canada, *Statement of the Government of Canada on Indian Policy*.

25 Rouland, *Les Inuit*, 9ff.

26 See Feit, "Negotiating Recognition," and La Rusic, Bouchard, et al., *Negotiating a Way of Life*.

27 Rouland, *Les Inuit*, 125ff.

28 "Les Cris de la Baie James et les Inuit du Québec cèdent, renoncent, abandonnent et transportent par les présentes tous leurs revendications, droits, titres et intérêts autochtones, quels qu'ils soient, aux terres et dans les terres du Territoire du Québec ... Le Québec et le Canada, la Société d'énergie de la Baie-James, la Société de développement de la Baie-James et la Commission hydro-électrique du Québec (Hydro-Québec) ... par les présentes, donnent, accordent, reconnaissent et fournissent aux Cris de la Baie-James et aux Inuit du Québec les droits, privilèges et avantages mentionnés aux présentes" (paras. 2.1 and 2.2 of the *Convention de la Baie-James et du Nord québécois*, quoted in Canada, *Traités en vigueur*, 45). "The Cree of James Bay and the Inuit of Quebec give up, renounce, abandon and hand over by virtue of this present document all their aboriginal claims, rights, titles, and interests, whatever they may be, to the land and in the land

within Quebec territory ... Quebec, Canada, the *Société d'énergie de la Baie James*, the *Société de développement de la Baie-James* and the *Commission hydro-électrique du Québec* (*Hydro-Québec*) ... by virtue of the present document, give, grant, recognize and supply to the Cree of James Bay and the Inuit of Quebec the rights, privileges, and advantages mentioned in the present document" (my translation).

29 "Un titre indien a existé. Sa nature véritable est difficile à cerner avec certitude, mais il semble être de caractère usufructuaire et surtout rattaché au droit traditionnel de chasse et de pêche lié aux nécessités de la subsistance ... Quoi qu'il en soit ... il faut trouver une formule de remplacement du "titre indien" sur les parties du territoire québécois qui peuvent en être affectées." "Il faut évidemment, au préalable ... reconnaître les droits territoriaux reliés au titre indien, en visant son extinction ... leur disparition, ensuite doit faire place à des droits, individuels ou collectifs selon le choix des Amérindiens, tels que ceux de chasser et de pêcher pour leur subsistance et celle de leur famille, l'octroi de terrains ... la jouissance de tous les bénéfices et prestations mises à la disposition des citoyens en général, en plus d'un fonds de développement spécial." Quebec, *Rapport de la Commission d'étude*, 4:363 and 377; my translation.

30 La Rusic, Bouchard, et al., *Negotiating a Way of Life*; Rouland, *Les Inuit*.

31 Canada, *Traités en vigueur*, iii and 48.

32 Scarman, *The Brixton Disorders*.

33 Broeker recounts pioneering British experiments with the Irish Peace Preservation Force and the imposition of martial law in early nineteenth-century Ireland. The Irish constabulary, which was to emerge from the Peace Preservation Force in the 1830s, came to be a significant influence in the development of the colonial police (Broeker, *Rural Disorder*, 202ff and 241–2, and Jeffries, *The Colonial Police*, 30–2). Bunyan suggests that policing in Britain is itself increasingly conforming to the colonial model (Bunyan, *The Political Police*, and "The police against the people"). Commissioners of the metropolitan police tend to have military or colonial experience, while the mobile armed special squads set up in the second half of the 1970s in London bear more than a passing resemblance to the mobile mounted detachments of the Peace Preservation Force of early nineteenth-century Ireland (Bunyan, *The Political Police*, 68 and 292).

34 Told, in suitably heroic terms, in Elliott, *The Frontier*.

CHAPTER SIXTEEN: ETHNICITY, RESISTANCE, AND NATIONHOOD

1 See above, chap. 15.

2 Morgan, *Ancient Society*, 58.

3 Tylor, *Primitive Culture*, 27.

4 See above, chap. 15.

5 See Althusser, "Idéologie," where he puts forward the notion of "inter-pellation." He does not, however, specifically relate it to the question of nationalism.

6 The following account owes much to Lyons' two works, *Culture and Anarchy in Ireland* and *Ireland since the Famine*.

7 Lyons, *Culture and Anarchy*, 8, and Jackson, *The Irish*, 2.

8 Hyde, "The Necessity," 135.

9 See, among others, Kenneth Jackson, *The Oldest Irish Tradition: A Window on the Iron Age* (Cambridge: Cambridge University Press 1964).

10 Lyons, *Ireland since the Famine*, 336.

11 Duffy, "The Revival," 42.

12 O'Grady, *Irish Bardic History*, 4.

13 Ibid., 92.

14 Ibid., 38.

15 Ibid., 46–7.

16 Ibid., 81.

17 Marcus quotes Yeats as having said, with reference to O'Grady, "I think it was his *History of Ireland, Heroic Period*, that started us all." Philip L. Marcus, *Standish O'Grady* (Lewisburg: Bucknell University Press, 1970), 7. On the significance of O'Grady's contribution to the revival of interest in early Irish literature and history, see Lyons, *Culture and Anarchy*, 33ff.

18 Hyde, "The Necessity," 159. On Douglas Hyde, see further Lyons, *Culture and Anarchy*, 35ff.

19 Lyons, *Ireland since the Famine*, 358ff.

20 Ibid., 376.

21 Quoted in ibid., 231.

22 Quoted in ibid., 331.

23 Quoted in ibid., 336.

24 "Praise God if this my blood fulfils the doom, when you, dark rose, shall redden into bloom"; quoted from Joseph Plunkett, *Poems*, (Dublin, 1916), in Lyons, *Ireland since the Famine*, 335.

25 Yeats, Lady Gregory, George Moore, and Edward Martyn founded the Irish Literary Theatre (later the Abbey Theatre) "to achieve through the theatre a sense of nationality which would transcend purely political values because it would restore to the nation its soul" (Lyons, *Culture and Anarchy*, 48).

26 Lyons, *Ireland since the Famine*, 115.

27 "Irish children grow up to learn that their culture, their own surrounding real local life is worth nothing" (Corkery, *Synge*, 14–15).

28 "By 1971, 60% of the total profits of publicly quoted companies in the South [of Ireland] were going to Britain" (Farrell, *Northern Ireland*, 328).

29 See the following Provisional IRA statement, "Ours is a socialism based on the native Irish tradition of *Comhar na gComharan* [neighbourly co-operation] which is founded on the right of worker-ownership and on our

Irish and Christian values" (*An Phoblacht* 1, no. 1 [Feb. 1970]), quoted by Farrell, *Northern Ireland*, 270.

30 Levasseur, *Loisir*, 58ff.

31 Linteau, Durocher, et al., *Histoire*, 610.

32 See Groulx, *La naissance*, passim.

33 Ibid., 116, 155–6.

34 Ibid., 269.

35 Ibid., 24ff.

36 "Rien en lui du demi-sauvage ou de demi-barbare ... un héros fait de simplicité, mais aussi d'idéal, de courage; un fondateur de pays et de race, un pionnier de la civilisation et de la foi et qui en a la dignité. Dans l'histoire de ces premiers temps qui sont les temps héroïques, son attitude est un peu celle qu'on lui a faite dans le bronze. Il faut le voir dans une attitude de foi et de labeur, tête nue sous le grand ciel, la faucille d'une main et, de l'autre, élevant vers le Créateur sa première gerbe de blé" (ibid., 153–4; my translation).

37 Ibid., 153.

38 "Un merveilleux instrument de culture, un élément de leur survivance" (ibid., 260; my translation).

39 "De tous les événements de l'histoire humaine, bien peu, sans doute, ont plus de prix aux yeux de Dieu, que la naissance des races et des peuples, vastes organisations spirituelles si fortement engagées dans les plans divins" (ibid., 106; my translation).

40 Corkery, *Synge*, 53.

41 Ibid., 19.

42 Ibid., *Synge*, 120.

43 Groulx, *La Naissance*, 82–3.

44 Synge, *The Aran Islands*, 127.

45 Corkery, *Synge*, 120.

46 Morris, *News from Nowhere*.

47 Wordsworth refers to the "pure commonwealth" that he discovered in the hills of the Lake District, "the members of which existed in the midst of a powerful empire, like an ideal society, or an organised community, whose constitution had been imposed and regulated by the mountains which protected it. Neither high born noblemen, knight nor esquire was here; but many of these humble sons of the hills had a consciousness that the land which they had walked over and tilled had, for more than five hundred years, been possessed by men of their name and blood" (quoted from Wordsworth's *A Description of the Scenery of the Lakes in the North of England*, in Mill, *Principles*, 1:247–8).

48 "All England may, if it so chooses, become one manufacturing town; and Englishmen ... may live diminished lives in the midst of noise, of dark-

ness, and of deadly exhalation. But the world cannot become a factory or a mine ... As the art of life is learned, it will be found at last that all lovely things are also necessary, the wild flower by the wayside, as well as the tended corn; and the wild birds and creatures of the forest, as well as the tended cattle" (Ruskin, *Unto this Last*, 93–4).

CHAPTER SEVENTEEN: MAKING
INEQUALITY POSSIBLE

1 Mitchell, "Perceptions," 25.
2 Thompson, "Eighteenth Century English society," 148.
3 See above, chap. 12.
4 See the discussion above, chap. 13.
5 See above, chap. 8.
6 Luckács, "Class Consciousness."
7 Ibid., 74.
8 Thompson, *The Making*.
9 Above, chap. 12.
10 Gutkind, "The View from Below."
11 Matza and Wellman, "The Ordeal."
12 Luckács, "Class Consciousness."
13 Again, a point that is central in Luckács's argument ("Class Consciousness").
14 Lewontin, Rose, et al., "Bourgeois Ideology."
15 See Godelier, "Infrastructures."
16 See above, chap. 5.
17 Weber, *Economy and Society*, 931. Weber's point is supported by Roethlisberger's classic study of labour-management relations at the Hawthorne plant of the Western Electric Company in Chicago in the 1920s and 1930s. The apparently favourable disposition of workers at the plant towards the directors of the company and upper management was matched by a hostile attitude towards the immediate representatives of that same management, the foremen and supervisors with whom they came into daily contact (Roethlisberger, *Management*, 335 and 339).
18 Hobsbawm, "Class Consciousness," 14.
19 "The working class, like the peasantry, consists almost by definition of people who cannot make things happen except collectively" (ibid., 14).
20 See above, chaps. 2 and 3.
21 Weber himself does not refer to this process as taking place in the context of class. See above, chap. 6, for the notions of "brotherhood" and "monopolistic closure."
22 See above, chap. 3.

CHAPTER EIGHTEEN:
THE TANGLED FOLIAGE

1 Porter, *The Vertical Mosaic*, 20.
2 Weber, *Economy and Society*, 20, and " 'Objectivity' in Social Science," 90.
3 Hindess and Hirst's two books, *Pre-Capitalist Modes of Production* (London: Routledge and Kegan Paul 1975) and *Mode of Production and Social Formation* (London: Macmillan 1977), are examples within Marxism of an overriding preoccupation with the improvement of general theory to the exclusion of any close empirical concern with the societies that that theory is held to be explaining.
4 See above, chap. 5.
5 "The women kneaded and pushed the cloth round and round the table with song after song. The one who sang the verse line would give turns and grace notes to take in all the syllables, always in absolute time and with a rhythm that was marvellous to me. When it was thought to be sufficiently shrunk and the feel of the texture right, one would measure the length with her third finger. If not yet shrunk enough they would give it another song, always keeping it moist. When ready at last it was rolled up tightly and two women would face across it and clapping the roll, would sing the *òran basaidh*, or clapping song, called in Glendale the *coileach*, in quick 2/4 time, which was for the purpose of finishing the *luadhadh* [waulking]" (description of a waulking observed in Glendale, South Uist, Outer Hebrides, in the 1930s, in Shaw, *Folksongs*, 6–7). See also John MacInnes, "Songs, Waulking, Metres of," in Thompson, ed., *The Companion*, 274.

Bibliography

Ahmad, Saghir. *Class and Power in a Punjabi Village*. New York: Monthly Review Press 1977.

Ahmed, Akbar S. *Pukhtun Economy and Society*. London: Routledge and Kegan Paul 1980.

Alavi, Hamza A. "The Politics of Dependence: A Village in West Punjab." *South Asian Review* 4, no. 2 (1971): 111–28.

Althusser, Louis. "Comment lire *Le Capital?*" (1969). In Louis Althusser, *Positions*. Paris: Editions sociales 1976.

– "Idéologie et appareils idéologiques d'Etat (notes pour une recherche)" (1970). In Louis Althusser, *Positions*. Paris: Editions sociales 1976.

Amos, Val, Paul Gilroy, and Errol Lawrence. "White Sociology, Black Struggle." In David Robbins, ed., *Rethinking Social Inequality*. Aldershot: Gower 1982.

Anderson, Alan B., and James S. Frideres. *Ethnicity in Canada*. Toronto: Butterworths 1981.

Anwar, Muhammad. *The Myth of Return: Pakistanis in Britain*. London: Heinemann 1979.

Arnold, Matthew. *Culture and Anarchy* (1869). Cambridge: Cambridge University Press 1932.

Aron, Raymond. "La Classe comme représentation et comme volonté." *Cahiers internationaux de sociologie* 38 (1965): 11–30.

Arrighi, Giovanni. "The Class Struggle in Twentieth Century Western Europe." Uppsala: Ninth World Congress of Sociology 1978 (mimeo).

Asad, Talal. "Market Model, Class Structure and Consent: A Reconsideration of Swat Political Organisation." *Man* 7 (1972): 74–94.

Avery, Donald. *Dangerous Foreigners, European Immigrant Workers and Labour Radicalism in Canada 1896–1932*. Toronto: McClelland and Stewart 1979.

Barth, Fredrik. *Political Leadership among Swat Pathans*. London: London School of Economics 1959.

– "Pathan identity and its maintenance." In Barth, ed., *Ethnic Groups and Bound-*

aries. London: George Allen & Unwin 1969.

Barthes, Roland. *Mythologies.* Paris: Seuil 1957.

Basran, G.S. "Racial and Ethnic Policies in Canada." In Bolaria and Li, eds. 1983.

Bell, Daniel. "Ethnicity and Social Change." In Glazer and Moynihan, eds. 1975.

Bernier, Bernard. "Main-d'oeuvre féminine et ethnicité dans trois usines de vête-ment à Montréal." *Anthropologie et sociétés* 3 (1979): 117-40.

Bernier, Bernard, Mikhael Elbaz, and Gilles Lavigne. "Ethnicité et luttes de classes." *Anthropologie et sociétés* 2, no.1 (1978): 15-60.

Berry, John W., Rudolf Kalin, and Donald M. Taylor. *Multiculturalism and Ethnic Attitudes in Canada.* Ottawa: Ministry of Supply and Services Canada 1977.

Bew, Paul, Peter Gibbon, and Henry Patterson. *The State in Northern Ireland 1921-1972.* Manchester: Manchester University Press 1979.

Bew, Paul, and C. Norton. "Class Struggle and the Unionist State: The Outdoor Relief Riots of 1932." *Economic and Social Review* 10 (1979): 255-65.

Black, R.D. Collison. *Economic Thought and the Irish Question 1817-1870.* Cambridge: Cambridge University Press 1960.

Blom, Jan-Petter. "Ethnic and Cultural Differentiation." In Barth, ed. 1969.

Bolaria, B.S. "Dominant Perspectives and Non-white Minorities." In Bolaria and Li, eds. 1983.

Bolaria, B.Singh, and Peter S. Li, eds. *Racial Minorities in Multicultural Canada.* Toronto: Garamond Press 1983.

Bonacich, Edna. "The Past, Present and Future of Split Labour Market Theory." *Research in Race and Ethnic Relations* 1 (1979): 17-64.

Bottomley, Gill, and Marie De Lepervanche, eds. *Ethnicity, Class and Gender in Australia.* Sydney: George Allen and Unwin 1984.

Bourque, Gilles. *Question nationale et classes sociales au Québec 1760-1840.* Montréal: Parti Pris 1970.

Bourque, Gilles, and Anne Legaré. *Le Québec, la question nationale.* Paris: Maspero 1979.

Brantenberg, Tom. "Ethnic Commitments and Local Government in Nain 1969-1976." In Paine, Robert, ed. 1977.

Breton, R., W.W. Isajiw, W. Kalbach, and J.G. Reitz. *Ethnic Pluralism in an Urban Setting: Conceptual and Technical Overview of a Research Project.* Toronto: Centre for Urban and Community Studies, University of Toronto 1981.

Bridges, Lee. "Keeping the Lid On: British Urban Social Policy 1975-1981." *Race and Class* 23 (1981): 171-85.

Brody, Hugh. *The People's Land: Eskimos and Whites in the Eastern Arctic.* Toronto: Penguin 1975.

Broeker, Galen. *Rural Disorder and Police Reform in Ireland, 1812-1836.* London: Routledge and Kegan Paul 1970.

Buckland, Patrick. *The Factory of Grievances: Devolved Government in Northern Ireland 1921-1939.* Dublin: Gill and Macmillan 1979.

Bunyan, Tony. *The Political Police in Britain.* London: Friedmann 1976.

– "The Police against the People." *Race and Class* 23 (1981): 153-70.

Canada. *Statement of the Government of Canada on Indian Policy*. Ottawa: Ministry of Indian Affairs and Northern Development 1969.

– *Report of the Royal Commission on Bilingualism and Biculturalism*. Ottawa: Queen's Printer 1970.

– *Un choix national: exposé du gouvernement du Canada sur une politique linguistique nationale*. Ottawa: Approvisionnements et Services Canada 1977.

– *Multiculturalism and the Government of Canada*. Ottawa: Ministry of Supply and Services Canada 1978.

– *Canadian Charter of Rights and Freedoms*. Ottawa: Government of Canada 1981.

– *Equality Now! Minutes of Proceedings and Evidence of the Special Committee on the Participation of Visible Minorities in Canadian Society*. Ottawa: Ministry of Supply and Services Canada 1984.

– *Traités en vigueur: ententes durables. Rapport du groupe d'étude de la politique des revendications globales*. Ottawa: Ministère des Affaires indiennes et du Nord canadien 1986.

– *Statement of Policy on Native Claims*. Ottawa: Department of Indian and Northern Affairs 1986.

Cassin, A. Marguerite, and Alison I. Griffith. "Class and Ethnicity: Producing the Difference That Counts." *Canadian Ethnic Studies* 13 (1981): 109–29.

Castles, Stephen. "The Social Time-Bomb: Education of an Underclass in West Germany." *Race and Class* 21 (1980): 369–87.

Castles, Stephen, and Godula Kosack. *Immigrant Workers and Class Structure in Western Europe*. Oxford: Oxford University Press 1973.

Clarke, Colin, David Ley, and Ceri Peach. *Geography and Ethnic Pluralism*. London: George Allen and Unwin 1984.

Cohen, Abner, ed. *Urban Ethnicity*. London: Tavistock 1974.

Cooper, John L. *The Police and the Ghetto*. New York: National University Publications 1980.

Corkery, Daniel. *Synge and Anglo-Irish Literature*. Cork: Mercier Press 1931.

Cregeen, Eric. "The Changing Role of the House of Argyll in the Scottish Highlands." In N.T. Phillipson and R. Michison, eds., *Scotland in the Age of Improvement*. Edinburgh: Edinburgh University Press 1970.

Dahlie, J., and T. Fernando, eds. *Ethnicity, Power and Politics in Canada*. Toronto: Methuen 1981.

Dahrendorf, Ralf. "Homo sociologicus" (1958). In Dahrendorf 1968.

– *Class and Class Conflict in Industrial Society*. Stanford: Stanford University Press 1959.

– "On the Origin of Inequality among Men" (1961). In Dahrendorf, *Essays in the Theory of Society*. Stanford: Stanford University Press 1968.

– *Life Chances: Approaches to Social and Political Theory*. Chicago: University of Chicago Press 1979.

Dahya, Badr. "Pakistani Ethnicity in Industrial Cities in Britain." In Cohen, ed. 1974.

Darling, Malcolm. *The Punjab Peasant in Prosperity and Debt*. 1925; Bombay: Oxford University Press 1947.

Davis, Nanciellen. *Ethnicity and Ethnic Group Persistence in an Acadian Village in Maritime Canada*. New York: AMS Press 1985.

Del Negro, Luciano. *Immigration et unité ouvrière*. Montréal: Confédération des syndicats nationaux 1981.

Dofny, Jacques, and Marcel Rioux. "Les Classes sociales au Québec." *Revue française de sociologie* 3, no. 3 (1963): 290-300.

Dollard, John. *Caste and Class in a Southern Town*. 1937; New York: Doubleday Anchor 1957.

Drummond, Lee. "The Cultural Continuum: A Theory of Intersystems." *Man* 15 (1980): 352–74.

Duffy, Charles Gavan. "The Revival of Irish Literature." Two addresses given before the London Irish Literary Society in 1892 and 1894. In Charles Gavan Duffy, George Sigerson, and Douglas Hyde, *The Revival of Irish Literature*. London: T.F. Unwin 1894, 9–60; repr. New York: Lemma Publishing Corp. 1973.

Dumont, Louis. "Caste: A Phenomenon of Social Structure or an Aspect of Indian Culture?" In A. De Reuck and J. Knight, eds., *Caste and Race*. London: Ciba Foundation 1967.

Dunk, Tom. "Indians, Racism and the 'People': The Dynamics of Class and Race in Northwestern Ontario." Paper presented at the annual meeting of the Canadian Ethnological Association 1984.

– "The Working Class and the Discourse on Indians: An Example from North-western Ontario." Paper presented at the WASA conference, Thunder Bay, Ontario, 1986.

Dupuy, Alex. "Class Formation and Underdevelopment in Nineteenth Century Haïti." *Race and Class* 24 (1982): 17–31.

Durkheim, Emile. *De la division du travail social* (1893). Paris: Presses Universitaires de France 1973.

Eidheim, Harald. "When Ethnic Identity Is a Social Stigma." In Barth, ed. 1969.

Elliott, J.G. *The Frontier 1839-1947: The Story of the North-West Frontier of India*. London: Cassell 1968.

Fanon, Franz. *Peau noire, masques blancs*. Paris: Seuil 1952.

Farrell, Michael. *Northern Ireland: The Orange State*. London: Pluto Press 1976.

Feit, Harvey. "Negotiating Recognition of Aboriginal Rights: History, Strategies, and Reactions to the James Bay and Northern Quebec Agreement." *Canadian Journal of Anthropology* 1 (1980): 159–72.

– "The Future of Hunters within Nation States: Anthropology and the James Bay Cree." In E.B. Leacock and R.B. Lee, eds., *Politics and History in Band Societies*. Cambridge: Cambridge University Press 1980.

Firth, Raymond. *We, the Tikopia*. 1936; Boston: Beacon Press 1957.

Foot, Paul. *Immigration and Race in British Politics*. Harmondsworth: Penguin 1965.

Frere, Sheppard. *Britannia: a History of Roman Britain*. 1967; London: Routledge and Kegan Paul 1978.

Friend, Andrew, and Andy Metcalfe. *The Politics of Mass Unemployment*. London: Pluto Press 1981.

Galaty, John. "Pollution and Pastoral Antipraxis: The Issue of Maasai Inequality." *American Ethnologist* 6 (1979): 803-16.

Galton, Francis. *Inquiries into Human Faculty and Its Development*. 1883; London: Dent 1907.

Gibbon, Peter. "The Dialectic of Religion and Class in Ulster." *New Left Review* 55. (1969): 20-41.

- *The Origins of Ulster Unionism*. Manchester: Manchester University Press 1975.

Glazer, Nathan, and Patrick Moynihan, eds. *Ethnicity: Theory and Experience*. Cambridge: Harvard University Press 1975.

Godelier, Maurice. "Infrastructures, sociétés, histoire." *Dialectiques 21* (1978): 41-53.

Goldmann, Lucien. *La Création culturelle dans la société moderne*. Paris: Denoël-Gonthier 1971.

Gonick, Marnina. "The Role of Gender, Ethnicity and Culture in Determining Métis Position in Fur-Trade Society." Research paper, 1985.

Gorer, Geoffrey. "English Identity over Time and Empire." In George De Vos and Lola Romanucci-Ross, eds., *Ethnic Identity*. London: Mayfield Publishing, 1975.

Goyder, John C. "Ethnicity and Class Identity: The Case of French- and English-speaking Canadians." *Ethnic and Racial Studies* 6 (1983): 72-89.

Groulx, Lionel. *La Naissance d'une race* (1918). Montréal: Librairie Granger Frères 1938.

Gutkind, Peter C.W. *Urban Anthropology*. Assen: Van Gorcum 1974.

- "The View from Below: Political Consciousness of the Urban Poor in Ibadan, Western Nigeria." *Cahiers d'études africaines* 57 (1975): 5-36.

Haaland, Gunnar. "Economic Determinants in Ethnic Processes." In Barth, ed. 1969.

Hannerz, Ulf. "Ethnicity and Opportunity in Urban America." In Cohen, ed. 1974.

Harris, Rosemary. *Prejudice and Tolerance in Ulster*. Manchester: Manchester University Press 1972.

Hechter, Michael. *Internal Colonialism*. Berkeley: University of California Press 1975.

Henry, Frances. *The Dynamics of Racism in Toronto*. Research report. Toronto: York University 1978.

Hobsbawm, E.J. "Class Consciousness in History." In I. Mészaros, ed., *Aspects of History and Class Consciousness*. London: Routledge and Kegan Paul 1971.

- "Capitalisme et agriculture: les réformateurs écossais au XVIIIe siècle." *Annales* 33, no. 3 (1978): 580-601.

Howe, Darcus. "From Bobby to Babylon: Blacks and the British Police." *Race Today* 12, no.5 (1980): 8-14, and 12, no.10 (1980): 31-41.

Hughes, Everett C. *French Canada in Transition*. Chicago: University of Chicago Press 1943.

Hunter, James. *The Making of the Crofting Community*. Edinburgh: John Donald 1976.

Huot, John. "In Defence of Toronto's Asians." *Race Today* 10, no.2 (1978): 33–8.

Hyde, Douglas. "The Necessity for De-anglicising Ireland. Lecture delivered before the Irish National Literary Society (Dublin) in 1892. In Charles Gavan Duffy, George Sigerson, and Douglas Hyde, *The Revival of Irish Literature*. London: T.F. Unwin 1894, 117–61; repr. New York: Lemma Publishing Corp. 1973.

Jackson, J.A. *The Irish in Britain*. London: Routledge and Kegan Paul 1963.

Jakobson, Roman, and Morris Halle. "Phonology and Phonetics" (1956). In Jakobson and Halle, *The Fundamentals of Language*. The Hague: Mouton 1971.

Jakubowicz, Andrew. "Ethnicity, Multiculturalism and Neo-conservatism." In Bottomley and De Lepervanche, eds. 1984.

Jamieson, Kathleen. *Indian Women and the Law in Canada: Citizens Minus*. Ottawa: Advisory Council on the Status of Women 1978.

Jeffries, Charles. *The Colonial Police*. London: Max Parrish 1952.

Jessop, Bob. "Recent Theories of the Capitalist State." *Cambridge Journal of Economics* 1 (1977): 353–73.

Jones, Greta. *Social Darwinism and English Thought*. Brighton: Harvester Press 1980.

Kennedy, J.C. "Local Government and Ethnic Boundaries in Makkovik, 1972." In Paine, ed. 1977.

Kerner, Otto. *Report of the National Advisory Commission on Civil Disorders*. Washington, DC: Government Printing Office 1968.

Knutsson, Karl Eric. "Dichotomisation and Integration – aspects of Inter-ethnic Relations in Southern Ethiopia." In Barth, ed. 1969.

Labelle, Micheline. *Idéologie de couleur et classes sociales en Haïti*. Montréal: Les presses de l'Université de Montréal 1978.

Labelle, Micheline, Danielle Lemay, Claude Painchaud. *Notes sur l'histoire et les conditions de vie des travailleurs immigrés au Québec*. Montreal: Perspectives 1980.

Labelle, Micheline, Geneviève Turcotte, Marianne Kempeneers, and Deirdre Meintel. *Histoires d'immigrées*. Montreal: Boréal 1987.

Laclau, Ernesto. "Fascism and Ideology." In Ernesto Laclau, *Politics and Ideology in Marxist Theory*. London: New Left Books 1977.

Laferrière, Michel. "Nationalisme québécois et conflits de classe." *Mondes en développement* 27 (1979): 477–97.

Lambert, John. *Crime, Police and Race Relations*. Oxford: Oxford University Press 1970.

Langlois, André. "Evolution de la répartition spatiale des groupes ethniques dans l'espace résidentiel montréalais, 1931–1971." *Cahiers de géographie du Québec* 29 (1985): 49–65.

La Rusic, Ignatius E., Serge Bouchard, Alan Penn, Taylor Brelsford, and Jean-Guy Deschênes. *Negotiating a Way of Life*. Montréal: SSDCC 1979.

Leach, Edmund. *Political Systems of Highland Burma* (1954). London: Athlone Press 1964.

– "Caste, Class and Slavery: The Taxonomic Problem." In A. De Reuck and

Jill Knight, eds., *Caste and Race*. London: Ciba Foundation 1967.

Lebow, Richard N. *White Britain and Black Ireland: the Influence of Stereotypes on Colonial Policy*. Philadelphia: Institute for the Study of Human Issues 1976.

Lee, David. "La Gaspésie de 1760 à 1867." *Cahiers d'Archéologie et d'histoire* 23 (1980): 170-9.

Legaré, Anne. *Les Classes sociales au Québec*. Montréal: Les Presses universitaires du Québec 1977.

Lenin, V.I. *The Development of Capitalism in Russia* (1899). Moscow: Foreign Languages Publishing House 1956.

- *State and Revolution*. 1917; New York: International Publishers 1932.

Levasseur, Roger. *Loisir et culture au Québec*. Montreal: Boréal Express 1982.

Lévi-Strauss, Claude. *Tristes tropiques*. Paris: Librairie Plon 1955.

Lewontin, Richard, Steven Rose, and Leo Kamin. "Bourgeois Ideology and the Origin of Biological Determinism." *Race and Class* 24 (1982): 1-16.

Ley, David. "Pluralism and the Canadian State." In Clarke, Ley, et al., eds. 1984.

Leys, Colin. *Underdevelopment in Kenya: The Political Economy of Neo-Colonialism 1964–1971*. Berkeley: University of California Press 1975.

Li, Peter S. "The Chinese Canadian Family." In Bolaria and Li, eds. 1983.

Linteau, Paul-André, René Durocher, and Jean-Claude Robert. *Histoire du Québec contemporain*. Montreal: Boréal Express 1979.

Lock, Margaret, and Pamela Dunk. "My Nerves Are Broken: The Communication of Suffering in a Greek Canadian Community." In D. Coburn, ed., *Health and Canadian Society, Sociological Perspectives*. Markham: Fitzhenry and Whiteside 1987.

Lukács, Georg. "Class Consciousness" (1920). In *History and Class Consciousness*. Cambridge: MIT Press 1971.

Lyons, Francis S.L. *Ireland since the Famine*. London: Weidenfeld and Nicholson 1971.

- *Culture and Anarchy in Ireland 1890-1939*. Oxford: Clarendon Press 1979.

McAll, Christopher. "Inégalité et différence." In Brigitte Dumas and Donna Winslow, eds., *Construction/destruction sociale des idées: Alternances, récurrences, nouveautés*. Montréal: Association canadienne-française pour l'avancement des sciences 1987.

McCormack, Ross. "Cloth Caps and Jobs: The Ethnicity of English Immigrants in Canada, 1900-1914." In Dahlie and Fernando, eds. 1981.

MacPherson, Alan G. *A Reconstruction of the Human Geography of Some Parts of the Scottish Highlands, 1747-1784*. PhD, McGill University 1969.

Mafeje, Archie. "The Ideology of Tribalism." *Journal of Modern African Studies* 9 (1971): 253-61.

Marx, Karl. *Der achtzehnte Brumaire*. 1852. In Karl Marx and Friedrich Engels, *Werke*, Band 8. Berlin: Dietz Verlag 1960. English translation: *The Eighteenth Brumaire*. In Karl Marx and Friedrich Engels, *Collected Works*, vol. 11. New York: International Publishers 1975.

- *Einleitung zur Kritik der Politischen Ökonomie*. 1852. In Marx and Engels, *Werke*,

Band 13. Berlin: Dietz Verlag 1974.

– *Pre-Capitalist Economic Formations*. 1857. English translation: New York: International Publishers 1965.

– *Das Kapital*, Band 1. 1867. In Marx and Engels, *Werke*, Band 23. Berlin: Dietz Verlag 1962. English translation: *Capital*, vol.1. London: Everyman's Library 1974.

– *Capital*, vol.3. 1894. English translation: New York: International Publishers 1967.

Marx, Karl, and Friedrich Engels. *Die deutsche ideologie*. 1845. In Marx and Engels, *Werke*, Band 3. Berlin: Dietz Verlag 1959.

– *Manifest der kommunistischen Partei*. 1848. In Marx and Engels, *Werke*, Band 4. Berlin: Dietz Verlag 1959. English translation: *The Manifesto of the Communist Party*. London: George Allen and Unwin 1948.

Mather, F.C. *Public Order in the Age of the Chartists*. Manchester: Manchester University Press 1959.

Matza, David, and David Wellman. "The Ordeal of Consciousness." *Theory and Society*. 9 (1980): 1–28.

Miliband, Ralph. *The State in Capitalist Society*. 1969; London: Quartet Books 1973.

– "Poulantzas and the Capitalist State." *New Left Review* 82 (1973): 83–92.

Mill, John Stuart. *Principles of Political Economy*. 1848; New York: Colonial Press 1899.

– *Considerations on Representative Government*. 1861; Indiana: Gateway Editions 1962.

Mills, C. Wright. *The Power Elite*. London: Oxford University Press 1956.

Millward, Pauline. "The Stockport Riots of 1852: A Study of Anti-Catholic and Anti-Irish Sentiment." In Swift and Gilley, eds. 1985.

Mitchell, J.C. "Perceptions of Ethnicity and Ethnic Behaviour: An Empirical Exploration." In Cohen, ed. 1974.

Moodley, Kogila. "Canadian Ethnicity in Comparative Perspective: Issues in the Literature." In Dahlie and Fernando, eds. 1981.

– "Canadian multiculturalism as Ideology." *Ethnic and Racial Studies* 6 (1983): 320–31.

Moreau, François. *Le Capital financier québécois*. Montréal: Albert Saint-Martin 1981.

Morgan, Lewis Henry. *Ancient Society*. 1877; Cambridge: Belknap Press 1964.

Morris, William. *News from Nowhere*. 1892; Lincoln: University of Nebraska Press 1971.

Myrdal, Gunnar. *An American Dilemma*. New York: Harper and Row 1944.

Nairn, Tom. "The Modern Janus." *New Left Review* 94 (1975): 3–29.

Ng, Roxana, and Judith Ramirez. *Immigrant Housewives in Canada*. Toronto: Immigrant Women's Centre 1981.

O'Grady, Standish. *Irish Bardic History*. 1878. In Standish O'Grady, *Selected Essays and Passages*. Dublin: Talbot Press 1918.

O'Tuathaigh, M.A.G. "The Irish in Nineteenth Century Britain: Problems of Integration." In Swift and Gilley, eds. 1985.

Paine, Robert, ed. *The White Arctic*. St John's: Memorial University of Newfoundland 1977.

Parekh, Bhikhu. "The Spectre of Self-consciousness" and "Postscript." In Parekh, ed., *Colour, Culture and Consciousness*. London: George Allen and Unwin 1974.

Parsons, Talcott. *The Social System*. Glencoe, Ill. Free Press 1951.

- "A Revised Analytical Approach to the Theory of Social Stratification." In Reinhard Bendix and Seymour M. Lipset, eds., *Class, Status and Power*. Glencoe, Ill. Free Press 1953.

- "Some Theoretical Considerations on the Nature and Trends of Change of Ethnicity." In Glazer and Moynihan, eds. 1975.

Peter, Karl. "The Myth of Multiculturalism and Other Political Fables." In Dahlie and Fernando, eds. 1981.

Piore, Michael J. *Birds of Passage: Migrant Labour in Industrial Societies*. Cambridge: Cambridge University Press 1979.

Porter, John. *The Vertical Mosaic*. Toronto: University of Toronto Press 1965.

Pospisil, Leopold. *Kapauka Papuans and Their Law*. New Haven: Yale University Press 1958.

Poulantzas, Nicos. "The Problem of the Capitalist State." *New Left Review* 58 (1969): 67–78.

- *Les Classes sociales dans le capitalisme d'aujourd'hui*. Paris: Seuil 1974.

Pryce, Ken. *Endless Pressure*. Harmondsworth: Penguin Books 1979.

Quebec. *Rapport de la Commission d'étude sur l'intégrité du territoire du Québec*. Quebec: Government of Quebec 1971.

- *Pour les familles québécoises, document de consultation sur la politique familiale*. Quebec: Government of Quebec 1984.

Rex, John. *Race, Colonialism and the City*. London: Routledge and Kegan Paul 1973.

Rex, John, and Robert Moore. *Race, Community and Conflict*. London: Oxford University Press 1967.

Rex, John, and Sally Tomlinson. *Colonial Immigrants in a British City*. London: Routledge and Kegan Paul 1979.

Rey, Pierre-Philippe. *Les Alliances de classes*. Paris: Maspero 1973.

Reynolds, Lloyd G. *The British Immigrant: His Social and Economic Adjustment to Canada*. Toronto: Oxford University Press 1935.

Ricardo, David. *On the Principles of Political Economy and Taxation*. 1817; Cambridge: Cambridge University Press 1966.

Rioux, Marcel. "Conscience Nationale et Conscience de Classe." *Cahiers internationaux de sociologie* 38 (1965): 99–108.

Roberts, P.E. *History of British India*. 1921; Oxford: Oxford University Press 1967.

Roethlisberger, F.J. *Management and the Worker*. Cambridge: Harvard University Press 1943.

Rooper, Alison, and Hazel Smith. "From Nationalism to Autonomy: The Ethnic Question in the Nicaraguan Revolution." *Race and Class* 27 (1986): 1–20.

Rouland, Norbert. *Les Inuit du Nouveau-Québec et la Convention de la Baie-James*. Quebec:

Association Inuksiutit Katimajiit and Centre d'études nordiques 1978.

Rousseau, Jérôme. "Classe et ethnicité." *Anthropologie et sociétés* 2, no.1 (1978): 61–9.

– "Kayan Stratification." *Man* 14 (1979): 215–36.

Rudé, George. *The Crowd in History*. New York: John Wiley 1964.

Ruskin, John. *Unto this Last*. 1860; Lincoln: University of Nebraska Press 1967.

Ryder, N.B. "The Interpretation of Origin Statistics." *Canadian Journal of Economics and Political Science* 21 (1955): 466–79.

Sahlins, Marshall D. *Social Stratification in Polynesia*. Seattle: University of Washington Press 1958.

– *Culture and Practical Reason*. Chicago: University of Chicago Press 1976.

St-Jean, Lise, and Marc-André Lemay. *Les Nations autochtones du Québec*. Montréal: Mouvement socialiste 1981.

Saul, John S. "The Dialectic of Class and Tribe." *Race and Class* 20 (1979): 347–72.

Saussure, Ferdinand de. *Cours de linguistique générale* (1915). Paris: Payot 1978.

Scarman, Lord. *The Brixton Disorders*. London: HMSO 1981.

Schneider, David M. *American Kinship*. Chicago: University of Chicago Press 1968.

Shaw, Margaret Fay. *Folksongs and Folklore of South Uist*. London: Routledge and Kegan Paul 1955.

Shils, E.A., and H.A. Finch, eds. *Max Weber on the Methodology of the Social Sciences*. Glencoe, Ill. Free Press 1949.

Simone, Nick. *Italian Immigrants in Toronto, 1890–1930*. Toronto: York University 1981.

Sivanandan, A. "Alien Gods." In Parekh, ed. 1974.

– "From Resistance to Rebellion: Asian and Afro-Caribbean Struggles in Britain." *Race and Class* 23 (1981): 111–52.

Siverts, H. "Ethnic Stability and Boundary Dynamics in Southern Mexico." In Barth, ed. 1969.

Sklar, Richard. "Political Science and National Integration – A Radical Approach." *Journal of Modern African Studies* 5 (1967): 1–11.

Smith, Adam. *An Inquiry into the Nature and Causes of the Wealth of Nations*. 1775; Edinburgh 1814.

Smith, Anthony D. *The Ethnic Revival*. Cambridge: Cambridge University Press 1981.

Stevens, P., and C.F. Willis. *Race, Crime and Arrests*. London: Home Office 1979.

Stymeist, David. *Ethnics and Indians*. Toronto: Peter Martin 1975.

Swift, Roger, and Sheridan Gilley. *The Irish in the Victorian City*. London: Croom Helm 1985.

Synge, J.M. *The Aran Islands*. 1909. In *Collected Works*, vol.2. London: Oxford University Press 1966.

Therborn, Göran. *Science, Class and Society*. London: New Left Books 1976.

Thompson, E.P. *The Making of the English Working Class*. Harmondsworth: Penguin 1963.

– "Eighteenth Century English Society: Class Struggle without Class?" *Social History* 3 (1978): 133–65.

- *The Poverty of Theory and Other Essays.* London: Merlin Press 1978.

Thomson, Derick S., ed. *The Companion to Gaelic Scotland.* Oxford: Blackwell 1983.

Tinker, Hugh. *A New System of Slavery, The Export of Indian Labour Overseas 1830-1920.* Oxford: Oxford University Press 1974.

Trigger, Bruce. "Pour une histoire plus objective des relations entre colonisateurs et autochtones en Nouvelle France." *Recherches amérindiennees du Québec* 11 (1980): 199-204.

Troubetzkoy, N. "La phonologie actuelle." *Journal de psychologie* 30 (1933): 227-46.

Trudel, Pierre. "Comparaison entre le Traité de la Baie James et la Convention de la Baie James." *Recherches amérindiennes au Québec* 9 (1979): 237-53.

Tylor, Edward Burnett. *Primitive Culture.* 1871; New York: Harper and Row 1958.

Upton, L.F.S. *Micmacs and Colonists: Indian-White Relations in the Maritimes, 1713-1867.* Vancouver: University of British Columbia Press 1979.

Van den Berghe, Pierre L. *The Ethnic Phenomenon.* New York: Elsevier 1981.

Vincent, Sylvie, and Arcand, Bernard. *L'Image de l'Amérindien dans les manuels scolaires du Québec.* Lasalle: Hurtubise 1979.

Wallerstein, Immanuel. "Ethnicity and National Integration in West Africa." *Cahiers d'études africaines* 1 (1960): 129-39.

Wallman, Sandra. "The Boundaries of 'Race': Processes of Ethnicity in England." *Man* 13 (1978): 200-17.

Wardhaugh, Ronald. *Language and Nationhood: The Canadian Experience.* Vancouver: New Star Books 1983.

Warner, W. Lloyd. "American Caste and Class." *American Journal of Sociology* 42 (1946): 234-7.

Weaver, Sally M. *Making Canadian Indian Policy: The Hidden Agenda.* Toronto: University of Toronto Press 1981.

Weber, Max. "'Objectivity' in Social Science and Social Policy." 1904. In Shils and Finch, eds. 1949.

- *Wirtschaft und Gesellschaft.* 1921; Tübingen: J.C.B.Mohr 1925. English translation: *Economy and Society.* Berkeley: University of California Press 1978.

Westergaard, John, and Henrietta Resler. *Class in a Capitalist Society.* Harmondsworth: Penguin 1975.

Whyte, John. "Interpretations of the Northern Ireland Problem: An Appraisal." *Economic and Social Review* 9 (1978): 257-82.

Wilson, Amrita. *Finding a Voice: Asian Women in Britain.* London: Virago 1978.

Wilson, Edward O. *On Human Nature.* Cambridge: Harvard University Press 1978.

Wright, Erik Olin. "Class Boundaries in Advanced Capitalist Societies." *New Left Review* 98 (1976): 3-41.

Youngson, A.J. *After the Forty-Five: The Economic Impact on the Scottish Highlands.* Edinburgh: Edinburgh University Press 1973.

Zubaida, Sami. "Theories of Nationalism." In G. Littlejohn, ed., *Power and State.* London: Croom Helm 1978.

Index